Berlin

WHAT'S NEW | WHAT'S ON | WHAT'S BEST

www.timeout.com/berlin

Contents

Berlin by Area

Essentials

Published by Time Out Guides Ltd
Universal House
251 Tottenham Court Road
London W1T 7AB
Tel: + 44 (0)20 7813 3000
Fax: + 44 (0)20 7813 6001
Email: guides@timeout.com
www.timeout.com

Managing Director Peter Fiennes
Editorial Director Ruth Jarvis
Business Manager Daniel Allen
Editorial Manager Holly Pick
Assistant Management Accountant Ija Krasnikova

Time Out Guides is a wholly owned subsidiary of Time Out Group Ltd.

© Time Out Group Ltd
Chairman Tony Elliott
Chief Executive Officer David King
Group Financial Director Paul Rakkar
Group General Manager/Director Nichola Coulthard
Time Out Communications Ltd MD David Pepper
Time Out International Ltd MD Cathy Runciman
Time Out Magazine Ltd Publisher/Managing Director Mark Elliott
Production Director Mark Lamond
Group IT Director Simon Chappell
Marketing & Circulation Director Catherine Demajo

Time Out and the Time Out logo are trademarks of Time Out Group Ltd.

This edition first published in Great Britain in 2010 by Ebury Publishing
A Random House Group Company
Company information can be found on www.randomhouse.co.uk
Random House UK Limited Reg. No. 954009
10 9 8 7 6 5 4 3 2 1

Distributed in the US by Publishers Group West
Distributed in Canada by Publishers Group Canada

For further distribution details, see www.timeout.com

ISBN: 978-1-84670-148-1

A CIP catalogue record for this book is available from the British Library.

Printed and bound in Germany by Appl.

The Random House Group Limited supports The Forest Stewardship Council (FSC), the
leading international forest certification organisation. All our titles that are printed on
Greenpeace approved FSC certified paper carry the FSC logo. Our paper procurement
policy can be found at www.rbooks.co.uk/environment.

Time Out carbon-offsets all its flights with Trees for Cities (www.treesforcities.org).

Berlin Shortlist

The **Time Out Berlin Shortlist** is one of a new series of guides that draws on Time Out's background as a magazine publisher to keep you current with what's going on in town. As well as Berlin's key sights and the best of its eating, drinking and leisure options, the guide picks out the most exciting venues to have recently opened and gives a full calendar of annual events. It also includes features on the important news, trends and openings, all compiled by locally based editors and writers. Whether you're visiting Berlin for the first time, or you're a regular, you'll find the *Time Out Berlin Shortlist* contains all you need to know, in a portable and easy-to-use format.

The guide divides central Berlin into seven areas, each of which contains listings for Sights & Museums, Eating & Drinking, Shopping, Nightlife and Arts & Leisure, with maps pinpointing all their locations. At the front of the book are chapters rounding up these scenes city-wide, and giving a shortlist of our overall picks in a variety of categories. We include itineraries for days out, plus essentials such as transport information and hotels.

Our listings give phone numbers as dialled from within Germany. From abroad, use your country's exit code followed by 49 (the country code for Germany) and the number given.

We have noted price categories by using one to four euro signs (€-€€€€), representing budget, moderate, expensive and luxury. Major credit cards are accepted unless otherwise stated. We have also indicated when a venue is NEW.

All our listings are double-checked, but places do sometimes close or change their hours or prices, so it's a good idea to call a venue before visiting. While every effort has been made to ensure accuracy, the publishers cannot accept responsibility for any errors that this guide may contain.

Venues are marked on the maps using symbols numbered according to their order within the chapter and colour-coded according to the type of venue they represent:

❶ Sights & Museums
❶ Eating & Drinking
❶ Shopping
❶ Nightlife
❶ Arts & Leisure

Map key	
Major sight or landmark	▮
Railway station	▮
Park	▮
Hospital/university	▮
Pedestrian Area	▮
Autobahn	▬
Main road	▬
Airport	✈
Church	✚
S-Bahn Station	Ⓢ
U-Bahn Station	Ⓤ
S-Bahn line	S1
U-Bahn line	U1
Course of Wall	▬
Area	MITTE

Time Out **Berlin** Shortlist

EDITORIAL
Editor Dave Rimmer
Deputy Editor Holly Pick
Researchers Ralf Oestereich, Mark Reeder
Proofreader Tamsin Shelton

DESIGN
Art Director Scott Moore
Art Editor Pinelope Kourmouzoglou
Senior Designer Henry Elphick
Graphic Designers Kei Ishimaru,
  Nicola Wilson
Advertising Designer Jodi Sher

Picture Editor Jael Marschner
Deputy Picture Editor Lynn Chambers
Picture Researcher Gemma Walters
Picture Desk Assistant Ben Rowe
Picture Librarian Christina Theisen

ADVERTISING
Commercial Director Mark Phillips
International Advertising Manager
  Kasimir Berger
International Sales Executive Charlie Sokol
Advertising Sales (Berlin) In Your Pocket

MARKETING
Sales & Marketing Director, North America
  & Latin America Lisa Levinson
Senior Publishing Brand Manager
  Luthfa Begum
Art Director Anthony Huggins
Marketing Intern Alana Benton

PRODUCTION
Production Manager Brendan McKeown
Production Controller Damian Bennett

CONTRIBUTORS
This guide was researched and written by Gavin Blackburn, Kimberly Bradley, Jenna Krumminga, Jenny Piening, Dave Rimmer and Nick Woods. The editor would like to thank the writers of *Time Out Berlin*.

PHOTOGRAPHY
Photography by Elan Fleisher, except pages 18, 46, 48, 122, 137, 156 Jael Marschner; page 31 Messe Berlin; page 32 Berlinale; page 34 courtesy Galerie Anselm Dreher, Berlin; pages 40, 47, 74, 96, 142, 155, 160, 170, 174, 176, 177 Britta Jaschinski; page 149 bpk Berlin, 2004.

The following images were provided by the featured establishment/artist: pages 100, 145.

Cover photograph: Hackescher Markt at night. Credit: Photolibrary.com

MAPS
JS Graphics (john@jsgraphics.co.uk).

About **Time Out**

Founded in 1968, Time Out has expanded from humble London beginnings into the leading resource for those wanting to know what's happening in the world's greatest cities. As well as our influential what's-on weeklies in London, New York and Chicago, we publish nearly 30 other listings magazines in cities as varied as Beijing and Mumbai. The magazines established Time Out's trademark style: sharp writing, informed reviewing and bang up-to-date inside knowledge of every scene.

Time Out made the natural leap into travel guides in the 1980s with the City Guide series, which now extends to over 50 destinations around the world. Written and researched by expert local writers and generously illustrated with original photography, the full-size guides cover a larger area than our Shortlist guides and include many more venue reviews, along with additional background features and a full set of maps.

Throughout this rapid growth, the company has remained proudly independent, still owned by Tony Elliott four decades after he started Time Out London as a single fold-out sheet of A5 paper. This independence extends to the editorial content of all our publications, this Shortlist included. No establishment has been featured because it has advertised, and no payment has influenced any of our reviews. And, for our critics, there's definitely no such thing as a free lunch: all restaurants and bars are visited and reviewed anonymously, and Time Out always picks up the bill.
For more about the company, see www.timeout.com.

Don't Miss

Reichstag

WHAT'S BEST
Sights & Museums

In 2010, Berlin celebrates the twentieth anniversary of German reunification. It's taken all that time to stitch the formerly divided city back together again, and though most of the major projects have been completed, the job still isn't quite finished yet. Berlin has been undergoing a massive infrastructural overhaul at every level, from public transport to the consolidation of its major public collections. Old landmarks have been renovated, a whole bunch of new ones commissioned and constructed, and others wiped out altogether – including what was once the most famous Berlin landmark of them all, the Wall.

The Brandenburg Gate is Berlin's signature sight, its Tower Bridge or Tour d'Eiffel, though these days it's facing competition in the urban icon

stakes from the Fernsehturm, the television tower on Alexanderplatz. To the north and south of the Brandenburg Gate, various new central landmarks now catch the eye: the postmodern towers of Potsdamer Platz; the undulating field of tilting concrete blocks that is the Denkmal für die ermordeten Jüden Europas (Memorial to the Murdered Jews of Europe); the new Bundeskanzleramt (Federal Chancellery) and government quarter. There's also Norman Foster's revamped Reichstag, complete with visitable glass cupola. A walk to the top is a must.

These new landmarks all lie along the line of the former Wall and, in one way or another, are intended to heal that wound of history and bind the city back together. On what is now merely the border of Mitte and

Tiergarten (the city's central park stretches away on the western side), the Brandenburg Gate was once the ceremonial entrance to Berlin as capital of Prussia. Unter den Linden, the grand avenue leading east, is dotted with the major neo-classical landmarks of the Imperial era, and winds up at Museumsinsel, an island in the River Spree. In October 2009, the Neues Museum (p56), complete with the famous bust of Nefertiti, reopened on this UNESCO World Heritage Site. It was the last of the island's five major institutions to undergo a huge makeover in a generation-long €1.5 billion project. Work is still not quite complete here, however. Parts of the Pergamonmuseum (p57) are still undergoing renovation, and a central walkway connecting all the island's museums has yet to be built. Elsewhere on the island, demolition of the Palast der Republik, once the building of the East German parliament, is now complete. While the city waits for the funding needed to reconstruct the old Stadtschloss (City Palace) that once stood on this site, the box-like Temporär Kunsthalle (p60) now proudly exemplifies the very Berlin principle of *Zwischennutzung* (interim usage).

While Museumsinsel is the biggest agglomeration of traditional landmarks – apart from its five major museums, it is also home to the Berliner Dom (p51), while the Staatsoper (p61) and the reunified Deutsches Historisches Museum (p56) are nearby on Unter den Linden – there are further cathedrals and concert halls to the south, around the Gendarmenmarkt.

Elsewhere around the city, other post-Wall additions to the landscape include the Jüdisches Museum (p118) in Kreuzberg, housed in a remarkable building by Daniel Libeskind; a whole slew of new embassies, mostly clustered

DON'T MISS

SHORTLIST

Best new
- Denkmal für die ermordeten Jüden Europas (p55)
- Sammlung Scharf-Gerstenberg (p153)

Best revamped
- Deutsches Historisches Museum (p56)
- Neues Museum (p56)
- Reichstag (p132)

Best modern museums
- Filmmuseum Berlin (p129)
- Jüdisches Museum (p118)

Best old-school
- Altes Museum (p51)
- Ethnologisches Museum (p150)
- Pergamonmuseum (p57)

Best World War II
- Gedänkstätte Haus der Wannsee-Konferenz (p151)
- Museum Berlin-Karlshorst (p152)

Best Cold War
- Allierten Museum (p148)
- Gedenkstätte Berliner Mauer (p150)
- Gedenkstätte Berlin-Hohenschönhausen (p150)
- Stasi Museum (p153)

Best for kids
- Deutsches Technikmuseum (p118)
- Gruselkabinett (p118)
- Haus am Checkpoint Charlie (p118)
- Zoologischer Garten (p134)

Best art
- Bauhaus Archiv (p128)
- Gemäldegalerie (p129)
- Hambuger Bahnhof (p67)
- Neue Nationalgalerie (p132)

south of the Tiergarten; the renovated Olympiastadion (p153) in the west of Charlottenburg; and the huge new Berlin Hauptbahnof, Europe's biggest railway station.

Neighbourhoods

Our book is organised according to area. Mitte is the city's historic centre. In the days of division it lay on the eastern side, but today it is once again the centre in every respect – historically, culturally, politically and commercially. Its southern reaches are full of big sights and grand avenues, major hotels and new department stores. Things get more bohemian at the borough's northern end, particularly around the Scheunenviertel, Berlin's historic Jewish quarter, whose narrow streets are dotted with cafés and restaurants, venues and galleries. In recent years, nightlife has been migrating even further north, and today the area around Brunnenstrasse and the Mitte end of Kastanienallee is probably the city's most happening 'hood.

Kastanienallee leads north into Prenzlauer Berg, east Berlin's most picturesque residential neighbourhood and Mitte's fashionable adjunct in terms of nightlife and gastronomy. The streets around Kollwitzplatz are inviting for a stroll, there is lots of activity in the 'LSD' neighbourhood around Lychener Strasse, Stargarder Strasse and Dunckerstrasse, and east Berlin's gay district is around the northern reaches of Schönhauser Allee.

Moving clockwise, we next come to Friedrichshain, the most 'eastern' in feel of the inner-city districts. Its spine is the broad, Stalin-era Karl-Marx-Allee, while the lively area around Simon-Dach-Strasse is the neighbourhood of choice for bohos and young radicals.

South over the river, we cross the former border into western Berlin and come to Kreuzberg, once the city's main alternative nexus and the capital of Turkish Berlin. Today, life is returning to the eastern area around Schlesisches Tor, while it never left the bustling western focal point of Bergmannstrasse. The borough's northern area, where it borders Mitte, contains some important museums, such as the Deutsches Technikmuseum (p118) and the Jüdisches Museum (p118) as well as the Cold War landmark Checkpoint Charlie.

West of Kreuzberg lies Schöneberg, a residential district centred around Winterfeldtplatz, with its popular twice-weekly market, and the historic gay district that stretches along and around Motzstrasse and Fuggerstrasse. Wittenbergplatz, at its north-western corner, is the location of KaDeWe (p126), continental Europe's biggest department store, and marks the beginning of Berlin's west end.

North of Schöneberg, Tiergarten is centred around the huge wooded

Neues Museum p9

park of the same name. The district contains the diplomatic quarter, as well as the new entertainment and commercial district of Potsdamer Platz, and the neighbouring Kulturforum that is home to institutions such as the Neue Nationalgalerie (p132) and the Philharmonie (p137).

Finally, there is the well-heeled district of Charlottenburg, Berlin's west end, whose main arteries are the Kurfürstendamm, an upmarket commercial avenue, and the parallel Kantstrasse. Most of the formal sights, such as the new Museum für Fotographie (p140) and the Kaiser-Wilhelm-Gedächtnis-Kirche (p138), are in the borough's eastern end.

Don't mention the Wall

'Is there anything left of the Wall?' That's the first question asked by many visitors. The answer is: not very much. A short section has been preserved on the border between Mitte and Wedding at the Gedenkstätte Berliner Mauer (p150). It's kept in inauthentically pristine condition (any graffiti is removed straight away) but is the only place where you can see what the various layers of defences looked like. A section of the inner Wall (the side that faced East Berlin) stands on the Friedrichshain bank of the Spree along Mühlenstrasse. Now known as the East Side Gallery, it was covered with paintings by international artists in the 1990s. And on Niederkirchnerstrasse, along the border between Kreuzberg and Mitte, there's a stretch preserved with graffiti and pockmarks inflicted by the hammers and chisels of souvenir-chipping 'Wall tourists' in the winter of 1989-90.

The area directly south of Niederkirchnerstrasse is known as the Topographie des Terror (p121), once the site of the Gestapo headquarters. It's just one of many landmarks relating to that other dark chapter in Berlin's history, the Nazi era. Only a few structures are left extant from that time, though the tragedy of the Holocaust is memorialised all over the city in a variety of different ways (p38 The Memorial Trail). The Olympiastadion (p153) is the biggest single Nazi-era building still standing.

Making the most of it

If you're planning to visit a lot of museums, then you may want to invest in a discount card. Most of the major museums and galleries are administered by the Staatliche Museen zu Berlin (SMPK), including the Altes Museum (p51), the Pergamonmuseum (p57), the Gemäldegalerie (p129) and the Ethnologisches Museum (p150). SMPK offers a three-day card (€19; €9.50 reductions), available from any of its museums. It doesn't cover temporary exhibitions, however. Most museums are closed on Mondays but open until 10pm on Thursdays, when they are free after 6pm. For more information, see www.smb.spk-berlin.de.

Another deal is the WelcomeCard, which combines free travel on public transport with discounted tours, boat trips and entry to museums, theatres and other attractions in both Berlin and Potsdam. WelcomeCards are available from Berliner Tourismus Marketing (p186), S-Bahn offices and many hotels. For fare zones A and B it costs €16.90 for 48 hours, €22.90 for 72 hours and €29.90 for five days; for a card including travel to and within Potsdam, it's €18.90 for 48 hours, €25.90 for 72 hours and €34.90 for five days. For more information, visit www.visitberlin.de/welcomecard.

Gendarmerie

WHAT'S BEST
Eating & Drinking

The summer 2009 opening of Josef Laggner's Gendarmerie (p65) in Mitte was a grand event for a grand new restaurant. Over 1,000 guests, including actors and ambassadors, politicians and painters, swanned into the lofty-ceilinged former banking hall, admired the custom-made central bar, oohed and aahed at the 14-metre-long, seven-ton painting on wood by Jean-Yves Klein, and tucked into free champagne, oysters and lobster.

This was quite literally a rare occasion – Berlin dining is almost never so showy – but even though the opening of Gendarmerie seems so far to have failed in its presumed objective of displacing the nearby Borchardt (p64) as Mitte's premier see-and-be-seen spot, it has established the Gendarmenmarkt neighbourhood as Berlin's prime locus for upscale dining. Apart from Gendarmerie and Borchardt, Lutter & Wegner (p65; also owned by Laggner), Malatesta (p65) and Vau (p65) are also around here. Not bad going for an area where it was hard to find much other than pork and cabbage a generation ago.

In a way, though, the same could be said for the whole of east Berlin, where pretty much the entire gastronomic infrastructure has been through an overhaul. Only a few places, such as Entweder Oder (p88), the Kellerrestaurant im Brecht-Haus (p67), Konnopke's Imbiss (p90) and Prater (p92) have survived in anything resembling their historic form, and all have benefitted from the relaxation of regulations and an improvement in ingredients. If you want a taste

of what dining was like before the Wall came down, Osseria (p91) is having a go at replicating the stodge and blandness of the communist days.

Berlin has in any case never been a great gastronomic capital, and that doesn't look likely to change anytime soon. But to say it doesn't rank up there with Paris or New York isn't to imply that you can't dine decently here, or that things haven't been steadily improving. Meanwhile, some cities would kill to have a café life as good as Berlin's, and its reputation as an excellent place for drinking is well deserved. The cafés serve breakfast all day, the bars stay open deep into the night, and restaurants tend to be relaxed, roomy and delightfully cheap compared to other western European capitals.

Surrounded by poor agricultural land, not much use for growing anything except cabbages and potatoes, Berlin's traditional dishes have always been of the meat-and-two-veg variety. *Eisbein* is the signature local dish – a leathery-skinned and extremely fatty pig's trotter, sometimes marinated and usually served with puréed peas. You won't find it on the menu, however, in anything but the most doggedly old-school establishments. Other regional cuisines from Germanic Europe are superior and probably better represented, such as south German (Schwarzwaldstuben, p76; Florian, p141; Alpenstueck, p71), Austrian (Austria, p115; Café Einstein, p135), Swiss (Nola am Weinberg, p75; Schneeweiss, p102) or Alsatian (Renger-Patzsch, p125; Gugelhof, p89). In the decidedly old-school atmosphere of Marjellchen (p142) you can even sample the cuisines of no-longer-German regions such as East Prussia, Silesia and

SHORTLIST

Best new
- AlpenStueck (p71)
- Cookies Cream (p64)
- Gendarmerie (p65)

Cocktails
- Bar am Lützowplatz (p135)
- Galerie Bremer (p141)
- Tausend (p69)
- Victoria Bar (p136)
- Würgeengel (p111)

Modern German
- Alpenstueck (p71)
- Florian (p141)
- Gugelhof (p89)
- Maxwell (p75)
- Renger-Patzsch (p125)
- Schwarzwaldstuben (p76)

Old-school
- Diener (p141)
- Grill Royal (p67)
- Henne (p110)
- Marjellchen (p142)
- Prater (p92)

See and be seen
- Borchardt (p64)
- Pan Asia (p75)
- Paris Bar (p142)

Sausages
- Konnopke's Imbiss (p90)
- Witty's (p125)

Breakfasts
- Anna Blume (p87)
- Barcomi's (p71)
- Café Einstein Stammhaus (p135)
- Honeypenny (p124)
- Schwarzes Café (p143)

Americana
- The Bird (p88)
- Julep's (p141)
- Links vom Fischladen (p90)
- Tartane (p69)

Tartane

Pomerania, while east and central European Jewish dishes are served at Restaurant Gabriel's (p142).

Tomorrow the world

The brevity of Germany's colonial experience has meant no deep-rooted link with a foreign cuisine, such as Britain's with India, or Morocco's with France. Turkish food, however, which arrived with post-war 'guest workers', is now deeply embedded in the western side of town, and Kreuzberg can claim to be the place where the doner kebab was invented in the early 1970s (Hasir, p110). Berlin's other post-war culinary innovation is also a snack at street level: the Currywurst, a pork sausage sliced and drenched in warm ketchup and curry powder. Try the traditional version under the railway arches at Prenzlauer Berg's venerable Konnopke's (p90), or the upmarket organic version (and the city's best chips) at west Berlin's Witty's (p125).

Reunification has meant a more well-travelled population,

and, in the beginning at least, lots of relatively cheap real estate where young restaurateurs could try out their ideas. With the arrival of the government to stimulate things at the high end, and an increasingly cosmopolitan population to encourage ethnic variety at street level, Berlin dining has been getting steadily more international.

Italian cuisine has long been well represented (Osteria No.1, p116; Sale e Tabbachi, p120; Trattoria Paparazzi, p93) and good quality Japanese food is now common (Kuchi, p74; Sachiko Sushi, p142; Ishin Mitte, p57), along with other East Asian cuisines such as Vietnamese (Monsieur Vuong, p75; Si An, p93), Thai (Mao Thai, p91; Edd's, p135), Chinese (Tai Ji, p143) and Indonesian (Good Time, p67). Indian food presents something of a problem; there are places all over town but most seem to have the same menu prepared to a similarly mediocre standard. If you're craving a curry, try Ashoka (p140) in Charlottenburg. There have also been a few

DON'T MISS

interesting attempts at east-west fusion cuisine, such as Der Imbiss W (p72) with its 'naan pizzas', 'rice shells' and 'international dressings'.

New immigrants, of course, have brought their own culinary traditions. An influx of Russians may not have had much to do with the fashionable borscht and vodka on offer at places such as Gorki Park (p73), Pasternak (p92), CCCP (p72) and Café Oberwasser (p72), but the ever-growing community of young Americans in east Berlin has certainly made its gastronomic mark with a wave of fancy burger joints such as the Bird (p88), Marien Burger (p91), Frittiersalon (p98), Links vom Fischladen (p90) and Tartane (p69).

Boundaries are blurred right across the whole spectrum of eating and drinking. Restaurants often have bars, which you're usually welcome to use even if you have no intention of eating, and bars, in their turn, often serve food. Cafés by day are popular for a long breakfast, light lunch or afternoon *Kaffee und Kuchen*

(coffee and cake) and then often turn into bars by night.

Berliners do like a drink. The capital's changing demographics mean that cocktail bars are on the increase. Tausend (p69) is currently setting the benchmark for avant-garde exclusivity, but perfectly mixed drinks can be found in every part of town at places such as Victoria Bar (p136), Greenwich (p74), Galerie Bremer (p141), Wurgeengel (p111) or Becketts Kopf (p88). There are also still plenty of characterful dives and unpretentious watering holes – just about one on every corner in some parts of town. In summer, café tables spread out on to the city's wide pavements, beer gardens begin to bustle, and beach bars spring to life in waterside locations across town (see box p103). This being Germany, beer is, of course, the main tipple, though local brews are poor in comparison to the best of Bavaria or Bohemia.

Tipping & etiquette

In restaurants, it's customary to tip around ten per cent. Tips are handed directly to the server (or you tell staff how much to take) rather than left on the table. At the moment of handing over the cash, don't say 'danke' unless you want them to keep the change.

In bars, people tend to pay their own way and drink at their own pace – partly because in many places bills are only totted up as you leave – but ceremonial rounds of tequila, vodka or Jägermeister are a feature of the Berlin night. Even though the general tendency is for bars to close earlier than they used to, hardly anywhere closes before 1am and most places stay open much later – many as long as there are still people in there.

Flohmarkt am Mauerpark p21

WHAT'S BEST

Shopping

The shopping landscape in Berlin is, like almost everything else in the city, a jumble of disparate elements unified not by geography but by a collective nod to innovation, individualism and experiment. In a city that prides itself on the spirit of creativity, lowbrow and highbrow, mainstream and avant-garde, designer chic and street style not only manage a harmonious co-existence, but interconnect, coming together in interesting juxtapositions.

A quirky independent bookshop might survive and thrive on the same block as a branch of a mega chain, and a cheap vintage store purveying communist kitsch can nestle comfortably among some of the city's most expensive boutiques. Even the recent influx of big-name brands into areas hithero dominated by the quirky and independent hasn't dampened the impulse of Berlin's progressives to keep things interesting. A lively independent shopping scene remains one of the city's strengths, ranging from designer kiosks offering an idiosyncratic selection of pop art knick-knacks on fashionable Kastanienallee to old-school but determinedly eccentric establishments such as Kreuzberg's Paul Knopf (p116), a labour of love reflecting the owner's lifelong fascination with buttons.

Berlin has never had one single downtown or retail focus, and these days things have become more mixed up than ever. Many of its treasures can be found in the least expected places, in courtyards or otherwise barren sidestreets scattered anywhere around the city. But the broad outlines of the retail picture have been clear ever since Berlin began sketching out its post-Wall infrastructure.

The west end has remained the upmarket showpiece it always was. Major department stores and the flagship outlets of international brands march westwards from KaDeWe (p126) on Wittenbergplatz and along the Kurfürstendamm, west Berlin's major shopping avenue. Luxury brands cluster on Fasanenstrasse while more discreet boutiques, interior design outlets and tasteful bookshops are scattered around the streets between the Ku-damm and Kantstrasse, in the area around Savignyplatz.

In the 1990s, newer department stores and still more international brands sprouted in the east along Friedrichstrasse, including interesting retail concepts such as the all-in-one cultural cornucopia that is Dussmann das Kulturkaufhaus (p69) and the high-end designer outlet Quartier 206 (p66), as well as an elegant branch of Galeries Lafayette (p65). Meanwhile, in between east and west there's also the big Arkaden mall at Potsdamer Platz. Over on the other side of Mitte, Alexanderplatz is also asserting itself as a retail hub, with the refurbishment of its Kaufhof (p84) department store, a new branch of the Saturn consumer electronics chain, and the Alexa mall to the south of the square.

The final big piece of the puzzle is also in Mitte: the complex of restored Jugendstil courtyards called the Hackesche Höfe. Berlin's attractive but modest answer to Covent Garden or Les Halles is the centrepiece of the Scheunenviertel and home to local designers and speciality stores as well as cafés, galleries and cabarets. The area that fans out from here has established itself as home to the adventurous and the eccentric, including local designers and labels such as Claudia Skoda (p76) and Respectmen (p78), as well as

SHORTLIST

Best newcomers
- AM1, AM2 & AM3 (p76)
- Zeha (p144)

Berlin designers
- Claudia Skoda (p76)
- Eisdieler (p92)
- Respectmen (p78)

Streetwear
- Big Brobot (p102)
- Depot 2 (p112)
- Skunkfunk (p94)

Discerning sounds
- Gelbe Musik (p144)
- Mr Dead & Mrs Free (p126)
- Space Hall (p116)

Reading matter
- Berlin Story (p59)
- Bücherbogen (p143)
- Dussmann das Kulturkaufhaus (p69)
- Marga Schoeller Bucherstube (p144)
- Saint Georges (p94)

Department stores
- Galeries Lafayette (p65)
- KaDeWe (p126)
- Kaufhof (p84)

Market days
- Flohmarkt am Mauerpark (p94)
- Trödelmarkt Boxhagener Platz (p104)
- Winterfeldt Markt (p126)

Notable eccentrics
- Another Country (p116)
- Paul Knopf (p116)
- RSVP (p78)

Chocoate city
- In't Veld Schockoladen (p90)
- Leysieffer (p144)

DON'T MISS

everything from retro-futurist furniture shops to stores selling Third World household gizmos.

But as we say, things are getting mixed up. The Scheunenviertel's reputation for style and daring has begun to draw the likes of Hugo Boss, Caharrt and Adidas to the area. Rising rents are also helping to chase small Berlin designers out of Mitte, mostly in the direction of Friedrichshain, though there have been signs that the streets around Savignyplatz and Bleibtreustrasse in Charlottenburg are beginning to reassert themselves as a centre of style. Interestingly, as we went to press the Zeha chain, an east German sportswear brand whose outlets were hitherto confined to the other side of town, was opening its first branch in the west (see box p145). Streetware shops and young urban brands are scattered all over town, such as Big Brobot (p102) in Friedrichshain, CherryBomb (p112) or Depot 2 (p112) in Kreuzberg, and Skunkfunk (p94) on Kastanienallee.

Other areas have more specialised characters. Since the late 1990s opening of the interior design mall Stilwerk (p144) in the west end, Kantstrasse has established itself as a clustering point for high-end household items. Nearby in Charlottenburg, Knesebeckstrasse, on either side of Savignyplatz, is good for bookshops, including the Marga Schoeller Bucherstube (p144) with its excellent English department, and the art and architecture bookshop Bucherbogen (p143). The Bergmannstrasse neighbourhood in Kreuzberg has everything from second-hand shops to small designer outlets, music stores, bookshops and delis.

A prematurely staid kind of stylishness prevails on and around Rykestrasse in Prenzlauer Berg; there are many useful shops in that area, though, such as Saint Georges

(p94) with its excellent selection of English second-hand books. Nearby Dunckerstrasse has probably now usurped Kreuzberg's Bergmann/ Zossener Strasse axis in terms of the best concentration of CD and DJ shops. In retail, as in nightlife, Kastanienallee is a thoroughfare of the alternative, connecting the north Mitte scene to that of Prenzlauer Berg, and it's around here that the art-meets-retail phenomenon of designer kiosks is evident in the miscellany offered by Kwik Shop (Kastanienallee 44, Mitte, 4432 4877, www.kwikshop.de), the rent-a-shelf platform for small Berlin designers that is Luxus International (Kastanienallee 101, Prenzlauer Berg, 4432 4877, www.luxus-international.de) or the coffee shop and knick-knack store Risi-Bisi Popshop (Brunnenstrasse 7, Mitte, 6677 3336, www.risi-bisi.de).

There are several interesting flea markets. Sunday's Flohmarkt am Mauer Park (p94) has the the most eclectic selection, though the Kunst und Trödel Markt (p136) is the best place for collectors. The Trödelmarkt Boxhagener Platz (p104) mixes bric-a-brac with the work of local artists and T-shirt designers.

Opening hours

Shops generally open at around 9am or 10am. More traditional and smaller stores tend to close around 6pm, but a relatively recent relaxation of laws means that places can now stay open until 10pm, and most bigger stores and the more adventurous smaller retailers stick it out at least until 8pm. It's also now possible to go shopping on Saturday afternoons. All but a few shops are closed on Sunday.

Credit cards are accepted ever more widely, but you'll still find a large number of places refusing to deal with plastic.

WMF

Nightlife

Berlin's reputation for decadence and nocturnal high jinks stretches all the way back to the 1920s, when apart from the cabaret scene of legend, it was also the first city to have anything one might recognise as a gay community in the modern sense. Nazism and war might have dampened its party spirit for a time, but even in the years of division East Berlin had more liberal licensing laws than London, while the western side of town teemed with draft-dodging youth and nihilistic artists, few of whom had anything important to get up for in the morning.

In reunified Berlin you can stay out until dawn pretty much any night of the week, there are late-night bars all over town, and bands and DJs will appear in just about any space large enough to accommodate a bar and stage. It has long been a city where music matters. Berlin concert audiences are some of the most enthusiastic in the world, every second person you meet seems to be some kind of DJ, and in any half-decent late-night bar the staff will have been chosen as much for their taste in tunes as their prowess with a cocktail-shaker.

From division to DIY

And as in most other aspects of city life, Berlin's all-too-vivid history has an effect still felt today. In the days of division, West Berlin was an island, remote from the musical mainstream; and East Berlin was remoter still. The feeling that nothing that came out of here would ever be commercial led to an attitude of confrontational experiment – if no one's going to buy it, we might as well do exactly what we want. This was epitomised by Einstürzende Neubauten, still not displaced as the city's signature band even long after their heyday. Though much has changed since that lot first started making music with hammers and drills, reflecting the city's post-war experience of rebuilding itself from ruin, you just know Berlin is never going to end up in thrall to any kind of fresh-faced pop scene.

It all kicked off after the fall of the Wall, as the West Berlin avant-garde collided with a party-starved East Berlin generation on makeshift dancefloors in spaces left accessible by the abandonment of border defences and the collapse of East German industry. The techno scene of the no-man's land years is long gone, but some of the DIY spirit of those days lives on in a variety of forms. There are the under-the-radar venues working on the edge of legality, such as Paloma Bar (p113), Villa (p154) or Zpyz (p114). Moveable parties, accessed via flyers or word-of-mouth, similarly exploit spaces that haven't yet been brought into the commercial mainstream. The tradition of imaginatively repurposed space survives and thrives in the latest incarnation of the venerable WMF (p85), triumphantly partying on in a former telecommunications office.

And then there is the continuing tradition of landmark clubs taking over now-obsolete power stations (see box p84). The first of these was the legendary E-Werk on Wilhelmstrasse back in the early 1990s. In recent years, the by now just-as-legendary Berghain (p104) has been occupying a former power station in Friedrichshain, its original fittings polished up

SHORTLIST

Best newcomers
- Dice Club (p84)
- Dot Club (p112)
- Suicide Circus (p105)
- Tresor.30 (p85)
- WMF (p85)

Goth heaven
- Duncker (p94)
- K17 (p105)

DIY aesthetic
- Paloma Bar (p113)
- Rosi's (p105)
- Villa (p154)
- Zpyz (p114)

Sophisticated disco
- Bohannon (p79)
- Goya (p126)

Life is a cabaret
- Café Theater Schalotte (p146)
- Chamäleon (p81)
- Kleine Nachtrevue (p126)
- Scheinbar Varieté (p127)

Have a ball
- Clärchens Ballhaus (p79)

All that jazz
- A-Trane (p146)
- B-Flat (p78)

Best gay joints
- Barbie Deinhoff's (p107)
- Haus B (p104)
- Möbel Olfe (p113)
- Roses (p113)

Techno thud
- Berghain (p104)
- Watergate (p113)

Rock the house
- Fritzclub im Postbahnhof (p104)
- Lido (p112)
- Maria am Ostbahnhof (p105)

into minimalist post-industrial detail. Across the river, Tresor.30 (p85), the latest incarnation of the post-Wall era's very first club, is installed in one corner of a gigantic former central-heating power station (the rest offers room for expansion into what is intended to be a multi-purpose cultural centre). And now the Dice Club (p84) has taken up residence in a disused transformer station near Alexanderplatz, once used to power Stasi facilities.

Berlin's recent restitution as Germany's capital has brought with it an influx of young professional types, who in turn have engendered the spread of a kind of bland, unchallenging stylishness. It's in increasingly upmarket Mitte that the trend towards fashion and exclusive door policies is most pronounced, but even there it's not hard to get in anywhere. The general approach to clubbing is incredibly laid-back.

Sounds of the city

Minimal techno (Ricardo Villalobos and Richie Hawtin remain the best local exponents) has begun to give way to electro (look out for Kaos or Ellen Allien) as the city's signature sound, but once a trend has started in Berlin it tends to stick around. Kreuzberg will forever be characterised by an anarcho-punk aesthetic. Buskers in Friedrichshain strum Beatles or Nirvana tunes. Disco is making a comeback in Mitte clubs such as Bohannon (p79). You'll still find a few clones in Schöneberg's gay quarter. And various scenes retain some kind of niche, such as goth at K17 (p105) or Duncker (p94), rockabilly at Roadrunners (p96), drum 'n' bass at Icon (p94), or even ballroom dancing at Clärchens Ballhaus (p79). Some

boundaries remain lurred, however. A place like Kaffee Burger (p79) might be literary salon one minute, live venue the next, and end the night as a debauched disco that keeps going until rush hour. Rock and dance have cross-pollinated, as exemplifed by the success of Canadian settler Peaches, or techno miscreants Modeselektor working with Thom Yorke.

Not many live venues in Berlin consistently book top acts, but quite a few are capable of hosting a great live show. Even so, it's impossible to recommend a single location – booking policies vary wildly and venue loyalty is unknown. Fritzclub im Postbahnhof (p104) is where the likes of Arcade Fire or Amy Winehouse might stop off, Dot Club is the place to catch hip hop

Clärchens Ballhaus

legends such as De La Soul or Grandmaster Flash, and stadium acts tend to appear at suburban arenas such as the Olympiastadion (p153) or the Waldbuhne.

Cabaret, meanwhile, is still alive and well, though don't go out looking for the reincarnation of Liza Minelli. The political satire sprinkled with songs and sketches that Berliners call Kabarett is largely impenetrable to outsiders. Acrobats, magicians and dancing girls are the staple of the form called Varieté – Chamäleon (p81) in the Hackesche Höfe is the best place to check this out. Drag cabaret, known as Travestie, isn't as common as many expect it to be, but you can still find a show in the old Berlin tradition at the friendly Kleine Nachtrevue (p126). A more daring kind of cabaret thrives in smaller, more out-of-the-way places such as Scheinbar (p127) in Schöneberg or Café Theater Schalotte (p146) in Charlottenburg.

Dot Club p25

Look out for acts such as Die O-Ton Piraten (clever drag musical theatre that montages famous film dialogues into irrelevant story lines), Gayle Tufts (charming American entertainer who mixes pop music with stand-up in a jumble of German and English) or Bridge Markland (gender-bending dance and poetry).

Finding the party

Though we've listed the best venues, much of what goes on here is beyond the scope of a book like this: once-a-week clubs in crumbling locations, temporary collectives throwing multi-act parties and the like. Much of the scene remains constantly on the move – even more so since the police began harassing improperly licensed venues. Many clubs don't update their websites, or only post the next week's events, and party promoters move from venue to venue.

Berlin's two fortnightly listings magazines, *tip* (www.tip-berlin.de) and *Zitty* (www.zitty.de), do a good job of covering the basics, but there's always something underground or last-minute going on. Look for flyers in shops, bars and cafés, where copies of the city's two free gay magazines, *Siegessäule* (www.siegessaeule.de) and *Blu* (www.blu.fm), can also be picked up. It might also be worth consulting *Exberliner* (www.exberliner.com), Berlin's rather overwritten English-language monthly. The website www.dorfdisco.de covers the local scene in both German and English. There's also plenty of information, though in German only, at www.berlinonline.de. Just remember that, although our listings were correct at the time of going to press, nothing stays the same for very long.

O2 World p30

Arts & Leisure

Though embarrassingly poor when it comes to sports, Berlin is a major performing arts capital with enough classical music and opera for any two normal cities, one of the world's most important film events, a rich and experimental theatre culture, a growing reputation for dance, and a calendar full of festivals. Recession and subsidy squeezes, however, mean that nothing much new is happening in this world.

Orchestral manoeuvres

The Berliner Philharmoniker (www.berliner-philharmoniker.de), based at the Philharmonie (p137) and currently going from strength to strength under the perennially popular Sir Simon Rattle, has long been one of the world's leading orchestras. But the Phil is only the tip of an iceberg that features six other major orchestras, a number of smaller ensembles, and no fewer than three opera houses. The Deutsches Symphonie Orchester (www.dso-berlin.de) is known for its avant-garde programme under the leadership of Ingo Metzmacher. Ground-breaking contemporary work is also the staple of the Rundfunk-Sinfonieorchester Berlin (www.rso-online.de) under Marek Janowski. The old masters are well served by the Konzerthausorchester Berlin (www.konzerthausorchester.de), which plays at the Konzerthaus (p66), though chief conductor Lothar Zagrosek has broadened the orchestra's scope to include some contemporary music. Of the smaller ensembles, the

Get the local experience

Over 50 of the world's top destinations available.

Deutsches Kammerorchester Berlin (www.dko-berlin.de) under manager Stefan Fragner, has an excellent reputation for working with rising-star conductors and soloists, while the Ensemble Oriol (www.ensemble-oriol.de) is a fine group that emphasises contemporary work.

The Staatsoper Unter den Linden (p61) is the grandest of the opera houses, and leaps from one success to another thanks to the popularity of general music director Daniel Barenboim. Musical performances of the highest quality are, however, sometimes marred by overly spectacular staging. Much-needed renovations will begin in 2010 and last for around three years, during which time the Staatsoper will camp out at the Schiller Theater (Bismarckstrasse 110, Charlottenburg). The Komische Oper (p59) has carved out its own niche with controversial and topical productions, while over in Charlottenburg the Deutsche Oper (p146) looks to find a distinctive artistic profile under new musical director Donald Runnicles. Among smaller ensembles, look out for Novoflot (www.novoflot.de), which usually presents its innovative productions at the Sophiensaele (p81).

There are also top-quality festivals throughout the year, including Zeitfenster (p32) and MaerzMusik (p32) in March, for baroque and contemporary music respectively, UltraSchall (p31) for new music, the Classic Open Air (p35) concert series in the Gendarmenmarkt each July, and MusikFest Berlin (p35) in September, which brings some of the world's finest orchestras to Berlin. For something a little different, look out for monthly Yellow Lounge events (www.yellowlounge.de), which feature

SHORTLIST

Best new venues
- O2 World (p105)
- Radialsystem V (p105)

Classic classical
- Konzerthaus (p66)
- Staatsoper Unter den Linden (p61)

Experimental
- HAU (p121)
- Schaubühne am Lehniner Platz (p146)
- Sophiensaele (p81)
- Volksbühne (p81)

Modern classics
- Berliner Ensemble (p70)
- Deutsches Theater (p70)
- Maxim Gorki Theater (p61)
- Philharmonie (p137)
- Renaissance (p146)

English entertainment
- Babylon-Kreuzberg (p114)
- CineStar Sony Center (p137)
- F40 (p117)
- Odeon (p127)

Essential cinemas
- Arsenal (p137)
- Babylon-Mitte (p80)
- Xenon (p127)

DON'T MISS

classical DJs, top-notch VJs and intimate live performances in a nightclub context.

Theatre meets dance

Berlin has long revelled in a reputation for cutting-edge theatre, which dates back to the days of Brecht and Piscator. A solid civic establishment is complemented by a lively fringe and such a general challenging of boundaries that these days it's almost impossible to draw a definite line between dance and theatre. The two forms cohabit under one roof at houses such as HAU (p121), the Sophiensaele (p81), and the Schaübühne am Lehniner Platz (p146). At the latter, Thomas Ostermeier, who has successfully combined dance with theatre for many years, now collaborates with choreographer Constanza Macras on productions such as a recent radical reinterpretation of *A Midsummer Night's Dream*. The rationalisation of three Kreuzberg houses under one artistic umbrella as the HAU (p121) has proved a great success. Elsewhere, the Volksbühne (p81) flies the flag for the avant-garde (look out for productions by Christoph Schlingensief), the Berliner Ensemble mixes modern productions of Brecht with the work of contemporary German-language writers and directors such as Robert Wilson, and the Deutsches Theater is renowned for its high-class productions of the classics. English-language theatre, meanwhile, thrives at F40 (p117) in Kreuzberg. In dance, look out for productions by Sasha Waltz at the new Radialsystem V (p105), and also for pieces by young choreographers Jerome Bel and Jochen Roller.

Cinema city

The Berlin International Film Festival (p32) is one of the world's major movie events, with an International Competition featuring star-studded premières complemented by a wide range of satellite events including a strong new focus on the business of film. But it's not the only film festival on the calendar. Summer's Fantasy Film Festival (p35) premieres the latest in fantasy, sci-fi and horror from around the world. The same bunch are behind Verzaubert: The International Queer Film Festival (p36), which showcases gay and lesbian cinema every November and December.

Mainstream Hollywood movies are mostly dubbed into German, but the CineStar Original in the Sony Center is a multiplex devoted to showing films in their original language. Movies in the original English can also be found at Schöneberg's Odeon Kino (p127) and the Babylon Kreuzberg (p114). Also in the Sony Center, the two-screen Arsenal (p137) has an eclectic programme of non-mainstream cinematic fare from every corner of the globe.

Sporting events

With just one team in the German top division, Hertha BSC (www. herthabsc.de), and no likely contenders in the lower leagues, the city that in 2006 hosted the FIFA World Cup Final has less decent football per capita than just about any comparable metropolis. It's difficult for the outsider to love Hertha, but it's not hard to get tickets for their games at the Olympiastadion (p153). Hertha usually place high enough to qualify for the UEFA Europa League.

By contrast, ALBA (www.alba berlin.de), the city's basketball team, are one of Germany's most successful, while EHC Eisbären Berlin (www.eisbaeren.de) compete creditably in the German ice-hockey league. Both ALBA and the Eisbären play their home games at the new O2 Arena. Major events on the Berlin sporting calendar are the Deutschland Pokal-Endspiel, the final of the German football cup at the Olympiastadion, and September's Berlin Marathon, one of the world's largest. The Qatar Telecom German Open, a clay-court women's tennis tournament that used to attract most of the big names, is, as of 2009, no more.

Calendar

Popkomm p35

The following are the pick of the annual events that take place in Berlin. Further information and exact dates can be found nearer the time in the city's two fortnightly listings magazines, *tip* and *Zitty*, or from leaflets and flyers regularly distributed to bars and restaurants around the city. Dates highlighted in **bold** are public holidays.

January

Ongoing Spielzeiteuropa (see Oct)

1 Neujahrstag (New Year's Day)

Early Jan **Tanztage**
Sophiensaele
www.tanztage.de
A two-week dance and choreography event highlighting new local talent.

Mid-late Jan **Internationale Grüne Woche**
Messegelände am Funkturm
www.gruenewoche.de

Overindulge, for ten whole days, on food and drink from all corners of Germany and around the world.

Mid Jan **UltraSchall**
Radialsytem V
www.radialsystem.de
Ten-day festival of new and avant-garde music at a new and avant-garde venue. Some concerts are broadcast live.

Late Jan **Bread & Butter**
Tempelhof airport
www.breadandbutter.com
The cutting-edge three-day fashion-industry trade fair has now returned to Berlin from Barcelona, and occupies some of the hangars of the former Tempelhof airport. See also July.

Late Jan **Lange Nacht der Museen**
Citywide
www.lange-nacht-der-museen.de
For one evening in January, around 200 museums stay open late for visitors and stage special events for the occasion. Shuttle buses connect the institutions.

February

Ongoing Spielzeiteuropa (see Oct)

Early Feb **Transmediale**
Akademie der Künste
www.transmediale.de
Massive three- to five-day event show-casing media art and digital culture.

Mid Feb **Berlin International Film Festival**
Various venues
www.berlinale.de
One of the world's most important film festivals attracts A-list stars, high-lights more obscure branches of film, and is a major business jamboree.

March

Mar (date varies) **MaerzMusik – Festival für aktuelle Musik**
Various venues
www.berlinerfestspiele.de
A festival of contemporary music from international avant-garde musicians and composers.

Mid Mar **International Tourism Fair**
Messegelände am Funkturm
www.itb-berlin.de
Tourism boards, travel agents and hotel chains have stalls at this huge five-day travel industry event.

April

Mar/Apr (date varies) **Karfreitag (Good Friday)**

Mar/Apr (date varies) **Oster Montag (Easter Monday)**

Apr **Zeitfenster – Biennale für alte Musik**
Konzerthaus
www.zeitfenster.net
A one-week biennial (2010, 2012) festival of music dating from the 16th and 17th centuries.

May

1 **Tag der Arbeit (Labour Day)**

May (date varies) **Himmelfahrt (Ascension Day)**

May (date varies) **Pfingstmontag (Whit Monday/Pentecost)**

Early May **Deutschland Pokal-Endspiel**
Olympiastadion
tickets@dfb.de
Germany's domestic football cup final in the nation's showpiece arena.

May (date varies) **Theatertreffen Berlin**
Haus der Berliner Festspiele
www.berlinerfestspiele.de
Performances by winners of contemporary German-speaking theatre competition, spread over three weeks.

May/June **Karneval der Kulturen**
Kreuzberg
www.karneval-berlin.de
A colourful four-day multicultural celebration with a huge Sunday parade. See box p33.

Berlin International Film Festival

Berlinale Palast

May/June **Haus der Kulturen der Welt**
www.hkw.de
Two-week festival of dance and performance from outside Europe.

June

June **Berlin Philharmonie at the Waldbühne**
Waldbühne
www.berlin-philharmonic.com
A candle-lit open-air classical concert in an atmospheric forest theatre closes the Berlin Phil's season.

Mid June **International Aerospace Exhibition & Conference**
Flughafen Schönefeld
www.ila-berlin.de
Popular biennial (2010, 2012) air show features exhibitors from 40 countries.

21 **Fête de la Musique**
Various venues
www.fetedelamusique.de
A summer solstice music event featuring a wide range of DJs and bands.

Weekend before Christopher Street Day **Schwul-Lesbisches Strassenfest**
Nollendorfplatz and around
www.regenbogenfonds.de
A gay and lesbian street fair that takes over Schöneberg every year.

Sat late June **Christopher Street Day Parade**
Route ending at Brandenburger Tor
www.csd-berlin.de
Berlin's big, bold gay and lesbian pride march ends up for the first time in 2010 at the Brandenburg Gate, where there's a concert and party. The new route had not been confirmed at press time.

July

July-Oct **Museumsinselfestival**
Museumsinsel and other venues
www.museumsinselfestival.info

Carnival culture

Equal parts multicultural showcase and raucous block party, the **Karneval der Kulturen der Welt** (Carnival of World Cultures; p32) takes place in May, mostly in Kreuzberg. Half a million non-Germans from more than 180 countries call Berlin home, and the capital has the highest percentage of immigrants of any city in Germany; established in 1996, this four-day street festival is a celebration of Berlin's cultural and ethnic diversity.

The event is replete with theatre, dance and music performances as well as an eclectic mix of international food, crafts and activities. Hundreds of associations and institutions participate, from theatres to art schools, community clubs to ethnic associations. Groups from over 70 countries dance and drum their way from Hermannplatz to the Yorckstrasse U-Bahn station in the half-day parade that is the event's main focus.

Although the diverse blend of food, music and costume is the basis of the event, it's also simply a joyous spring bash. Near the end of the parade, party-floats from Berlin's hippest clubs roll slowly through the Kreuzberg streets, gathering revellers in their wake. The whole shebang ends in cacophonous carousing at Yorckstrasse station. A perfect overture for the Berlin summer party season.

DON'T MISS

Art Forum Berlin

As hyped as Berlin's art world is, it's never been a city with a lot of local art-collector cash. But that doesn't mean that art's commercial side doesn't deserve an annual marketplace.

Taking place each autumn, **Art Forum Berlin** (p35) began as the German capital's first fair for international contemporary art back in 1996. Since then, the long, late September weekend on which the Forum takes place has exploded into a city-wide art extravaganza that both attracts and takes advantage of visiting collectors, curators and art-lovers from all over the world.

In recent years, satellite fairs such as Preview (www.preview berlin.de), Berliner Liste (www. berliner-liste.org) and Berliner Kunstsalon (www.kunstsalon.de) have also sprung up to show emerging work. The two-year-old Art Berlin Contemporary (www. artberlincontemporary.com), or ABC, stages high-concept exhibitions – in 2009, each participating gallery featured one artist's work on a two-metre by one-metre table. Then there are big museum shows, or special exhibitions in galleries that aren't participating in the fair but want a piece of the action. Parties go down in bunkers, glass buildings or other unusual venues.

It all sounds fabulous, and it can be. But in 2008, Art Forum Berlin hit some obstacles. The art-market bubble was imploding along with the world economy, sales were down, and some galleries were grumbling about how the fair was run. Enter new management in 2009. Peter Vetsch and Eva-Maria Häusler from Art Basel expanded the event's focus to include a section on works dating back to 1960, another featuring galleries younger than five years old, and another that showcases outdoor displays and installations. Along with setting a more professional tone, the new leaders have aimed to attract a serious clientele.

Berlin has long been known as a 'producers' city', meaning this is a place where artists come to create their work. Considering the local economy, it's unlikely to become a town for collectors any time soon. But Art Forum weekend shows that Berlin is happy to roll out the red carpet for them anyway.

Season of open-air performances, from rock and classical concerts to readings, plays and film screenings.

Early July **Classic Open Air**
Gendarmenmarkt
www.classicopenair.de
This four- to seven-day big-name classical music concert series is held in Berlin's most exquisite square.

Early July **Yoga-Festival Berlin**
Kulturpark Kladow
www.yogafestival.de
Om-tastic weekend with sessions led by teachers from around the world, plus music and a market.

Mid July **Bread & Butter**
Tempelhof airport
www.breadandbutter.com
The summertime edition of the January fashion fair, over three days (see Jan).

August

Ongoing Museumsinselfestival (see July)

Aug (date varies)
young.euro.classic
Konzerthaus
www.young-euro-classic.de
Two weeks of concerts by youth orchestras from around Europe.

1st weekend Aug **Internationales Berliner Bierfestival**
Karl-Marx-Allee
www.bierfestival-berlin.de
Hundreds of beers from 60 countries, served at stalls.

Early Aug **Fantasy Film Festival**
CinemaxX Potsdamer Platz
www.fantasyfilmfest.com
The latest in splatter, science-fiction, fantasy, thriller and horror films.

2nd half Aug **Tanz im August**
Various venues
www.tanzimaugust.de

Germany's leading modern dance festival offers big names and new trends.

Late Aug/early Sept **Kreuzberger Festliche Tage**
Viktoriapark
www.kreuzberger-festliche-tage.de
Two weeks of music, games, beer, food and family fun.

September

Ongoing Kreuzberger Festliche Tage (see Aug), Museumsinselfestival (see July)

Sept (date varies) **Popkomm**
Messegelände am Funkturm
www.popkomm.de
After a year off in 2009, this major music industry event is scheduled to return in a new format in 2010. There's a trade fair and concerts all over town.

Early Sept **Lange Nacht der Museen**
Citywide
www.lange-nacht-der-museen.de
Around 200 museums stay open late and stage special events.

Early Sept **Musikfest Berlin**
Philharmonie
www.berlinerfestspiele.de
The Berlin Symphony Orchestra collaborates with the Berlin Philharmonic in this two-week festival, which also includes orchestras from Europe and the US.

Mid Sept **Internationales Literaturfestival Berlin**
Haus der Berliner Festspiele
www.literaturfestival.com
Big names and new authors in a major literary feast of readings, symposia and discussions over two weeks.

Late Sept/early Oct
Art Forum Berlin
Messegelände am Funkturm
www.art-forum-berlin.de

Five-day contemporary art trade fair bringing together gallerists and artists. See box p34.

Last Sun **Berlin Marathon**
Citywide
www.berlin-marathon.com
Berlin's marathon route takes runners past most of the city's major sights.

October

Ongoing Art Forum (see Sept)

Oct-Feb **Spielzeiteuropa**
Haus der Berliner Festspiele
www.berlinerfestspiele.de
Five months of new theatre and dance from across Europe.

3 **Tag der Deutschen Einheit (Day of German Unity)**

Mid Oct **Venus Berlin**
Messegelände am Funkturm
www.venus-berlin.com
Three-day trade fair and awards ceremony for the adult entertainment industry.

Late Oct **Berliner Märchentage**
Various venues
The Berlin Fairytale Days celebrate tales from around the world with some 400 storytelling and music events.

Late Oct/early Nov **JazzFest Berlin**
Various venues
www.berlinerfestspiele.de
A wide-ranging four-day jazz event with internationally renowned artists.

November

Ongoing Spielzeiteuropa (see Oct)

1 **All Saints' Day**

Nov-Dec **Christmas markets**
Various locations
www.weihnachtsmarkt-deutschland.de

Gallons of mulled wine and stalls selling toys, gifts and sausages spread a festive mood across the city.

Late Nov **Buss- und Bettag (Day of Repentance and Prayer)**

Late Nov **Worldtronics**
Haus der Kulturen der Welt
www.hkw.de
Three-day festival showcasing electronic music from around the world, plus trade fair and exhibition.

Late Nov-mid Dec **Verzaubert: International Queer Film Festival**
Kino International, Karl-Marx-Allee
www.verzaubertfilmfest.com
The latest gay and lesbian films from around the world.

December

Ongoing Christmas markets (see Nov), Spielzeiteuropa (see Oct), Verzaubert: International Queer Film Festival (see Nov)

24 **Heiliger Abend (Christmas Eve)**
Almost everything closes from early evening as Germans retreat indoors to feast and exchange gifts.

25 **Weihnachten (Christmas Day)**

26 **Stephanstag (St Stephen's Day/Boxing Day)**

31 **Berliner Silvesterlauf**
Starts in the Grunewald
www.berlin-marathon.com
Traditional New Year's Eve fun run for the fit and the fearless.

31 **Silvester (New Year's Eve)**
Citywide
Mayhem at the Brandenburg Gate with crazed revellers tossing firecrackers all over the place, but Berlin's parks offer plenty of more sedate – and safer – events.

Itineraries

The Memory Trail

Berlin's tumultuous 20th-century history has proven fertile ground for a thriving culture of remembrance, and its position in the present as a node of global creativity has translated into a memorial landscape as challenging as it is diverse. The spectrum ranges from impromptu, low-budget projects by avant-garde artists to expansive, government-funded affairs built by world-renowned architects. Some are conceptual, others concrete; some are experimental, others traditional. They commemorate a wide range of people, victims and events, and have sparked political controversy and public debate.

Allow a day for this itinerary, which focuses on World War II-era memorials in the city centre. You will be passing through areas heavily frequented by both locals and tourists, so there will be no shortage of refreshment stops along the way.

It begins at the **Denkmal für die ermordeten Juden Europas** (Memorial to the Murdered Jews of Europe; p55); if you need a rendezvous point, there is a row of cafés along Cora-Berliner-Strasse on its eastern side. Berlin's most central and arguably most ambitious monument, this undulating grid of tilting stelae spreads across 19,000 square metres of prime real estate just south of the Brandenburg Gate. Designed by Peter Eisenman and inaugurated in May 2005, the €25 million construction serves as the city's principal Holocaust memorial, complete with a subterranean Place of Information with a sombre and powerful exhibition.

Cross the street towards the Tiergarten at the south-west corner of the memorial, where Ebertstrasse meets Hannah-Arendt-Strasse. Follow a short dirt path into the park to find Michael Elmgreen and Ingar Dragset's **Memorial to the Homosexual Victims of**

Denkmal für die ermordeten Juden Europas

National Socialism, a concrete slab erected among the trees in May 2008. Take a moment to watch the video loop inside the unadorned cuboid before heading back on to Ebertstrasse and walking north towards the Brandenburg Gate.

Turn left on to the broad unnamed path leading back into Tiergarten, just past the Strasse des 17. Juni. Notice the double line of cobblestones that cuts through the intersection, marking the route of the Wall that once stood here. Walking into **Tiergarten**, you'll see on the right the site of a planned memorial to the Roma and Sinti victims of Nazism. Though ground has already been broken, the only thing standing is a wooden sign announcing the coming memorial – testament to the often contentious politics of memory that has stalled the project for years.

Detour briefly down the path that diverges to the left, and you'll find the 1945 **Sowjetisches Ehrenmal** (Soviet War Memorial), or just keep heading straight until you reach the **Reichstag**. Out front, you'll see an arrangement of stone tablets. This is

a **memorial to the murdered Members of Parliament** – 96 opposition party politicians killed by the Nazis. Walk clockwise around the building and notice the bullet holes and graffiti scrawled by Soviet soldiers, purposely left as reminders of a violent past. At the north-east corner of the building, you'll find **two small memorials** – a plaque thanking Hungary for opening its western border to East Germans in 1989, and a slab of the wall of Gdansk shipyard, birthplace of the Polish trade union Solidarity – both of which made crucial contributions to the end of the Cold War and German reunification. Look down towards the water, and you'll see a memorial of **seven white crosses** dedicated to those killed trying to escape from East to West Berlin.

Coming around the building, you'll find yourself back at Ebertstrasse. Follow it to the Brandenburg Gate, walk through, and continue on to Unter den Linden. Here you can walk a few blocks (which means you can stop for refreshment at **Café Einstein** on the corner of Neustadtkirchstrasse; p135) or take a bus two stops (to Staatsoper, and then walk back a few yards in the direction you have just come) to arrive at **Bebelplatz** on the south side of Unter den Linden. At its centre, you'll find a glass plate set into the ground, through which you can view an underground room of empty white bookcases. This is Israeli artist Micha Ullman's **Bibliotek**, a memorial to the notorious Nazi book-burning that took place here in 1933. A line from Heinrich Heine is engraved several times around the perimeter of the square: 'Where they burn books, they ultimately burn people.'

Across the street, you'll find the **Neue Wache**. A neoclassical

ITINERARIES

Missing House

building by Schinkel dating from 1816, it was rededicated in 1993 as the Central Memorial of the Federal Republic of Germany to the Victims of War and Tyranny. The single room houses a moving enlarged replica of a Käthe Kollwitz sculpture called *Mother with Dead Son*, under which the remains of an unknown German soldier and unknown concentration camp victim are enshrined.

Keep heading east along Unter den Linden, which soon becomes Karl-Liebknecht-Strasse. Take a left on to a small side street called Rosenstrasse, and enter the park on your left. There, you'll find Ingeborg Hunzinger's **Block der Frauen** (Block of Women), a memorial to the thousands of non-Jewish women in mixed marriages who gathered at this site in February 1943 to demand the release of their husbands, who were being detained by the Nazis in a Jewish community building. After five days of protest, the men were miraculously released back to their loved ones.

Cutting diagonally across the park, you come to the **site of Berlin's oldest synagogue**, where a commemorative plaque tells the history of the building

that stood here from 1714 to 1945. Take a right out of the park on to Heidereutergasse and walk back towards Rosenstrasse, where you'll see a **rose-coloured advertising column** bearing information (in German only) about the events that took pace here.

Next stop is the **Gedenkstätte Stille Helden** (Silent Heroes Memorial) near the Hackescher Höfe. To get there, walk north down Rosenstrasse away from the park and take a right on An der Spandauer Brücke. Follow this street until you reach Rosenthaler Strasse, on to which you'll take a right. On the left side, just past Starbucks, you'll see something called **Cinema Courtyard**, with a sign for the Anne Frank Center. As you walk in the courtyard, notice the Stolpersteine ('stumbling stones'), set into the pavement at your feet. These small brass plaques, found all over Berlin, mark the homes of people persecuted by the Nazis and are engraved with the name, birth date and death date (if known) of the person who lived there. The project was conceived by sculptor Gunter Demnig in 1996.

As you enter the courtyard, you'll see a small door on your left. Take this up to the **Silent Heroes Memorial**, a permanent exhibition commemorating those who hid and otherwise helped Jews persecuted by the Nazi regime. Free of charge, the two-storey centre is full of compelling documentation of heroism and resistance.

Deeper into the courtyard, you'll find the **Museum Blindenwerkstatt Otto Weidt** (Museum of Otto Weidt's Workshop for the Blind), where a free exhibition documents the story of one such silent hero and the Jewish employees he risked his life to protect. Consisting of five small rooms and a short film, the museum

Der Verlassene Raum

is informative and manageable. You can stop for beer or tea at the cosy Café Cinema on your way out of the courtyard.

When you re-emerge on to Rosenthaler Strasse, turn right and walk to the corner, then right again on to Oranienburger Strasse. Take the first right on to Grosse Hamburger Strasse and on the right you'll find the remains of Berlin's **oldest Jewish Cemetery**, first dedicated in 1672 and still the last resting-place of German-Jewish philosopher Moses Mendelssohn. There's a plaque commemorating the Jewish old-age home that once stood here, an information board detailing the history of the cemetery, and a memorial to the 55,000 Jews who were held here by the Gestapo before deportation to Auschwitz and Theresienstadt. Notice that the ground on which the memorial stands pays homage to the fallen building: red bricks follow the lines of the original foundation, and rubble from the demolished home was deliberately left in the spaces between the lines.

Further down Grosse Hamburger Strasse, you'll find the **Missing House** on the left. The empty space was once home to an apartment building destroyed during World War II. When French artist Christian Boltanski came across the site in 1990, he learned that many of the building's former residents had been Jews; in their honour, he dedicated this memorial to 'absence'. The signs on the adjacent buildings show the names of the former residents along with their dates of birth and death, their occupations, and the approximate locations of their apartments within the building.

Follow Grosse Hamburger Strasse even further north, and you'll wind up at **Koppenplatz**, the last stop on this itinerary. At the far end of the small park is **Der Verlassene Raum** (The Deserted Room), a simple but effective bronze sculpture by Karl Biedermann erected in commemoration of Kristallnacht. Across the park at Koppenplatz 6, a plaque hanging in the building's courtyard offers lines from the Baal Shem Tov: 'To forget is banishment. To remember is salvation.' A family tree is painted on the wall behind the plaque, a memorial to the building's former Jewish owners, most of whom lost their lives in the Holocaust.

Strausberger Platz

Socialism Safari

In the 20 years since German reunification in 1990, much of east Berlin, especially in its central areas, has received a westernising makeover. But four decades of communism, during which most of the city was raised from post-war rubble, has left its mark. Districts such as Lichtenberg and Hohenschönhausen don't feature much in guidebooks, but it's here that you get the feeling that the Wall might never have fallen, and you don't have to travel far out of the city centre to get a taste of what life was like behind the Iron Curtain.

Leave a day free for our tour through some of the more notable remnants of the former German Democratic Republic (GDR). We start at **Alexanderplatz**, the focal point of east Berlin, and a good place to begin is at the **Weltzeituhr** (World Time Clock) on the east side of the square. Topped with a sort of giant atom and showing the time in an

assortment of locations that citizens of communist Berlin were never allowed to visit, this has long been a popular meeting point.

There's still enough communist architecture around here to get a flavour of what the GDR was like: the towering Park Inn hotel, the eye-catching fountain and, of course, the iconic Fernsehturm (TV Tower; p82). But renovation has robbed the Galeria department store of its communist character, the new Saturn store disrupts the square's former sightlines, and the modernist buildings near the Weltzeituhr, between which the tram lines pass, date from the 1920s rather than the 1960s.

Facing the Saturn store and with the Weltzeituhr behind you, bear right and cross Grunerstrasse towards the Alexa mall; on the other side, turn left. You are on the corner of the **Berliner Congress Center**, a beautiful domed building that was the GDR's main exhibition hall. With the Alexa behind you, continue to the next building, the **Haus des Lehrers**. A landmark work of socialist-realist architecture, it's remarkable for the period mosaic on the façade idealising the hardworking citizens of the GDR.

Continue past the Haus des Lehrers and take a right. You are now on the wide, tree-lined **Karl-Marx-Allee**. This monumental boulevard, built between 1951 and 1954 in Russian socialist-realist style, was originally named Stalinallee and re-christened Karl-Marx-Allee in 1961. Centrepiece of communist cityscaping, this is one of east Berlin's main axes. After about five minutes' walk you'll reach U-Bahn Schillingstraße. On the opposite side of the street is **Kino International**, once the main cinema for East Berlin showing movies from the socialist states. The roof of the block to the right of the cinema bears two rare surviving examples of period advertising; signs for LKW Tatra and Motkov cars. Standing opposite the cinema you are beside the former Café Moskau. In the early 1960s, this was a lively café and haunt of the GDR art scene. If you need to refuel, cross the street; next to Kino International is a row of cafés snuggled under shady trees.

Switch back to the south side of Karl-Marx-Allee and continue walking away from Alexanderplatz. You'll soon reach a large roundabout, **Strausberger Platz**. This marks a change in architecture from minimalist buildings to an earlier, more ornamental style. Keep right and make your way over the pedestrian crossings to head directly over the roundabout. At the other side on your right is a bust of Karl Marx. The GDR – indeed, most of the eastern bloc – was once filled with

statues of communist heroes; this is one of the few remaining in Berlin. Continue along the boulevard and, just after you pass Andreasstrasse, you will reach the **Karl Marx Buchhandlung**, once the biggest book store in East Berlin. Although it is now the offices of the Architectural Association, you can still peer inside and see the original fittings. This was the place used as a bookshop location at the ending of the film *The Lives of Others*.

If it's clocking lunchtime, cross Karl-Marx-Allee and head to the furthermost entrance to U-Bahn Weberwiese. There's a row of nice restaurants here, including Mexican and Greek places, and the Czech restaurant **Prager Hopfenstube** (p102), which perhaps best suits the theme of our tour. A block beyond is the former **Kosmos Kino**, which still has its original striking façade.

Continue down the street and you'll soon reach a busy intersection marked on either side by green-domed towers. This is **Frankfurter Tor**. From this point there's a change in architecture and atmosphere. The street narrows, boasts more shops and bars and is filled with more people. To dive back into the real GDR, jump on to the U5 at U-Bahn Frankfurter Tor, take the train in the direction of Hönow, and hop off after three stops at U-Bahn Magdalenenstrasse. Follow the signs for Ruschestrasse and you will emerge from the station into **Frankfurter Allee**; carry straight on and take the first right into **Ruschestrasse**. In this street is the former headquarters of the **Ministry for State Security** (Stasi). Once the most secure area in East Berlin, it is now a museum; however, it's badly signposted. Once you turn into Ruschestrasse stay on the right-hand side.

ITINERARIES

Landsberger Allee

Halfway up the street between Frankfurter Allee behind you and Normannenstrasse ahead is what looks, on the right, like the entrance to a hospital. A walk to the back of this yard brings you to the imposing façade of the former Stasi headquarters and the entrance to the **Stasi Museum** (p153), more properly known as the Forschungs- und Gedänkstätte Normannenstrasse. Here you can while away an hour or two investigating espionage in East Germany in a building largely untouched since the GDR collapsed – the offices of former spy boss Erich Mielke have been left exactly as they were. Once you're done learning about one of the world's densest surveillance networks, leave the museum and retrace your steps back to Frankfurter Allee.

Here you can simply wander back towards Alexanderplatz on foot (the Fernsehturm is always in sight ahead to guide your way), or jump back on to the U5; Alexanderplatz is the last station on this line. If you're hungry for more GDR delights, then, with

U-Bahn Magdalenestrasse behind you, head down Frankfurter Allee and turn right into **Möllendorffstrasse**. Here you'll see a tram stop (S + U Frankfurter Allee). Take the M13 (direction Wedding/Virchow Klinikum) north through the Lichtenberg district. Enjoy the ride through residential east Berlin with its wealth of communist-era *Plattenbauten* (tower blocks); some are very striking, such as the blue and white checked block on the right just as the tram crosses Herzbergstrasse. Ride this tram for six stops – approximately ten minutes – and jump off at the stop for Hohenschönhausenstrasse/ Weissenseer Weg.

You are now in the residential district of **Hohenschönhausen**, a jungle of blocky, socialist architecture. The outskirts of just about every city in communist eastern Europe were rebuilt pretty much like this. When you get off the tram, turn left into Hohenschönhausenstrasse and you'll find another tram stop. Here catch the M6 heading towards

Hellersdorf/Riesaer Strasse. This tram snakes through still more tower blocks interspersed with communal parkland. Ride for three stops, disembarking at **Genslerstrasse**. Here you have the opportunity to learn more about the Stasi by visiting its former remand prison. It's about a five-minute walk (approximately 450 metres) from the tram stop. Once you leave the tram, turn right, cross the tracks and bear right along the front of the shopping centre. At the end, turn left into Genslerstrasse and follow the street. East Berlin suddenly changes here; the hulking tower blocks are replaced by cobbled streets and cute, detached houses. You are actually walking into yet another former high security zone. This area was inhabited by Stasi officers – and mostly still is today.

You will soon arrive at the forbidding walls and observation towers of the former Hohenschönhausen prison, today the **Gedänkstätte Berlin-Hohenschönhausen** (p150). Here you can learn about Stasi surveillance and interrogation as well as being shown around the cells and interrogation rooms. Most of the original fixtures and fittings remain intact and the 90-minute guided tours (English ones can be arranged in advance, or otherwise take place at 2pm on Saturdays and 2.30pm on Wednesdays) are conducted by former inmates who can speak about prison conditions and interrogation techniques. It all adds up to a bleakly authentic experience.

Afterwards, retrace your steps to the tram stop. Jump on to the M6 (direction Plugstrasse) and use this 20-minute journey back to Mitte to enjoy the sights of east Berlin. Directly opposite the tram stop is a giant pumping station of the **Berliner Wasserbetriebe**

Osseria

(water board). Built in the late 1800s, this Gothic red-brick compound provides an interesting contrast to the grey, post-war architecture that dominates this area. The tram takes you along **Landsberger Allee** (once Leninallee), lined with trees and yet more *Plattenbauten*. You'll gradually see the change from the bare, residential districts of the GDR to brighter, more commercial areas as the tram heads west. Keep your eyes open at the Landsberger Allee/Petersburger Strasse stop; on the right is the spectacular zig-zag architecture of the SEZ sports centre, built in the 1980s, a popular workout area for east Berliners. Stay on this tram for a further five stops (approximately ten minutes), and you'll arrive back to **Alexanderplatz**.

If you haven't yet had a bellyful of communism, you can always hop on an M3 tram and head up to Weissensee and the **Osseria** restaurant, where you can try the nearest thing to an authentic communist-era dinner that Berlin currently has to offer. See box p95.

ITINERARIES

Fernsehturm p48

The U2 Tour

The U2 underground line connects the centres of east and west Berlin, juxtaposing their sights, department stores and sausage stands, stopping off at the new, unifying quarter that is Potsdamer Platz. On the central stretch – the oldest portion of the Berlin U-Bahn – there are some beautiful stations and something interesting to be found near just about every stop. Here we present the highlights. How much you cram into one day is a matter of stamina, specific interest and the amount of shopping you manage to acquire along the way.

First you need a ticket. The standard €2.10 BVG fare will buy you two hours' travel in one direction. A day pass for the central zones is €6.10. Either is available from any of the ticket machines at any of the stations.

Start at **Zoologischer Garten** – more commonly known as 'Bahnhof Zoo' or 'Zoo Station', and as such the

title of a song by the other U2. It's no longer a stop for intercity and international trains, but for decades this was where arrivals from the West would emerge to find – after transit through the drabness of East Germany – a surprisingly colourful commercial downtown.

It's still the centre of west Berlin. **Stilwerk** (p144), the interior design mall, is a short walk along Kantstrasse. Glitzy **Kurfürstendamm**, main avenue of the west, begins two blocks to the south. And west Berlin's signature sight, the **Kaiser-Wilhelm Gedächtnis-Kirche** (p138), a church left partially ruined to memorialise wartime destruction, is around the corner. Allow an hour or two if you want to explore the actual **Zoo** (p134), across the busy bus interchange outside the station. On the other side of the tracks, the new **Museum für Fotografie** (p140) and home to the Helmut Newton Foundation is on Jebenstrasse.

Wittenbergplatz, next station east, is a nicely restored art nouveau building. **KaDeWe** (p126), continental Europe's largest department store, is right outside. Its legendary sixth-floor foodhall has a number of stands where you can snack on oysters or drink a glass of champagne. Opposite, on the north-west corner of the square, more down-to-earth fare can be consumed at **Witty's** (p125), a sausage stand offering fine organic Currywurst and possibly the best chips in Berlin. On this side of the square on Thursdays, there's also a small farmers' market.

The train surfaces before **Nollendorfplatz**, main station for the western gay district – **Motzstrasse**, leading south-west, is its main thoroughfare. The theatre on the square was the legendary Metropol club in the 1980s, and venue for Erwin Piscator's political theatre experiments in the 1920s. It currently houses **Goya** (p126). There are cafés and boutiques along lively Maasenstrasse, and a splendid, popular market in **Winterfeldtplatz** (p126) every Wednesday and Saturday. Erich Kästner's *Emil and the Detectives* was mostly set in Nollendorfplatz, and Christopher Isherwood lived around the corner at Nollendorfstrasse 17 when living through the times that he would later fictionalise in *Goodbye to Berlin*, the novel that provided the basis for the movie *Cabaret*. On the south-facing wall of the station is a **memorial plaque** to gay and lesbian victims of the Nazis.

Between **Bülowstrasse** and **Gleisdreieck**, look north for a wide-angle view of Potsdamer Platz's postmodern skyline. U2 the group recorded *Achtung Baby!* – as Bowie recorded *Heroes* – at Hansa Studios, Köthener Strasse 38, a block away from Mendelssohn-

Friedrichstrasse p48

Bartholdy-Park station. The studios are now the Meistersaal, a small concert hall for chamber music. After here, we pass from east to west and the U2 line goes back underground. This section was closed while the Wall was up, and Potsdamer Platz station lay unused under no-man's land.

Alight here to view the single biggest architectural project of the post-Wall era, a whole new city quarter, intended to bring together east and west, but part of neither. Helmut Jahn's tented Sony Center has become a popular public space, and contains two key cinemas: the **Cinestar** multiplex (p137), where Hollywood product is shown in original English, and the **Arsenal** (p137), cineastes' favourite. There are plenty of places to stop and snack around here, and more in the Daimler Quarter and Arkaden mall on the other side of Potsdamer Strasse. From here it's a short walk up Ebertstrasse to the **Denkmal für die Ermordeten Juden Europas** (p38).

One exit from **Stadtmitte** station emerges on to

Alexanderplatz

ITINERARIES

Friedrichstrasse, mainstream shopping mile of the east, close to Galeries Lafayette (p65) and Quartier 206 (p66). The other exit is at the south-west corner of the **Gendarmenmarkt**. Here are the **Deutscher Dom** (p63) and the **Französischer Dom/ Huguenottenmuseum** (p63) and a profusion of upmarket venues for lunch, including **Borchardt** (p64), **Lutter & Wegner** (p65) and **Vau** (p65).

Three stops further east, the platforms at **Märkisches Museum** station are tiled with maps showing the growth of Berlin. Just east of the next stop, **Klosterstrasse**, are the only remains of the medieval Berlin wall, the Stadtmauer. Set into the 14th-century ruins is the 17th-century pub Zur Letzten Instanz. It takes its name from the nearby law court, from which there was no further appeal. At the north end of Klosterstrasse are the ruins of the Franciscan Klosterkirche, an unrestored victim of World War II.

Alexanderplatz station is the most complex on the network and it's easy to get lost in its warren of

tunnels. This is the hub of east Berlin and, overground, the busy square, dominated by the iconic **Fernsehturm** (p82), still retains some of the atmosphere of a communist-era showpiece.

Rosa-Luxemburg-Platz is the stop for the east end of the fashionable Scheunenviertel. From here you can walk down Rosa-Luxemburg-Strasse, past the impressive modernist bulk of east Berlin's landmark avant-garde theatre, the **Volksbühne** (p81), browse the boutiques of Münzstrasse and Alte and Neue Schönhauser Strasse, dip into the Jugendstil courtyards of the **Hackesche Höfe** and, if you're getting hungry, seek East Asian refreshment at hip **Monsieur Vuong** (p75) or **Pan Asia** (p75).

The U2 continues north into Prenzlauer Berg. From the next stop, **Senefelderplatz**, a short walk up **Kollwitzstrasse** leads into the chic neighbourhood around Kollwitzplatz. The line emerges overground before the stop after that, **Eberswalder Strasse**, which stands at the nexus of several crucial thoroughfares. **Kastanienallee** to the south-west is the alternative artery connecting the scenes of Prenzlauer Berg and north Mitte. Danziger Strasse runs to the east, and a left turn up Lychener Strasse leads into what's known, after the initials of its main thoroughfares, as the **'LSD' district**. In both of these directions there are too many cafés, bars and restaurants to list right here, but it's a perfect place to end the day, or kick off an evening. You can also sample an eastern-style Currywurst at the eternally popular **Konnopke's Imbiss** (p90), which has been serving sausages under the overhead tracks just south of the station under the same family management since the 1930s.

Berlin by Area

Berliner Dom

Mitte

BERLIN BY AREA

The centre of Berlin – historically, culturally, scenically and administratively – Mitte is what it says it is: the 'middle'. Unter den Linden and Friedrichstrasse are its two main axes, running respectively east–west and north–south. Friedrichstrasse is a narrow and busy commercial artery. The Linden is a grand avenue lined with solemn public buildings, and arrives in the east, after changing its name, at Alexanderplatz – centre of old East Berlin and a key urban hub. South and east of here are scattered points of interest. The main action is to the north of the borough, in the lanes of the Scheunenviertel and beyond.

Unter den Linden & Museumsinsel

Unter den Linden runs east from the Brandenburg Gate, passing museums and embassies, opera houses and cathedrals. The name comes from the lime trees (Linden) that shade the central walkway. Its 18th- and 19th-century neoclassical and baroque buildings were mostly rubble after World War II, but the majority have been restored. The Linden arrives at Museumsinsel, the island in the Spree where Berlin was born and, as the name suggests, home to some important collections. It was also the site of the recently demolished Palast der Republik, East Germany's parliament building. The site is currently home to the Temporäre Künsthalle (see box p60) and will eventually be replaced by a reconstruction of the old Prussian Stadtschloss that stood here until the 1950s.

Sights & museums

Alte Nationalgalerie

Bodestrasse 1-3 (266 424 242/www. alte-nationalgalerie.de). S5, S7, S9, S75

Hackescher Markt. **Open** 10am-6pm Tue, Wed, Fri-Sun; 10am-10pm Thur. **Admission** €8; €4 reductions. No credit cards. **Map** p53 D3 ❶

With its ceiling and wall paintings, fabric wallpapers and marble staircase, the Old National Gallery is a sparkling home to one of the largest collections of 19th-century art and sculpture in Germany. Among the 440 paintings and 80 sculptures, which span the period from Goethe to early Modern, German artists such as Adolph Menzel, Caspar David Friedrich, Max Liebermann and Carl Spitzweg are well represented. There are also some first-rank early Impressionist works from Manet, Monet and Rodin. Although it's well worth a visit, don't expect to see the definitive German national collection.

Altes Museum

Am Lustgarten (2090 5245/www. smb.museum). S3, S5, S7, S9, S75 Hackescher Markt. **Open** 10am-6pm Tue, Wed, Fri-Sun; 10am-10pm Thur. **Admission** €8; €4 reductions. No credit cards. **Map** p53 D3 ❷

Opened as the Royal Museum in 1830, the Old Museum originally housed all the art treasures on Museumsinsel. It was designed by Schinkel and is considered one of his finest buildings, with a particularly magnificent entrance rotunda beyond the monumental ionic columns of the portico where vast neon letters now declare that 'All Art has been Contemporary', an installation by Maurizio Nannucci. The Altes Museum shares the Collection of Classical Antiquities with the nearby Pergamonmuseum – the Greek collection is on the ground floor – and at press time was hauling Etruscan artefacts out of storage to replace the Egyptian Museum, now moved to the Neues Museum, on the upper floor.

Berliner Dom

Am Lustgarten (2026 9133/guided tours 2026 9119/www.berliner-dom.de). S5, S7, S9, S75 Hackescher Markt.

Open *Apr-Sept* 9am-8pm Mon-Sat; noon-8pm Sun. *Oct-Mar* 9am-7pm Mon-Sat; noon-7pm Sun. **Admission** €5; €3 reductions; free under-14s. No credit cards. **Map** p53 D3 ❸

The dramatic Berlin Cathedral is now finally healed of its war wounds and celebrated its centenary in 2005. Built in Italian Renaissance style, it was destroyed during World War II and remained a ruin until 1973, when extensive restoration work began. It has always looked fine from the outside, but now that the internal work is complete, it is fully restored to its former glory. Crammed with Victorian detail and containing dozens of statues of eminent German Protestants, its lush 19th-century interior is hardly the perfect acoustic space for the frequent concerts that are held here, but it's worth a visit to see the crypt containing around 90 sarcophagi of notables from the Hohenzollern dynasty, or to clamber up for splendid views from the cupola. Call to book a guided tour.

Bode Museum

Monbijoubrücke (266 3666/www.smb. museum). U6, S1, S2, S5, S7, S9, S75 Friedrichstrasse or S5,S7,S75,S9 Hackescher Markt. **Open** 10am-6pm Mon-Wed, Fri-Sun; 10am-10pm Thur. **Admission** €8; €4 reductions. No credit cards. **Map** p52 C3 ❹

Built by Berlin architect Ernhard von Ihne in 1904, the Bode Museum reopened after a thorough renovation in 2006. It was originally intended by Wilhelm von Bode as a home for art from the beginnings of Christendom, and now contains the Byzantine Collection, Sculpture Collection and the Numismatic Collection. The neobaroque Great Dome, the Basilica hall and the glorious Cupola have been carefully restored to keep up with modern curatorial standards, but they retain their magnificence. Most impressively, despite one of the world's largest sculpture collections and more than half a million pieces in the coin collection, the

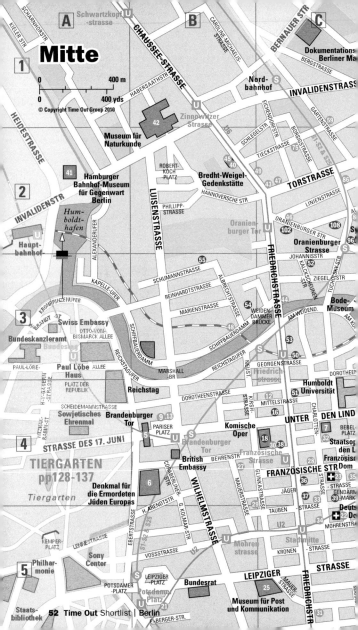

Mitte

0   400 m

0   400 yds

© Copyright Time Out Group 2010

A   Schwartzkopf-strasse

SCHARNHORSTSTR

KIELER STR

HEIDESTRASSE

CHAUSSEE-STRASSE

HABERSAATHSTR

B

Caroline-Michaelis-Strasse

BERNAUER STR

C

Dokumentations Berliner Ma

BERGSTRASSE

Nord-bahnhof

INVALIDENSTRASS

Zinnowitzer Strasse

EICHENDORFST

SCHLEGELSTR

TIECKSTRASSE

BORSIGSTRASSE

GARTENSTRASSE

59

S-S2 & S

42

Museum für Naturkunde

45
40

Brecht-Weigel-Gedenkstätte

49

43 47

TORSTRASSE

75

86

ROBERT-KOCH-PLATZ

41

Hamburger Bahnhof-Museum für Gegenwart Berlin

INVALIDENSTR

LUISENSTRASSE

PHILLIPP-STRASSE

Hannoversche Str

LINIENSTRASSE

46

Oranien-burger Tor

102

ORANIENBURGER STR

108

A

96

Humboldt-hafen

Haupt-bahnhof

ALEXANDERUFER

Oranienburger Strasse

52

JOHANNISSTR

KALCK-SCHEUNEN-STR

55

SCHUMANNSTRASSE

KAPELLE-UFER

REINHARDTSTRASSE

ALBRECHTSTRASSE

ZIEGEL-STR

TUCHOLSKY-STR

Bode-Museum

MARIENSTRASSE

54

WEIDEN-DAMMER BRÜCKE

AM WEIDEND.

FRIEDRICHSTRASSE

AMKO

BRANDT

KRONPRINZENUFER

Swiss Embassy

OTTO-VON-BISMARCK ALLEE

SCHIFFBAUERDAMM

SCHIFFBAUERDAMM

53

GEORGENSTRASSE

50

Bundeskanzleramt

Bundestag

REICHSTAGUFER

REICHSTAGUFER

Friedrich strasse

S

DOROTHEEN

PAUL-LÖBE

Paul Löbe Haus

PAUL-LÖBE ALLEE

MARSHALL BR

NEUST

Humboldt Universität

51

PLATZ DER REPUBLIK

Reichstag

DOROTHEENSTRASSE

12

MITTELSTRASSE

UNTER DEN LIND

7

BEBEL-PLATZ

Staatsop den L

SCHEIDEMANNSTRASSE

KIRSH STR

CHARLOTTEN

SCHEIDEMANN

Sowjetisches Ehrenmal

Brandenburger Tor

9 13

PARISER PLATZ

16

Komische Oper

18

Französisc

VITZAU RABIN-ST

STRASSE DES 17. JUNI

5

U

Brandenburger Tor

BEHRENSTR

30 38

28

Französisc Dom

TIERGARTEN

pp128-137

British Embassy

EBERTSTRASSE

6

CORABURGER STR

WILHELMSTRASSE

Französische Strasse

FRANZÖSISCHE STR

27

GLINKASTRASSE

MAUERSTRASSE

23

GENDARM

MARK

Tiergarten

Denkmal für die Ermordeten Jüden Europas

H. ARENDTSTR

G. KOLMAR STR

JÄGER

36

37

33

STRASSE

29

TAUBEN - STRASSE

34

Deuts
Do

S-S2 & S28

U2

MOHRENSTR.

U

Mohren strasse

KEMPER-PLATZ

LENNESTRASSE

VOSSSTRASSE

Stadtmitte

KRONEN - STRASSE

Philhar-monie

5

Sony Center

POTSDAMER-PLATZ

S

LEIPZIGER-PLATZ

Bundesrat

LEIPZIGER

25

STRASSE

FRIEDRICHSTR

Staats-bibliothek

U

Potsdamer Platz

21

E.-BERGER-STR.

Museum für Post und Kommunikation

MAUER-STR

31

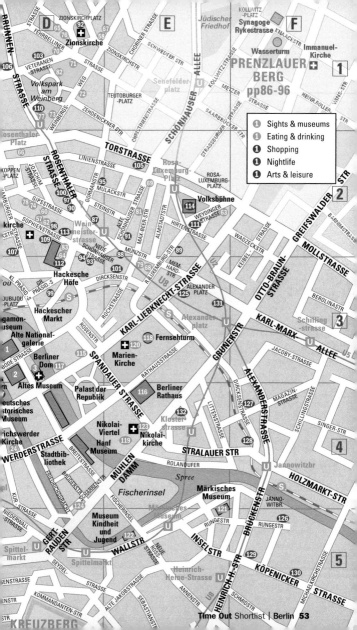

Legend:

① Sights & museums
① Eating & drinking
① Shopping
① Nightlife
① Arts & leisure

Whatever your carbon footprint, we can reduce it

For over a decade we've been leading the way in carbon offsetting and carbon management.

In that time we've purchased carbon credits from over 200 projects spread across 6 continents. We work with over 300 major commercial clients and thousands of small and medium sized businesses, which rely upon our market-leading quality assurance programme, our experience and absolute commitment to deliver the right solution for each client.

Why not give us a call?

T: London (020) 7833 6000

museum somehow retains a totally uncluttered feel and the sculptures stand free from off-putting glass cases. In particular, make sure you look out for the wall-length Apse Mosaic from 545 AD and the 14th-century Mannheim High Altar.

Brandenburger Tor

Pariser Platz. U55, S1, S2 Brandenburger Tor. **Map** p52 B4 ❺
Constructed in 1791, and designed by Carl Gotthard Langhans after the Propylaea gateway into ancient Athens, the Brandenburg Gate was built as a triumphal arch. The Quadriga statue, a four-horse chariot driven by Victory and designed by Johann Gottfried Schadow, sits on top. It has had an eventful life. When Napoleon conquered Berlin in 1806 he carted the Quadriga off to Paris and held it hostage until his defeat in 1814. The Tor was badly damaged in World War II, and during subsequent renovations, the GDR removed the Prussian Iron Cross and turned the Quadriga around so that the chariot faced west. The current Quadriga is a 1958 copy, and was stranded in no-man's land for 30 years. The Tor was the scene of much celebration while the Wall came down, and after that there had to be further repairs. The Iron Cross was replaced and the Quadriga was turned back to face into Mitte again.

Denkmal für die ermordeten Juden Europas

Cora-Berliner-Strasse 1 (2639 4336/ www.holocaust-denkmal.de). U2, S1, S2, S26 Potsdamer Platz. **Open** *Field of stelae* 24hrs daily. *Information centre* 10am-8pm Tue-Sun. **Admission** free. **Map** p52 B4 ❻
After many years of controversy, Peter Eisenmann's 'field of stelae' – 2,711 of them, arranged in undulating rows on 19,704sq m (212,000sq ft) of city block – with its attendant information centre to memorialise the Murdered Jews of Europe, was opened in 2005. Each of the concrete slabs has its own foundation,

Bode Museum p51

and they tilt at differing angles. The effect is (no doubt deliberately) reminiscent of the packed headstones in Prague's Old Jewish Cemetery. There's no vantage point or overview; to engage with the thing you need to walk into it. It's spooky in places, especially on overcast days and near the middle of the monument, where many feel a sense of confinement. The information centre is at the south-east corner of the site, mostly underground. It's like a secular crypt, containing a sombre presentation of facts and figures about the Holocaust's Jewish victims.

Deutsche Guggenheim Berlin

Unter den Linden 13-15 (202 0930/ www.deutsche-guggenheim.de). U6 Französische Strasse. **Open** 10am-8pm Mon-Wed, Fri-Sun; 10am-10pm Thur. **Admission** €4; €3 reductions; free under-12s. Free to all Mon. **Map** p52 C4 ❼
In partnership with the Deutsche Bank (and housed in one of its buildings), this

is the least impressive European branch of the Guggenheim. The modest exhibition space was designed by Richard Gluckman, and houses four exhibitions a year, usually alternating single-artist retrospectives with themed shows. Utopia Matters runs Jan-Apr 2010.

Deutsches Historisches Museum

Zeughaus, Unter den Linden 2 (203 040/www.dhm.de). U6 Französische Strasse. **Open** 10am-6pm daily. **Admission** €5; free under-18s. **Map** p53 D4 ⑧

The permanent exhibition in the Zeughaus finally opened in July 2006 and provides an exhaustive blast through German history from 100 BC to the present day, divided chronologically into significant eras. The museum originally had trouble raising the funds to buy historical objects, but there's enough here now for the exhibits to work on their own, without the need for an overarching narrative. German nationalism becomes the focus once you enter the 19th century and later on more than one room is dedicated to the Nazi era. The DHM has succeeded admirably in looking the past straight in the eye, although the attempt to be impartial means that it is sometimes factual to the extreme. Temporary exhibitions are housed in the new Pei building.

Kennedys

NEW *Pariser Platz 4A (2065 3570/ www.thekennedys.de). U55, S1, S2 Brandenburger Tor.* **Open** 10am-6pm daily. **Admission** €7; €3.50 reductions. No credit cards. **Map** p52 B4 ⑨

This small museum celebrates the 'special relationship' between Berlin and the Kennedy family, cemented by John F Kennedy's iconic 'Ich bin ein Berliner' speech in June 1963. With photos and memorabilia, the museum tells the history of the family, beginning with immigration from Ireland in the late 19th century and ending at the deaths of John and Robert Kennedy. It all looks wonderful in a minimalist setting, but that might also be down to the limits of the subject matter. Don't expect to learn anything new.

Neues Museum

Bodestrasse 3 (266 424 242/ www.smb.museum). S5, S7, S9, S75 Hackescher Markt. **Open** 10am-6pm Mon-Wed, Sun; 10am-8pm Thur-Sat. **Admission** €10; €5 reductions. No credit cards. **Map** p53 D3 ⑩

Mostly in ruins since 1945, the Neues Museum was, at press time, after an 11-year, $250 million makeover by English architect David Chipperfield, finally about to reopen. It's now the permanent home of the Ägyptische Museum (Egyptian Museum), whose most celebrated exhibit is the bust of Nefertiti, dating from around 1350 BC. The collection also includes a series of characterful model faces, and the vivid 'Berlin Green Head', plus papyruses and statuary aplenty. The building, which follows the floorplan of Friedrich August Stüler's original mid-19th-century design, but

Deutsches Historisches Museum

Hackescher Markt

with substantial sections completely reinvented by Chipperfield, also now hosts the collection of the Museum für Vor- und Frühgeschichte (Museum of Prehistory and Early History).

Pergamonmuseum

Am Kupfergraben (2090 5566/ www.smb.museum). U6, S1, S2, S5, S7, S9, S75 Friedrichstrasse. **Open** 10am-6pm Tue, Wed, Fri-Sun; 10am-10pm Thur. **Admission** €10; €5 reductions; free under-16s. No credit cards. **Map** p53 D3 ⓫

One of the world's major archaeological museums, the Pergamon should not be missed. Its treasures, comprising some of the Antikensammlung (Collection of Classical Antiquities; the rest is in the Altes Museum) and the Vorderasiastisches Museum (Museum of Near Eastern Antiquities), contain three major draws. The first is the Hellenistic Pergamon Altar, dating from 170-159 BC; huge as it is, the museum's partial re-creation represents only one third of its original size. In an adjoining room, and even more architecturally impressive, is the towering two-storey Roman Market Gate of Miletus (29m/95ft wide and almost 17m/56ft high), erected in AD 120. This leads through to the third of the big

attractions – the extraordinary blue and ochre tiled Gate of Ishtar and the Babylonian Processional Street, dating from the reign of King Nebuchadnezzar (605-562 BC). There are plenty of other gems in the museum that are also worth seeking out, including some stunning Assyrian reliefs.

The museum is also now home to the Museum für Islamische Kunst (Museum of Islamic Art), which takes up some 14 rooms in the southern wing. The collection is wide ranging, including applied arts, crafts, books and architectural details from the eighth to the 19th centuries. Entrance is included in the overall admission price, as is an excellent audio guide.

There are temporary exhibitions too. Return of the Gods, images of the Graeco-Roman pantheon, runs until April 2010. Note that the Pergamon is currently undergoing renovation, which is happening in stages.

Eating & drinking

Ishin Mitte

Mittelstrasse 24 (2067 4829/ www.ishin.de). U6, S1, S2, S5, S7, S9, S75 Friedrichstrasse. **Open** 11am-8pm Mon-Fri; 11am-6pm Sat. **€€**. No credit cards. **Japanese**. **Map** p52 C4 ⓬

Discover the city from your back pocket

Essential for your weekend break, 25 top cities available.

Roomy but crowded, with a constant stream of happy hour-style discounts, this is probably the best money-for-quality sushi deal in Berlin. The fish is fresh, with specials offered daily, and portions are generous: when was the last time you actually received more food than the photos on the menu suggested?

Margaux
Unter den Linden 78 (2265 2611/ www.margaux-berlin.de). U55, S1, S2 Brandenburger Tor. **Open** 7-10.30pm Mon-Sat. €€€€.
French. Map p52 B4 ⑬
This top-flight place features Michael Hoffman's slightly avant-garde take on classic French cooking, such as stewed shoulder of venison seasoned with coriander, anise and saffron. The spacious interior is lit by glowing columns of honey-hued onyx, which reflect in black marble floors. The restaurant is named for its extraordinary wine list, which includes some 30 vintages of Château Margaux. Service is first-rate.

Operncafé im Opernpalais
Unter den Linden 5 (202 683/ www.opernpalais.de). U6 Französische Strasse. **Café**. Map p53 D4 ⑭
A traditional coffee and cake stop in literally palatial surrounds. Choose from a huge selection of beautifully displayed cakes, then relax over a Milchkaffee in the elaborate interior, or sit outside in summer and watch Unter den Linden go by.

Tadshikische Teestube
In the Palais am Festungsgraben, Am Festungsgraben 1 (204 1112). U6, S1, S2, S5, S7, S9, S75 Friedrichstrasse. **Open** 5pm-midnight Mon-Fri; 3pm-midnight Sat, Sun. No credit cards.
Café. Map p52 C3 ⑮
An improbable gift from the Soviet Union to the people of the DDR back in the early 1980s, the Tajik Tearoom is an extraordinary throwback. Sip exotic teas while lounging on the floor with

samovars, low tables, rugs and cushions. It's a little faded nowadays, but worth the detour. Excellent snacks and light meals, and for less agile guests, there are a few conventional tables. Booking recommended. It's in the same building as the Maxim Gorki theatre.

Shopping

Berlin Story
Unter den Linden 26 (2045 3842/ www.berlin-story.de). U6, S1, S2, S5, S7, S9, S75 Friedrichstrasse. **Open** 10am-7pm daily. Map p52 C4 ⑯
You won't find a better selection of Berlin-related books in German, English and other languages: everything from novels with Berlin settings to non-fiction volumes on history and culture. Historical maps, posters, videos, CDs, postcards and souvenirs are also available.

Kunst und Nostalgie Markt
Am Zeughaus (0171 710 1662). U6, S1, S2, S5, S7, S9, S25, S75 Friedrichstrasse. **Open** 11am-5pm Sat, Sun. Map p53 D3 ⑰
On the riverbank by the Deutsches Historisches Museum, Kunst und Nostalgie Markt is one of the few places in Berlin where you can still find genuine DDR relics, with anything from old signs advertising coal briquettes to framed pictures of Honecker. Also paintings, prints, candles, leatherwork, books and CDs.

Arts & leisure

Komische Oper
Behrenstrasse 55-57 (202 600/ tickets 4799 7400/www.komische-oper-berlin.de). U55, S1, S2, S25 Brandenburger Tor. Map p52 C4 ⑱
Despite its name, the Komische Oper puts on a broader range than just comic works, and, after its founding in 1947, made its reputation by breaking with the old operatic tradition of

Interim art

Temporäre Kunsthalle Berlin

There's a German word that's been batted around Berlin for 20-odd years: *Zwischennutzung*. It means 'interim usage' – think clubs in bunkers or art exhibits in former parliamentary buildings. The place in question is used, often creatively, until the city or investor decides it's time for something more permanent.

Perched all by itself on Schlossplatz is the ultimate in *Zwischennutzung*: what looks like an outsize shipping container is the **Temporäre Kunsthalle Berlin** (Schlossplatz, 2045 3650, www.kunsthalle-berlin.com, open 11am-6pm Mon-Wed, Fri-Sun, 11am-9pm Thur). Designed by Austrian architect Adolf Krischanitz and privately funded, the structure went up in September 2008, and is slated to come down in September 2010. Its purpose? To showcase Berlin-based artistic talent in large-scale rotating exhibitions (and prove to city authorities that Berlin needs a new contemporary art centre, but that's another story).

So why the time limit? It's all about taking advantage of urban planning. The Palast der Republik, the building housing the East German parliament, was once located here; dismantling was completed in December 2008. But reconstruction of the Prussian Stadtschloss planned for this site has yet to begin. The gap is an opportunity for the organisers of the last exhibition shown in the Palast (interim usage again) to lobby for a place to show home-grown art in the centre of the city.

Year one saw the Kunsthalle mount four solo shows and find itself a little bit embroiled in city and art-world politics; year two is dedicated to more involved group exhibitions (with newly free admission). All of the artists featured live and work in Berlin.

The Kunsthalle has also provided a venue for lectures, films and DJ parties. It even has a museum-quality bookshop and a great outdoor café terrace from which visitors can meditate on what is likely the only vast empty space in any European city centre. None of this will last, so catch it while you can.

'costumed concerts' – singers standing around on stage – and putting an emphasis on 'opera as theatre'. Most of its productions are sung in German. Discounted tickets are sold immediately before performances.

Maxim Gorki Theater

Am Festungsgraben 2 (box office 2022 1115/information 2022 1129/ www.gorki.de). U6, S1, S2, S5, S7, S9, S75 Friedrichstrasse. **Map** p52 C3 ⑲
Intendant Armin Petras with a young and new ensemble has been breathing life into this jewel of a theatre over the last few years. The programming features new interpretations of classical and modern dramas as well as adaptations from films and novels, with the result that the atmosphere alone is often enough to transcend the language barrier.

Staatsoper Unter den Linden

Unter den Linden 7 (203 540/tickets 2035 4555/www.staatsoper-berlin.de). U2 Hausvogteiplatz. **Map** p52 C4 ⑳
The Staatsoper was founded as Prussia's Royal Court Opera for Frederick the Great in 1742, and designed along the lines of a Greek temple. Although the present building dates from 1955, the façade faithfully copies that of Knobelsdorff's original, twice destroyed in World War II. The elegant interior gives an immediate sense of the house's past glory, with huge chandeliers and elaborate wall paintings. Chamber music is performed in the small, ornate Apollo Saal, which is housed within the main building. Unsold tickets are available for €10 half an hour before the performance.

South of Unter den Linden

Before getting into its ceremonial stride, the Linden crosses Friedrichstrasse. By day, this

is a bustling commercial street of grand hotels and new department stores. By night, there's not much going on except for trade from the clutch of fine restaurants on and around the Gendarmenmarkt, the area's sightseeing centrepiece. Friedrichstrasse continues south into Kreuzberg at what was once Checkpoint Charlie.

Sights & museums

Dali – Die Austellung

NEW *Leipziger Platz 7 (3254 6873/ www.daliberlin.de). U2, S1, S2 Potsdamer Platz.* **Open** noon-8pm Mon-Sat; 10am-8pm Sun. **Map** p52 B5 ㉑
Formerly a temporary exhibition on the Kurfürstendamm, this has now turned into a permanent private museum on Leipziger Platz. Don't expect any large canvases or major works here; it's all engravings, numbered print series and the occasional limited-edition statuette – early art marketing of the kind that led André Breton to rechristen Dali with the scornful anagram, Avida Dollars.

Friedrichswerdersche-Kirche/ Schinkel-Museum p63

Bags packed, milk cancelled, house raised on stilts.

You've packed the suntan lotion, the snorkel set, the stay-pressed shirts. Just one more thing left to do – your bit for climate change. In some of the world's poorest countries, changing weather patterns are destroying lives.

You can help people to deal with the extreme effects of climate change. Raising houses in flood-prone regions is just one life-saving solution.

**Climate change costs lives.
Give £5 and let's sort it *Here & Now***

www.oxfam.org.uk/climate-change

Be Humankind (R) Oxfa

Deutscher Dom

Gendarmenmarkt, entrance in Markgrafenstrasse (2273 0431). U2, U6 Stadtmitte. **Open** 10am-10pm Tue; 10am-6pm Wed-Sun. *Guided tours* 11am, 1pm, 4pm daily. **Admission** free. **Map** p52 C5 ㉒

Both this church and the Französischer Dom were built in 1780-85 by Carl von Gontard for Frederick the Great, in imitation of Santa Maria in Montesanto and Santa Maria dei Miracoli in Rome. The Deutscher Dom was intended for Berlin's Lutheran community. Its neo-classical tower is topped by a 7m (23ft) gilded statue representing Virtue. Inside is a permanent exhibition on the history of Germany's parliamentary system, but there are no English translations.

Französischer Dom/ Hugenottenmuseum

Gendarmenmarkt (229 1760/ www.franzoesischer-dom.de). U2, U6 Stadtmitte. **Open** noon-5pm Tue-Sat; 11am-5pm Sun. **Admission** €2; €1 reductions. No credit cards. **Map** p52 C4 ㉓

Built in the early 18th century for Berlin's 6,000-plus-strong French Protestant community, the church was later given a baroque tower, which offers fine views over Mitte. The tower is purely decorative and unconsecrated – and, therefore, not part of the church, which is known as the Französischen Friedrichstadt Kirche (noon-5pm Mon-Sat; after service-5pm Sun).

An exhibition on the history of the French Protestants in France and Berlin-Brandenburg is displayed within the building (the modest church has a separate entrance at the western end). It chronicles the religious persecution suffered by Calvinists and their emigration to Berlin after 1685. One part of the museum is devoted to the church's history, particularly the effects of World War II – it was bombed during a Sunday service in 1944 and remained a ruin until the mid 1980s.

Friedrichswerdersche-Kirche/Schinkel-Museum

Werderscher Markt (208 1323/ www.smb.spk-berlin.de). U2 Hausvogteiplatz. **Open** 10am-6pm Tue-Sun. **Admission** free. **Map** p53 D4 ㉔

This church, designed by Karl Friedrich Schinkel, was completed in 1831. Its war wounds were repaired in the 1980s and it reopened in 1987 as a homage to its architect. Inside are statues by Schinkel, Schadow and others, bathed in soft light from stained-glass windows.

Museum für Kommunikation

Leipziger Strasse 16 (202 940/ www.museumsstiftung.de/berlin). U2 Mohrenstrasse or U2, U6 Stadtmitte. **Open** 9am-5pm Tue-Fri; 10am-6pm Sat, Sun. **Admission** €3; €1.50 reductions. **Map** p52 C5 ㉕

A descendant of the world's first postal museum (founded in 1872), this collection covers a bit more than mere stamps. It traces the development of telecommunications up to the internet era, though philatelists might head straight to the basement and the 'Blue Mauritius', one of the world's rarest stamps.

Sankt-Hedwigs-Kathedrale

Hinter der katholischen Kirche 3 (203 4810/www.hedwigs-kathedrale.de). U2 Hausvogteiplatz or U6 Französische Strasse. **Open** 10am-5pm Mon-Sat; 1-5pm Sun. **Admission** free. *Guided tours* €1.50. **Map** p53 D4 ㉖

Constructed in 1747 for Berlin's Catholic minority, this circular Knobelsdorff creation was bombed out during the war and only reconsecrated in 1963. Its modernised interior contains a split-level double altar. The crypt holds the remains of Bernhard Lichtenberg, who preached here against the Nazis, was arrested, and died while being transported to Dachau in 1943.

Stasi: Die Ausstellung

Mauerstrasse 38 (2241 7470/ www.bstu.bund.de). U2 Mohrenstrasse *or U6 Französische Strasse*. **Open** 10am-6pm Mon-Sat. **Admission** free. **Map** p52 B4 ㉗

A small but extremely informative exhibition about the Stasi on the ground floor of the Stasi documentation centre. Ingenious spy equipment and rows of jarred 'bodily smells' taken from interrogation chairs illustrate the terrible extent of Stasi surveillance. The exhibition is in German, but if you ring beforehand you can get a very knowledgeable guide in English.

Eating & drinking

Borchardt

Französische Strasse 47 (8188 6262). U6 Französische Strasse. **Open** 11.30am-1am daily. **€€€**. **French**. **Map** p52 C4 ㉘

In the late 19th century, the original Borchardt opened next door at no.48. It became the place to be for politicians and society folk, but was destroyed in World War II. Now Roland Mary and Marina Richter have reconstructed a highly fashionable, Maxim's-inspired bistro serving respectable French food. So why not snarf down a dozen oysters and tuck into a fillet of pike-perch or beef after a cultural evening nearby?

Café Nö!

NEW *Glinkastrasse 23 (201 0871/ www.cafe-noe.de). U6 Französische Strasse*. **Open** noon-1am Mon-Fri; 7pm-1am Sat. **€€**. No credit cards. **International**. **Map** p52 B4 ㉙

This unassuming but right-on wine bar with wholesome meals is owned by a former DDR rock musician now continuing his family's gastronomy tradition, and given the mostly bland or overpriced restaurants around here, this is a genuine pearl. Snacks include bruschetta and marinated plums baked with bacon; Alsatian flammkuchen and lamb ragout are among the dinners. All the food goes well with an intelligent, international wine list.

Cookies Cream

NEW *Behrenstrasse 55 (2067 4829/ www.cookiescream.de). U6 Französische Strasse*. **Open** 7pm-midnight Tue-Sun. **€€€**. **Vegetarian**. **Map** p52 C4 ㉚

Meander through the delivery area between Westin Grand and Komische Oper to a blank door with flickering light bulbs. Upstairs is a warm, rough-edged dining-room with open kitchen, where chef Stephan Hentschel (that's him with the red hair) is rethinking vegetarian cuisine with an inspiringly cliché-free menu. Tofu and pasta are

Gendarmenmarkt

shunned for dishes such as parmesan dumplings with cilantro carrots and Amalfi lemon sauce or pine nut and potato roll with beetroot carpaccio. Mostly backless seating is the only downside in this annexe of the Cookies nightclub complex.

Entrecôte

Schutzenstrasse 5 (2016 5496/ www.entrecote.de). U2, U6 Stadtmitte. **Open** noon-midnight Mon-Fri; 6pm-midnight Sat; 6-11pm Sun. **€€€**. **French. Map** p52 C5 ③

Steak and frites in a brasserie ambience close to Checkpoint Charlie. The food is simple but well prepared and Fred's Special Sauce, a mixed herb remoulade, is excellent. The long wine list encompasses all French regions, and there are half bottles too. Service is very professional.

Gendarmerie

NEW *Behrenstrasse 42 (7677 5270/ www.gendarmerie-berlin.com).* U6 Französische Strasse. **Open** 11am-2am daily. **€€€€**. **French/German. Map** p52 C4 ②

The latest venture by Josef Laggner, the man behind Lutter & Wegner and some 20 other restaurants and bars, opened in a former bank building in May 2009. The dining room is truly grand, with a huge, custom-made central bar, leather banquettes, high ceilings and a specially commissioned 14m by 5m (46ft by 16ft) painting by Jean-Yves Klein. Less spectacular but just as well executed is a menu of regional and French dishes. Downstairs in the former vault, the 'Oyster Bank' is open to VIPs only.

Lutter & Wegner

Charlottenstrasse 56 (202 9540/ www.lutter-wegner-gendarmenmarkt.de). U2, U6 Stadtmitte. **Open** 11am-3am daily. **€€€**. **Modern European. Map** p52 C4 ③

This place has it all: history (an early Berlin wine merchant, its sparkling wine became known as 'Sekt', now the common German term); a lovely atmosphere in its airy, elegant rooms; great German/Austrian/French cuisine; and excellent service. The wine list is justifiably legendary, and if the prices look high, head for the bistro, where the same list holds sway along with perfect salads, cheese and ham plates, plus excellent desserts.

Malatesta

Charlottenstrasse 59 (2094 5071/ www.ristorante-malatesta.de). U2, U6 Stadtmitte. **Open** noon-midnight daily. **€€€**. **Italian. Map** p52 C5 ③

This nicely located, first-rate Italian is spread out over two floors. Downstairs there's a small bar for an aperitif or coffee. Starters such as grilled artichoke hearts and antipasto misto, familiar home-made pastas, daily fish specialities and meat dishes such as oxtail filled with truffles are among the reasons to linger upstairs. Service is attentive but not intrusive.

Vau

Jägerstrasse 54-55 (202 9730/ www.vau-berlin.de). U6 Französische Strasse. **Open** noon-2.30pm, 7-10.30pm Mon-Sat. **€€€€**. **Modern European. Map** p52 C4 ③

Love of innovation and inspiration from all corners of the globe make chef Kolja Kleeberg's menu one of the best in town. His lobster with mango and black olives with tapenade, and braised pork belly with grilled scallops, are complemented by an extensive wine list. Downstairs, the fake library bar (the 'books' are bricks of coal) is great for special occasions. Booking essential.

Shopping

Galeries Lafayette

Friedrichstrasse 76-78 (209 480/www. lafayette-berlin.de). U6 Französische Strasse. **Open** 10am-8pm Mon-Sat. **Map** p52 C4 ③

This elegant glass complex designed by French superstar Jean Nouvel offers

BERLIN BY AREA

great clothes, frequent sales on the upper floors, a good selection of accessories and cosmetics at street level and a basement gourmet food hall where you'll feel transported to Paris. For local flair, check out the store's Labo Mode section, which showcases collections from young, up-and-coming Berlin designers.

Quartier 206

Friedrichstrasse 71 (2094 6800/www. quartier206.com). U6 Französische Strasse. **Open** 10.30am-7.30pm Mon-Fri; 10am-6pm Sat. **Map** p52 C4 ③⑦ Reminiscent of New York's Takashimaya, this upmarket store offers not just the most lusted-after designers, but the definitive items from those labels. Cult cosmetics and perfumes are on the ground floor; upstairs is devoted to women's and men's fashion, lingerie, jewellery and shoes, plus a home-living section stocked with sinfully expensive design items.

Nightlife

Crush

Behrenstrasse 55 (280 8806). Friedrichstrasse 164. U6, S1, S2, S5, S7, S75, S9 Friedrichstrasse. **Open** 11pm-late Tue, Thur, Sat. No credit cards. **Map** p52 C4 ③⑧ This blank canvas of a venue hosts various club nights, including the superhot Cookies on Tuesdays and Thursdays (accessed via a different entrance at Friedrichstrasse 164; www.cookies-berlin.de), which has been attracting the Beautiful People for years. A catacomb of concrete passageways opens on to a vast concert room resembling a cross between a school gym and a bingo hall, complete with huge, ostentatious chandeliers. A somewhat understaffed island bar serves all manner of drinks – eventually.

Music can vary but anything with a thumping bass and an electro slant goes. Weekends are occasionally worth a look, with a more diverse selection of

parties; Fashion Week after-shows, art exhibitions, hip hop nights… anything goes. The interior is usually completely transformed depending on the theme of the night.

Arts & leisure

Konzerthaus

Gendarmenmarkt 2 (2030 92101/ www.konzerthaus.de). U6 Französische Strasse. **Map** p52 C4 ③⑨ Formerly the Schauspielhaus am Gendarmenmarkt, this 1821 architectural gem by Schinkel was all but destroyed in the war. Lovingly restored, it was reopened in 1984 with three main spaces for concerts. Organ recitals in the large concert hall are a treat, played on the massive Jehmlich organ at the back of the stage. The Konzerthausorchester is based here, presenting a healthy mixture of the classic, the new and the rediscovered, and the Rundfunk-Sinfonieorchester Berlin and Staatskapelle Berlin also feature.

North along Friedrichstrasse

North of Unter den Linden, Friedrichstrasse begins to fizzle a little after passing the station and former border post of the same name. There are several theatres dotted about as it runs on, forming the boundary between the Scheunenviertel to the east and the government quarter to the west.

Sights & museums

Brecht-Weigel-Gedenkstätte

Chausseestrasse 125 (200 571 844). U6 Oranienburger Tor. **Open** *Guided tours* Every 30mins 10-11.30am, 2-3.30pm Tue; 10-11.30am Wed, Fri; 10am-11.30am, 5-6.30pm Thur; 10am-3.30pm Sat. **Admission** €3; €1.50 reductions. No credit cards. **Map** p52 B2 ④⓪

Brecht's home from 1948 until his death in 1956 has been preserved exactly as he left it. Tours of the house (phone in advance for an English one) give interesting insights into the life and reading habits of the playwright. The window at which he worked overlooked the grave of Hegel in the neighbouring cemetery. Brecht's wife, actress Helene Weigel, continued living here until her death in 1971, and the Kellerrestaurant near the exit serves Viennese dishes according to her recipes.

Hamburger Bahnhof – Museum für Gegenwart

Invalidenstrasse 50-51 (397 8340/ www.hamburgerbahnhof.de). U55, S5, S7, S9, S75 Hauptbahnhof. **Open** 10am-6pm Tue-Fri; 11am-8pm Sat; 11am-6pm Sun. **Admission** €8; €4 reductions. No credit cards. **Map** p52 A2 ㊶

The Hamburg Station Museum of Contemporary Art opened in 1997 within a huge and expensive refurbishment of a former railway station. The exterior features a stunning fluorescent light installation by Dan Flavin. Inside, the biggest draw is the gradual unveiling of the Friedrich Christian Flick Collection – a staggering 2,000 works from around 150 artists, mostly of the late 20th century. Flick, from a steel family whose fortune was tainted with Nazi-era controversy, has paid for the refurbishment of the Rieckhalle – an adjacent 300m (984ft) warehouse – to accommodate works from his collection, many of them large-scale, as they are doled out in temporary, themed exhibitions. There are other exhibitions too; Die Kunst ist Super! runs until February 2010.

Museum für Naturkunde

Invalidenstrasse 43 (2093 8550/ www.museum.hu-berlin.de). U6 Zinnowitzer Strasse or S1, S2, S25 Nordbahnhof. **Open** 9.30am-5pm Tue-Fri; 10am-6pm Sat, Sun. **Admission** €5; €3 reductions. No credit cards. **Map** p52 B4 ㊷

Berlin's recently renovated Natural History Museum is a real treasure trove. The biggest draw is the skeleton of a Brachiosaurus, which weighed 50 tons at death and is as high as a four-storey house. 'Oliver', as the dinosaur has been nicknamed, is one of the world's largest known land animals and was discovered in the early 1900s. Four renovated exhibition rooms were reopened in 2007, including the new 'Evolution in Action'. The glorious fossil and stone collections downstairs are worth a look.

Eating & drinking

Good Time

Chausseestrasse 1 (2804 6015/www. goodtime-berlin.de). U6 Oranienburger Tor. **Open** noon-midnight daily. €€€. **Indonesian**. **Map** p52 C2 ㊸

Indonesian food is rare in Berlin, and this friendly place does it well. The rijstafel, the soup and the rendang are all excellent. German tastes are catered to with a wide range of noodle dishes and there are Thai specialities too.

Grill Royal

Friedrichstrasse 105B (2887 9288/ www.grillroyal.com). U6, S1, S2, S5, S7, S9, S25, S75 Friedrichstrasse. **Open** 6pm-1am daily. €€€€. **International**. **Map** p52 C3 ㊹

With its entrance on the promenade by the Spree below the Weidendammer Brücke, this comfortably cavernous restaurant is more reminiscent of London or Paris than Berlin. In the beginning it seemed full of what pass for celebrities in Germany's capital, but has now settled into a functioning eaterie for a well-heeled but more anonymous crowd. They come to enjoy fine steaks of Irish, French or Argentine provenance, plus a few other meat and fish dishes. Reservations essential.

Kellerrestaurant im Brecht-Haus

Chausseestrasse 125 (282 3843/www. brechtkeller.de). U6 Oranienburger Tor.

BERLIN BY AREA

Discover
the world's
greatest cities

New book available at **timeout.com/shop**

Open 6pm-1am daily. €€€.

Central European. Map p52 B2 ④⑤
Bertholt Brecht got that sleek, well-fed look from the cooking his partner Helene Weigel learned in Vienna and Bohemia. This atmospheric place, crammed with model stage sets and Brecht memorabilia, serves a number of her specialities, including Fleischlabberln (spicy meat patties) and a mighty Wiener Schnitzel. In summer, the garden doubles capacity.

Mirchi

Oranienburger Strasse 50 (2844 4480/ www.mirchi.de). U6 Oranienburger Tor. **Open** noon-1am daily. €€€.
South Asian. Map p52 C2 ④⑥
An ambitious 'Singapore fusion' concept sees Indian, Chinese, Thai and Malay ideas mingling on a creative menu. The hearty Thai-Indian soups show the kitchen at its simple, tasty best. Nice entrance, lots of space, useful location.

Tartane

NEW *Torstrasse 225 (4472 7036/ www.tartane.org). U6 Oranienburger Tor.* **Open** 6pm-2am daily. €€. No credit cards. **American**. Map p52 C2 ④⑦
Basically a burger joint, but one serving up a gourmet version of the American classic that keeps even snooty Mitte film-industry types trooping back for more – it's high on both flavour and looks. Other hearty, Americanesque fare – such as caesar salads, chicken wings and quesadillas – are also on offer in a slick and quirky interior. There aren't many seats, and while the service is very pretty, it can be slow.

Tausend

NEW *Schiffbauerdamm 11 (4171 5396/ www.tausendberlin.com). U6, S5, S7, S9, S75 Friedrichstrasse.* **Open** 9pm-late Tue-Sat. **Bar**. Map p52 B3 ④⑧
An elegant bar/lounge for 'grown ups' – that's what founder Till Harter had in mind for this high-design, upscale establishment. With unmarked

entrance – look for the iron door under the train overpass – and strict entrance policy, it's also as exclusive as Berlin gets. Here's where the well-heeled see and are seen while sipping innovative drinks in a tubular, steel-ceilinged interior lit by eerily eye-like 3D installations. Try a bracing Wasabi cocktail in summer or a malt whisky served with local pine honey in winter.

Weinbar Rutz

Chausseestrasse 8 (2462 8760/www. rutz-weinbar.de). U6 Zinnowitzer Strasse. **Open** 6.30pm-midnight Mon-Sat. €€€€. **German**. Map p52 C2 ④⑨
The impressive ground-floor bar has a whole wall showcasing wines from around the globe – not obscure New World vintages, but the best of the best. There are no tasting notes on the list, however. The second-floor restaurant serves a limited nouvelle menu, all dishes are beautifully presented. Snacks downstairs. Booking essential.

Shopping

Berliner Antik- & Flohmarkt

Bahnhof Friedrichstrasse, S-Bahnbogen 190-203 (208 2655/www.antikmarkt-berlin.de). U6, S1, S2, S5, S7, S9, S25, S75 Friedrichstrasse. **Open** 11am-6pm Mon, Wed-Sun. Map p52 C3 ⑤⓪
In renovated arches under the S-Bahn tracks, scores of dealers sell furniture, jewellery, paintings and vintage clothing. Be warned: it's not cheap.

Dussmann das KulturKaufhaus

Friedrichstrasse 90 (2025 1111/www. kulturkaufhaus.de). U6, S1, S2, S5, S7, S9, S75 Friedrichstrasse. **Open** 10am-midnight Mon-Sat. Map p52 C4 ⑤①
Intended as a 'cultural department store', this spacious five-floor retailer offers books, CDs, videos, magazines, DVDs and everything in between. You can borrow reading glasses (€10 deposit) or a portable CD player (€50 deposit) while you're in the store.

Nightlife

Kalkscheune

Johannisstrasse 2 (5900 4340/www.
kalkscheune.de). U6 Oranienburger
Tor. No credit cards. **Map** p52 C3 **52**
Though it mostly holds Schlager parties and cabaret nights, this elegantly
restored 19th-century factory building
occasionally presents a few interestingly offbeat artists, such as Devendra
Banhart and Nouvelle Vague.

Arts & leisure

Admiralspalast

Friedrichstrasse 101 (3253 3130/tickets
4799 7499/www.admiralspalast.de).
U6, S1, S2, S5, S7, S9, S75
Friedrichstrasse. **Map** p52 C3 **53**
This combination spa and theatre has a
long history dating back to 1873, and in
its 1920s heyday was a 24-hour 'amusement palace' with a steam sauna, bowl-
ing alley, casino, restaurants, cafés, club,
cinema and even a bordello. Having survived World War II it served operetta
through the communist years, and has
now been superbly remodelled to stage
musical theatre, concerts, cabaret and
other events on three separate stages.
At press time the staff were promising
that the Roman-style baths would also
open soon.

Berliner Ensemble

Bertolt-Brecht-Platz 1 (2840 8155/
www.berliner-ensemble.de). U6, S1,
S2, S5, S7, S9, S75 Friedrichstrasse.
Map p52 B3 **54**
This theatre is best known for its association with Brecht – first during the
Weimar period (*The Threepenny Opera*
was premiered here in 1928) and later
under the communists when Brecht ran
the place from 1948 until his death in
1956. Artistic director Claus Peymann
focuses on contemporary theatre and
original productions as well as direct-
ing classics with an updated point of
view. Expect a repertoire where modern productions of Brecht rub shoulders

with pieces by living artists and directors such as Robert Wilson.

Deutsches Theater

Schumannstrasse 13A (284 410/tickets
2844 1225/www.deutschestheater.de).
U6, S1, S2, S5, S7, S9, S75
Friedrichstrasse. **Map** p52 B3 **55**
Within the DT's two adjoining buildings are three venues displaying new
and experimental work, from one-man
shows and concerts to modern interpretations of Gogol, Shakespeare and
Büchner. The four in-house directors –
Barbara Frey, Dimiter Gotscheff,
Jürgen Gosch and Michael Thalheimer
– are all innovators; Thalheimer in particular has received countless awards.

Scheunenviertel & Mitte Nord

Sights & museums

Neue Synagoge

Centrum Judaicum, Oranienburger
Strasse 28-30 (8802 8451/www.
cjudaicum.de). S1, S2 Oranienburger
Strasse. **Open** *Mar-Oct* 10am-8pm
Mon, Sun; 10am-6pm Tue-Thur; 10am-
5pm Fri. *Nov-Feb* 10am-6pm Mon-Thur,
Sun; 10am-2pm Fri. **Admission** €3;
€2 reductions. No credit cards.
Map p52 C2 **56**
Built in 1857-66 as the Berlin Jewish
community's showpiece, it was the New
Synagogue that was attacked during
Kristallnacht in 1938, but not too badly
damaged – Allied bombs did far more
harm in 1945. The façade remained
intact and the Moorish dome has been
rebuilt. There's an exhibition about
Jewish life in Berlin and a glassed-in
area protecting the sanctuary ruins.

Sammlung Hoffmann

Sophienstrasse 21 (2849 9120/www.
sophie-gips.de). U8 Weinmeisterstrasse.
Open (by appointment only) 11am-4pm
Sat. **Admission** €6. No credit cards.
Map p53 D2 **57**

This is Erika and Rolf Hoffmann's private collection of international contemporary art, including a charming floor installation work by Swiss video artist Pipilotti Rist and work by Douglas Gordon, Felix Gonzalez-Torres and AR Penck. The Hoffmans offer guided tours through their apartment every Saturday by appointment – felt slippers supplied.

Eating & drinking

103

Kastanienallee 49 (4849 2651/ www.agentur103.de). U8 Rosenthaler Platz. **Open** 9am-2am daily. No credit cards. **Bar. Map** p53 D1 ⑱
Well lit and pleasantly airy (for Berlin), this L-shaped bar competes with Schwarzsauer to be the primary Kastanienallee hangout. The food, an odd mix of Asian and Italian, is generally excellent. But more importantly, it's the perfect summer location to sit outside with a beer and watch well-coiffed local freaks strut their stuff.

AlpenStueck

NEW *Gartenstrasse 9 (2175 1646/ www.alpenstueck.de). S1, S2, S25 Nordbahnhof.* **Open** 6pm-1am daily. €€€. **German. Map** p52 C1 ⑲
Artsy but not pretentious, this restaurant offers Austrian and south German classics served in a cool ambience. Everything from the strudel crust to the bread is handcrafted; the entrées, including a roast beef smothered in crispy onions and medallions of pork with rösti potatoes and endive salad, are at the level where you just can't help talking about flavours and textures. The pasta, including noodles and peas with cherry tomatoes as a starter, is especially memorable. The wine list and desserts are good too.

Altes Europa

Gipsstrasse 11 (2809 3840/ www.alteseuropa.com). U8 Weinmeisterstrasse/bus N2,

N5, N8. **Open** noon-1am daily. No credit cards. **Bar. Map** p53 D2 ⑳
The gentle minimalism of the decor – big picture windows, basic furnishings and nothing but a few old maps and prints on the walls – is a relief in an increasingly pretentious neighbourhood, and this spacious place is good for anything from a party to a private conversation. The bar serves light meals, Ukrainian vodka and draught Krusovice in both dark and light varieties to a mixed, youngish crowd.

Bandol sur Mer

Torstrasse 167 (6730 2051). U8 Rosenthaler Platz. **Open** 6pm-late daily. €€€. No credit cards. **French. Map** p52 C2 ㉑
Offering French bistro fare in a low-key yet Gallic-elegant atmosphere, this teensy restaurant has space for only 22 diners, but Berliners line up for its exquisite entrecôte, innovative seafood and an extensive selection of excellent French and German wines. Everything comes fresh from the market and the chefs aren't afraid to add slight twists to the classics. The specials are handwritten in chalk on the wall, and reservations are mandatory for the two sittings. Even Brad Pitt's a fan.

Barcomi's

Sophienstrasse 21, Sophie-Gips-Höfe, 2 Hof (2859 8363/www.barcomi.de). U8 Weinmeisterstrasse. **Open** 8am-9pm Mon-Sat; 9am-9pm Sun. No credit cards. **Café. Map** p53 D2 ㉒
Prominent in the renovated courtyard just downstairs from the Sammlung Hoffmann (p70), and serving snacks, light meals and American-style coffee, Barcomi's is a popular stop for lunch or an afternoon break. Decent but over-rated and often packed.

Bar 3

Weydingerstrasse 20 (2804 6973). U8 Rosa-Luxemburg-Platz. **Open** 9pm-late Tue-Sat. No credit cards. **Bar. Map** p53 E2 ㉓

BERLIN BY AREA

Nestled in a cul-de-sac near the Volksbühne, this low-lit bar has wrap-around windows, a slick black interior, a spacious U-shaped bar and inexpensive wine and beer. Try the Kölsch brew from Cologne or small servings of wine that go for €2.50. It's popular with the over-30 art crowd and a great place to both theorise and throw back a few drinks in a sleek but unpretentious atmosphere. It also sells Walkers crisps.

Café Aedes East

Hof II, Hackesche Höfe, Rosenthaler Strasse 40-41 (285 2103). S5, S7, S9, S75 Hackescher Markt. **Open** 10am-midnight daily. **Café**. Map p53 D2 ⑥④
This small and stylish Hackesche Höfe café fills with insiders who know that the food here is better – and better-priced – than the stuff in the larger places in the first Hof. Expect a mixture of people from the nearby theatres, bars and offices.

Café Oberwasser

Zionskirchstrasse 6 (448 3719). U8 Bernauer Strasse/M1 Zionskirchplatz. **€€€**. **Open** 5pm-late daily. No credit cards. **Russian**. Map p53 D2 ⑥⑤
This cosy bistro-type restaurant with dim lighting and overstuffed furniture may look a bit second-hand but after a drink or two it starts to look like the attic of some faded aristocrat. The food is a combination of Russian and non-Russian cuisine, freshly prepared to order by a hostess who seems to be the only person on the job. Things go slow, but plan to make an evening of it and you won't be sorry.

CCCP

Torstrasse 136 (0179 692 913). U8 Rosenthaler Platz. **Open** 6pm-late Tue-Thur; 10pm-late Fri, Sat. No credit cards. **Bar**. Map p53 D2 ⑥⑥
CCCP is a celebration of all things Russian. This means copious amounts of vodka – straight or mixed – quaffed by locals and a few other shady

characters rubbing shoulders in the small, dark space. A crimson colour scheme, seedy vibe and kitschy decorations complete the picture. The doorman might refuse entry to large groups or anyone who looks too touristy.

Der Imbiss W

Kastanienallee 49 (4849 2657). U8 Rosenthaler Platz. **Open** noon-midnight daily. **€**. No credit cards. **International**. Map p53 D1 ⑥⑦
This vogueish place is named for Gordon W, a minor celebrity chef from Canada, who devised its wacky fusion menu of 'naan pizzas', 'rice shells' and international 'dressings'. The food is clever but it's not always that well executed and the open kitchen can be a bit much in the small space. Grab an outside table in summer.

Dolores

Rosa-Luxemburg-Strasse 7 (2809 9597/www.dolores-berlin.de). U2, U5, U8, S5, S7, S9, S75 Alexanderplatz. **Open** 11.30am-10pm Mon-Sat; 1-10pm Sun. **€€**. No credit cards. **American/Mexican**. Map p53 E3 ⑥⑧
For fans of the Northern California-style burrito, this is a true haven. Black beans and lime rice mix with fresh greens and a choice of fillings, such as grilled chicken, marinated beef and tofu. The guacamole is always fresh and perfectly spicy.

Erdbeer

Max-Beer-Strasse 56 (8643 6941/ www.erdbeer.de). U8 Rosa-Luxemburg-Platz. **Open** 4pm-late daily. No credit cards. **Bar**. Map p53 E2 ⑥⑨
The name means strawberry, and this dark, spacious (and a bit dingy) bar off Rosa-Luxemburg-Platz has earned a reputation for its powerful and delicious fresh fruit drinks. There are other eccentric mixtures on offer, as well as the usual beers, both bottled and from the Fass. Nightly DJs are of wildly differing styles and quality.

Forum

FC Magnet

*Veteranenstrasse 26 (0177 291 6707/
www.fcmagnetbar.de). U8 Rosenthaler
Platz.* **Open** 7pm-late daily. No credit
cards. **Bar. Map** p53 D1 ⑳
A few years ago, Berliners began transforming old-style East Berlin social
clubs into fancy new bars. The slacker
entrepreneurs behind FC Magnet have
taken it a step further, creating a fashionable football bar complete with its
own team. Though the drinks aren't
exceptional, people pack in at weekends
to play Kicker (table football) under a
giant photo of Franz Beckenbauer.

Forum

*Fehrbelliner Strasse 57 (440 6983/
www.weinerei.com). U8 Rosenthaler
Platz.* **Open** 11am-midnight daily.
No credit cards. **Bar. Map** p53 D1 ㉑
Resembling a shabbily comfortable living room, Forum's main draw is the
pay-what-you-want policy after 8pm.
You 'rent' a glass for €1 and hit the
wine bar and modest buffet. When it's
time to go, throw what you want to pay
into a big jar – but expect dirty looks
if you've been drinking all night and
then contribute only a fiver. It can get

rowdy in the evening; by day it's a laid-
back café serving reasonably priced
soups, snacks and coffee.

Galão

*Weinbergsweg 8 (4404 6882/
www.galao-berlin.de). U8 Rosenthaler
Platz.* **Open** 7.30am-8pm Mon-Fri; 8am-
8pm Sat; 9am-7pm Sun. No credit cards.
Café. Map p53 D1 ㉒
Serves the best panini in the area, with
delicious Milchkaffee to accompany.
It's small but makes a virtue of it by
tossing a few cushions on to the steps,
transforming what could be a cramped,
table-less restaurant into an outdoor
meeting place in summer.

Gorki Park

*Weinbergsweg 25 (448 7286/
http://gorki-park.de). U8 Rosenthaler
Platz.* **Open** 9.30am-2am Mon-Sat;
10am-2pm Sun. No credit cards.
Café. Map p53 D1 ㉓
Gorki Park is a tiny Russian-run
café with surprisingly tasty and
authentic snacks – blini, borscht and
the like. Guests range from students
and loafers to the occasional guitar-
toting Ukrainian and scenesters

BERLIN BY AREA

having a quiet coffee before heading down to pose at more centrally located bars. The vodka selection is strangely disappointing.

Greenwich

Gipsstrasse 5 (2809 5566). U8 Weinmeisterstrasse. **Open** 8pm-6am daily. No credit cards. **Bar.** Map p53 D2

It's not long since east Berlin nightlife was mostly squats serving cheap beer and industrial vodka. But when club pioneer Cookie opened this place, the city began its half-hearted romance with glam-flecked exclusivity. The interior looks like a set from Barbarella. Increasingly a yuppie hangout, but the cocktails are top-notch and the clientele is easy on the eyes.

Maxwell

Honigmond

Borsigstrasse 28 (2844 5512/ www.honigmond-berlin.de). U6 Zinnowitzer Strasse. **Open** 7am-1am Mon-Fri; 8am-1am Sat, Sun. €€. **German.** Map p52 C2

This quiet neighbourhood place serves up traditional German food alongside an innovative menu that ranges from kangaroo to fondue. Noteworthy are the Königsberger Klöpse (east Prussian meatballs in a creamy caper sauce) and a very good caesar salad. Excellent wine list and remarkable home-made bread (and butter!). It's also a hotel (p164).

Kapelle

Zionskirchplatz 22-24 (4434 1300/ www.cafe-kapelle.de). U8 Rosenthaler Platz/bus N2, N8, N84. **Open** 9am-3am daily. No credit cards. **Café/bar.** Map p53 D1

A comfortable, high-ceilinged café/bar across from the Zionskirch, Kapelle takes its name from Die Rote Kapelle, 'the Red Orchestra'. This was a clandestine anti-fascist organisation and in the 1930s and '40s the Kapelle's basement was a secret meeting place for the resistance. The regularly changing menu features organic meat and vegetarian dishes, and the proceeds are donated to local charities and social organisations.

Kim

Brunnenstrasse 10 (no phone). U8 Rosenthaler Platz. **Open** 9pm-late daily. No credit cards. **Bar.** Map p53 D1

Kim perfectly captures that unfinished look with which Berlin's fashionable set is so enamoured. Kim has been a favourite since it opened in 2007. The door is unmarked; just look for an all-glass façade and crowds sporting New Romantic haircuts and skinny jeans. The dimly lit, white-walled space is DIY: under a geometric dropped ceiling are stackable chairs and tables that guests can arrange as they like. Cheap drinks and a rotating roster of neighbourhood DJs add to a don't-give-a-damn aesthetic.

Kuchi

Gipsstrasse 3 (2838 6622/www.kuchi.de). U8 Weinmeisterstrasse. **Open** noon-midnight Mon-Sat; 6pm-midnight Sun. €€. **Japanese.** Map p53 D2

It's the quality of the ingredients at this Japanese that makes the food special.

And it isn't just fish in the sushi rolls: one maki is filled with chicken, mandarin oranges and poppy seeds. Delicate tempura, yakitori chicken hearts or shiitake mushrooms are all excellently served by a young, cool and multinational team. Packed at lunch.

Lebensmittel in Mitte

Rochstrasse 2 (2759 6130). U2 Weinmeisterstrasse. **Open** 11am-midnight Mon-Fri; 10am-midnight Sat. *Food served* noon-4pm Mon-Fri; 1-11pm Sat. No credit cards. **German. Map** p53 E3 **79**

This deli/restaurant offers fine cheeses, rustic bread, organic veggies, sausage, even Austrian pumpkin seed oil to take away. But guests can also settle into long wooden benches under the antlers on the wall, and dine on southern German specialities such as Leberkäse, tongue, rösti and cheese spätzle, accompanied by a broad selection of southern German and Austrian wines or authentic Bavarian beer.

Maxwell

Bergstrasse 22 (280 7121/ www.mxwl.de). U8 Rosenthaler Platz or S1, S2, S25 Nordbahnhof. **Open** 6pm-midnight daily. €€€. **Modern European. Map** p52 C1 **80**

Set in a beautiful neo-Gothic former brewery, tucked away in a peaceful courtyard with great summer tables, chef and proprietor Uwe Popall presides over a relaxed and tasteful atmosphere while offering a light, eclectic menu. His stress on local, seasonal ingredients (the spring asparagus menu is always a treat) and philosophy of colourful simplicity is popular with the art scene and younger diplomatic crowd.

Monsieur Vuong

Alte Schönhauser Strasse 46 (9929 6924/www.monsieurvuong.de). U8 Weinmeisterstrasse. **Open** noon-midnight daily. €€. No credit cards. **Vietnamese. Map** p53 E2 **81**

Something of an institution, serving fresh and tasty Vietnamese soups and noodles. A couple of daily specials supplement a handful of regular dishes. Once you've tried the glass noodle salad, you'll understand why less is more. Chic, cheap and cheery, but often packed.

Nola's am Weinberg

Veteranenstrasse 9 (4404 0766/ www.nola.de). U8 Rosenthaler Platz. **Open** 10am-1am daily. €€€. **Swiss. Map** p53 D1 **82**

Swiss food in a former park pavilion, with a quiet terrace as well as a spacious bar and dining room. It's hearty fare, such as venison goulash with mushrooms and spinach noodles, or rösti with spinach and cheese with fried eggs. The goat's cheese mousse with rocket starter is big enough for two and it's worth noting that, with a little thought, it's possible to eat quite cheaply here.

Pan Asia

Rosenthaler Strasse 38 (2790 8811/www.panasia.de). U8 Weinmeisterstrasse or S5, S7, S9, S75 Hackescher Markt. **Open** noon-midnight daily. €€. **Asian. Map** p53 D2 **83**

Hidden in a pleasant courtyard off busy Rosenthaler, with tables outside in summer, this is a fashionably minimalist place to see, be seen and eat modern Asian food. Japanese beers and Chinese teas complement excellent wun tun, kimchi salad and a variety of soups and wok dishes. Downsides? Self-conscious crowd, inconsistent service.

Papà Pane di Sorrento

Ackerstrasse 23 (2809 2701/ www.papapane.de). U8 Rosenthaler Platz or S1, S2, S25 Nordbahnhof. **Open** noon-midnight daily. €€€. No credit cards. **Italian. Map.** p53 D1 **84**

Streetside windows, an open, high-ceilinged dining room and lots of Italian-restaurant bustle provide a perfect frame for excellent pizzas and delicious pastas. Papà Pane is a lunchtime favourite for gallerists and creative types working nearby. At night, the art crowd often convenes here in large groups to see and be seen in a casual, open atmosphere.

Salumeria Culinario

Tucholskystrasse 34 (2809 6767/ www.salumeria-culinario.de). S1, S2 Oranienburger Strasse. **Open** 10am-11pm Mon-Sat; 11am-midnight Sun. **€€**. No credit cards. **Italian**. **Map** p52 C2 ❻❺

The daily lunch menu is a great way to recharge after a morning of shopping or gallery hopping. Pick up a bottle of wine, some cheese, olives and salami, or ponder the panettoni in the Italian import section, or simply grab a plate to go. There's space for 60 at the busy beer tables on the pavement.

Schwarzwaldstuben

Tucholskystrasse 48 (2809 8084). S1, S2 Oranienburger Strasse. **Open** 9am-11pm Mon-Fri; 9am-midnight Sat, Sun. **€€€**. No credit cards. **German**. **Map** p52 C2 ❻❻

This Swabian place is a casually chic affair, and wears its mounted deer head ironically. The food is excellent. The soups are hearty, standout main courses include the Schäuffele with sauerkraut and potatoes, and Flammkuchen (a sort of German pizza). Rothaus Tannenzapfle beer on tap.

Shopping

Absinthe Depot Berlin

Weinmeisterstrasse 4 (281 6789/ www.erstesabsinthdepotberlin.de). U8 Weinmeisterstrasse. **Open** 2pm-midnight Mon-Fri; 1pm-midnight Sat. No credit cards. **Map** p53 D2 ❻❼

This place stocks the best and most potent absinthes from across the world – including, of course, the good Czech stuff. If you're lucky, the owner might even invite you for a sampling session and history lesson.

AM1, AM2 & AM3

Münzstrasse 21-23 (3088 1945/ www.andreasmurkudis.net). U8 Weinmeisterstrasse. **Open** noon-8pm Mon-Sat. **Map** p53 E2 ❻❽

Three concept shops hidden in a court-yard, AM 1-3 offer a reverently presented selection of cutting-edge, luxury designers, many of them local. The shop is run by Andreas Murkudis, brother of famous German fashion designer Kostas Murkudis – several of whose items can be found in the stores.

Blush

Rosa-Luxemburg-Strasse 22 (2809 3580/www.blush-berlin.com). U2 Rosa-Luxemburg-Platz or U8 Weinmeisterstrasse. **Open** noon-8pm Mon-Fri; noon-7pm Sat. **Map** p53 E2 ❻❾

Beautiful lingerie in lace and silk. Imports from France and Italy, as well as German brands.

Calypso

Rosenthaler Strasse 23 (2854 5415/ www.calypsoshoes.com). U8 Weinmeisterstrasse. **Open** noon-8pm Mon-Sat. **Map** p53 D2 ❾❶

See box p77.

Claudia Skoda

Alte Schönhauser Strasse 35 (280 7211/www.claudiaskoda.com). U8 Weinmeisterstrasse. **Open** noon-8pm Mon-Fri; 11am-7pm Sat. **Map** p53 E2 ❾❶

Berlin's most established womenswear designer has extended her range to include clothes for men – items for both sexes are showcased in this loft space. Made with high-tech yarns and innovative knitting techniques, the collections bear her signature combination of stretch fabrics and graceful drape effects.

Farmers' Market at Zionskirchplatz

Zionskirchplatz (394 4073). U2 Senefelderplatz or U8 Rosenthaler

First-class second-hand

Calypso

Being cool in Berlin means a mix-and-match of new and second-hand clothing to create an individual look. There is no stigma attached to wearing someone else's cast-offs; in fact, in this city it's a sign of sartorial savvy, if you can pull it off.

Berlin has lots of vintage and second-hand clothes stores and a good, varied selection of them are situated close together in Mitte, which means you can zip through them quickly if time is tight.

Most of these outlets have some kind of theme, so you can tailor your trail to your desired look. **Sterling Gold** (p78) in the Heckmann-Höfe, for example, is where ladies can dress to impress with one of the elegant US cocktail frocks and ball gowns, from the 1950s to the 1980s, that cram the stands. Vintage glamour comes at a price, however; expect to fork out around €200 per dress.

Two other gems are just around the corner. **Waahnsinn** (p78) has a vibrant stock of vintage clothing from the 1950s to '70s,

including a great range of classic hats. The shop prides itself on its theatrical/risqué edge – this is where to come for sequinned hot pants for men.

Footwear emporium **Calypso** (p76), just down the road, has a colourful collection of shoes for men and women and is no less idiosyncratic than Waahnsinn. The footwear dates from the 1930s, though most is from the 1960s to '80s, a great place to pick up a zany pair of platform heels to give your new outfit a lift.

For more everyday jeans, sports or casual gear, the best of it can be found at one of Berlin's second-hand superstores. **Made in Berlin** (p78), near Hackescher Markt, specialises in casual clothing from the 1960s to '90s – much of it with name brands. On Tuesdays you can take advantage of its 'happy hours', when the kilo price is reduced by 20 per cent from noon to 3pm, so you can splash out on all kinds of cool, classic or quirky items and return home without later having to tighten your belt.

BERLIN BY AREA

Platz. **Open** 11am-6pm Thur.
Map p53 D2 **92**

Regional growers sell fruit and veggies, fresh fish and home-made jams, breads and cheeses. Farmers set up their stands on the cobblestone walkway surrounding one of Berlin's most beautiful churches, making this a truly picturesque market throughout the year.

Made in Berlin

Neue Schönhauser Strasse 19 (212 30 601/www.kleidermarkt.de). S5, S7, S75, S9 Hackescher Markt or U8 Weinmeisterstrasse. **Open** 12pm-8pm Mon-Sat. **Map** p53 D3 **93**
See box p77.

RespectMen

Neue Schönhauser Strasse 14 (283 5010/www.respectmen.de). U8 Weinmeisterstrasse. **Open** noon-8pm Mon-Fri; noon-7pm Sat.
Map p53 D2 **94**

Dirk Seidel, Karin Warburg and Alfred Warburg's menswear seems traditionally tailored on the rail, yet reveals a body-conscious, contemporary cut when worn. Trousers, jackets, suits and coats can be made to order. Also stocks labels like Drykorn and Franco Ziche.

RSVP

Mulackstrasse 14 (2809 4644/ www.rsvp-berlin.de). U8 Weinmeisterstrasse. **Open** noon-7pm Tue-Sat. **Map** p53 D2 **95**

Stationery for the aesthete: art deco scissors, exotic erasers, paper from Italy, Polish notebooks, G Lalo boxes and Caran d'Ache pens.

Sterling Gold

Heckmann-Höfe, Oranienburger Strasse 32 (2809 6500/www. sterlinggold.de). U6 Oranienburger Tor or S1, S2, S25, S26 Oranienburger Strasse. **Open** noon-8pm Mon-Fri; noon-6pm Sat. **Map** p52 C2 **96**
See box p77.

Waahnsinn

Rosenthaler Strasse 17 (282 0029/ www.waahnsinn-berlin.de). U8 Weinmeisterstrasse. **Open** noon-8pm Mon-Sat. No credit cards.
Map p53 D2 **97**
See box p77.

Whisky & Cigars

Sophienstrasse 8-9 (282 0376/ www.whisky-cigars.de). S5, S7, S9, S75 Hackescher Markt. **Open** 11am-7pm Mon-Fri; 11am-6pm Sat.
Map p53 D2 **98**

Two friends with a love of single malts are behind this shop, which stocks 450 whiskies and cigars from Cuba, Jamaica and Honduras, among others. They hold regular tastings and will deliver.

Nightlife

Bang Bang

Neue Promenade 10 (6040 5310/ www.bangbang-club.net). U8 Weinmeisterstrasse or S5, S9, S75 Hackescher Markt/bus N5. **Open** 9pm-late Tue-Sat. **Admission** €3-€8. No credit cards. **Map** p53 D2 **99**

Located smack dab in touristy Hackescher Markt and decorated with enormous photo prints of 1960s and '70s icons, Bang Bang is a small yet inviting club and live venue. Booking policy veers towards avant-garde or Britpop acts, with soul and Baile-funk DJs often as not entertaining the miniscule dancefloor.

B-Flat

Rosenthaler Strasse 13 (283 3123/www.b-flat-berlin.de). U8 Weinmeisterstrasse. **Open** from 9pm daily. No credit cards.
Map p53 D2 **100**

Maintaining a large piano-bar feel, this jazz venue pulls in a decent local hero once in a while, but its strongest nights tend to feature singers. It holds free Wednesday night jam sessions from 9pm.

Bohannon

Dircksenstrasse 40 (6950 5287/
www.bohannon.de). U2, U5, U8, S5,
S7, S9, S75 Alexanderplatz or S5, S7,
S9, S75 Hackescher Markt. **Open**
10pm-late Mon, Thur-Sat. No credit
cards. **Map** p53 E3 🔟🏧
The club's name, a nod to funk legend
Hamilton Bohannon, indicates its driving musical principle. Billed as offering 'soulful electronic clubbing', this
basement location features two dancefloors and regular sets by the likes of
dancehall DJ Barney Millah and excellent Friday night soul parties.

Café Zapata in Tacheles

Oranienburgerstrasse 54-6A (281
6109/www.cafe-zapata.de). U6
Oranienburger Tor. **Open** varies.
Admission varies. No credit cards.
Map p52 C2 🔟🏧
Though part of the squatted Tacheles
complex, Café Zapata stands on its
own as a live venue, booking top-flight
folk and indie artists like Joanna
Newsom, local hero Bruno Adams and
Omaha, Nebraska's The Good Life.
The small space opens on to a beer
garden in summer.

Calabash Club

Veteranenstrasse 21 (7346 3838/
www.myspace.com/calabashclub).
U8 Rosenthaler Platz or S1, S2,
S25 Nordbahnhof. **Open** 10pm-late
Tue, Fri-Sun. No credit cards.
Map p53 D1 🔟🏧
A massive complex, containing a
cinema, theatre and gallery, operated
by a Berlin arts collective.
There's also a party floor with a
playlist mostly devoted to reggae,
breakbeat and drum 'n' bass; the
dingy bar is a popular spot for the
city's stoners. The cinema programme
is interesting, consisting mostly of
independent and low-budget films.

Clärchen's Ballhaus

Auguststrasse 24 (282 9295/
www.ballhaus.de). S1, S2

Oranienburger Strasse. **Open** 10am-late
daily. No credit cards. **Map** p53 D2 🔟🏧
This old-school dancehall has been frequented by nimble-footed Berliners
since it opened in 1913, and under new
management is now more popular than
ever. There are two ballrooms – the
upstairs Mirror salon is the grander, but
both still sport vintage details – and a
programme of tango, swing or salsa.
You can also just stop by for a pizza.

Kaffee Burger

Torstrasse 60 (2804 6495/www.
kaffeeburger.de). U2 Rosa-Luxemburg-
Platz. **Open** 8pm-late Mon-Thur; 9pm-
late Fri, Sat; 7pm-late Sun. No credit
cards. **Map** p53 E2 🔟🏧
Best known as home of the popular
twice-monthly Russendisko, Kaffee
Burger's programme runs the cultural
gamut. Early evenings may see readings, film screenings or live music.
Later on, DJs play anything from old-
school country to Balkan beats or
Britpop. The club's decor has been left
intact from GDR days, and relatively
bright lighting facilitates interaction
with strangers... as do the cheap drinks.

King Kong Klub

Brunnenstrasse 173 (9120 6860/
www.king-kong-klub.de). U8 Rosenthaler
Platz. **Open** 9pm-late daily. No credit
cards. **Map** p53 D1 🔟🏧
King Kong Klub is unpretentious, with
pudgy leather sofas, subdued red lighting and rock 'n' roll and B-movie paraphernalia scattered about. The music
policy mainly covers rock and electro.
It's popular with student-types and
local eccentrics.

Mudd Club

Grosse Hamburger Strasse 17 (4403
6299/www.muddclub.de). S5, S7, S9,
S75 Hackescher Markt. No credit cards.
Map p53 D2 🔟🏧
NYC Mudd Club founder Steve Mass
has rebirthed his venture in a brick-
lined Berlin basement that resounds to
Russendisko rather than No Wave.

BERLIN BY AREA

Indeed, Mudd self-consciously attempts to ape the popular Kaffee Burger, hiring DJs with moustaches and stocking Russian beer. Booking favours loveable outsiders such as Mark Lanegan or the Dirty Three.

Rodeo

Auguststrasse 5A (0163 162 0168/ www.rodeo-berlin.de). U6 Oranienburger Tor or S1, S2, S25 Oranienburger Strasse. **Open** 8pm-late Fri, Sat. No credit cards. **Map** p52 C2 **108**

Rodeo is one of Berlin's most stylish venues. Opening around 7pm, the church-like main room, with its stunning domed ceiling and arched windows, acts as a restaurant where guests are seated at long communal tables. Once the meals are over, the tables are cleared away and the DJ takes to the decks. Music policy tends to be electro/rock based.

Sophienclub

Sophienstrasse 6 (282 4552/ www.sophienclub-berlin.de). U8 Weinmeisterstrasse or S5, S7, S9, S75 Hackescher Markt. **Open** 10pm-late Tue-Sat. No credit cards. **Map** p53 D2 **109**

A survivor from the old East, this space has a reputation for ignoring musical trends. If you are looking for 'ladies' night' or what the German's call 'Blackclassics', this is your place. It's not a complete desert, though: the boys from Karrera Klub are now doing their indie/Britpop thing here on Tuesdays. Other nights feature disco, house and R&B.

ZMF (ZurMoebelFabrik)

Brunnenstrasse 10 (no phone/www. zurmoebelfabrik.de). U8 Rosenthaler Platz or S5, S9, S75 Hackescher Markt. **Open** 10pm-6am Fri, Sat. No credit cards. **Map** p53 D1 **110**

The initials 'ZMF' stand for 'ZurMoebelFabrik', and the building used to be a furniture factory before this cosy club took over the basement. A bare-brick and concrete dancefloor leads into a spacious lounge with a liberal supply of comfy beaten-up sofas. A highlight at ZMF is the Neon Raiders party, a monthly event with a solid queer following and a sexy, open-minded crowd cutting up the dancefloor to an impressive line-up of international DJs.

Arts & leisure

Babylon-Mitte

Rosa-Luxemburg-Strasse 30 (242 5969/www.babylonberlin.de). U2, U5,

Alexanderplatz

ALEXANDERP

U8, S3, S5, S7, S75 Alexanderplatz or U2 Rosa-Luxemburg-Platz. No credit cards. **Map** p53 E2 ⑪

Housed in a restored landmark building by Hans Poelzig, this cinema focuses on new German independent film, but English-language fare is on the up, particularly in its regular Schräge Filme (Weird Films) programme, and its foreign films tend to have English subtitles. Tuesdays are silent film nights, with live musical accompaniment.

Chamäleon

Hackesche Höfe, Rosenthaler Strasse 40-41 (tickets 400 0590/www. chamaeleonberlin.de). S5, S7, S9, S75 Hackescher Markt. **Performances** 8.30pm Mon, Wed, Thur; 8.30pm, midnight Fri, Sat; 7pm Sun. No credit cards. **Map** p53 D3 ⑫

This beautiful old cabaret theatre with a whiff of decadence about it is located in the famous courtyards of the Hackesche Höfe. The focus is on stunning acrobats combined with music theatre. It attracts a diverse audience and is Berlin's most comfortable and affordable revue house.

Sophiensaele

Sophienstrasse 18 (information 2789 0030/tickets 283 5266/ www.sophiensaele.com). U8 Weinmeisterstrasse or S5, S7, S9, S75 Hackescher Markt. No credit cards. **Map** p53 D2 ⑬

This former club house for craftsmen and DDR theatre workshop now presents a contemporary programme of dance, theatre, music and opera, with up-and-coming groups from around the world. If avant-garde is ever crowd-pleasing, then it's here. The largest of the off-theatres, the Sophiensaele is also the perfect venue for an assortment of theatre and dance festivals.

Volksbühne

Linienstrasse 227 (2406 5777/ www.volksbuehne-berlin.de). U2 Rosa-Luxemburg-Platz. **Map** p53 E2 ⑭

The provocative interpretations, four-hour productions and alternative operettas staged by Frank Castorf, one of the most talked-about and controversial directors in town, restored the popularity of the 'People's Stage', but his deconstructions and modernisations of Russian novels and American plays have become a bit predictable. Yet the theatre continues to uphold its tradition, under his direction, of presenting the unexpected. The theatre is also home to a gallery, a small studio theatre (Parasit), and the hip, eclectic Roter and Grüner Salons. Former after-hours hangouts for the East German theatre elite, these two very different halls retain their old-style decor.

Alexanderplatz & South-east Mitte

With the **Fernsehturm** (Television Tower) visible from all over the city and with its role as a major public transport hub, Alexanderplatz is a point of orientation. The **Rotes Rathaus** on its western side is the city's (red) town hall. Alexanderplatz proper is the square on the other side of the S-Bahn tracks, a vast open space whose communist and Weimar buildings are still being renovated. Among the housing blocks to the south, a huge mall is under construction. There are scattered points of interest between here and Kreuzberg, and east along Karl-Marx-Allee to Friedrichshain.

Sights & museums

AquaDom & Sea Life

Spandauer Strasse 3 (992 800/ www.sealife.de). S5, S7, S9, S75 Hackescher Markt. **Open** 10am-6pm daily. **Admission** €15.95; €11.95 reductions. No credit cards. **Map** p53 D3 ⑮

Billed as two attractions in one: Sea Life leads you through 13 themed aquaria offering fish in different habitats; the AquaDom is the world's largest free-standing aquarium – a spacey stucture that looks like it might just have landed from some extremely watery planet. You take a lift up through the middle of this giant cylindrical fishtank – a million litres of saltwater that is home to 2,500 colourful creatures, and enfolded by the atrium of the Radisson Hotel.

Berliner Rathaus

Rathausstrasse 15 (902 60/guided tours 9026 2523). U2, U5, U8, S5, S7, S9, S7, Alexanderplatz. **Open** 9am-6pm Mon-Fri. *Guided tours* by appointment. **Admission** free. **Map** p53 E4 ⓶⓺

This magnificent building was constructed of terracotta brick during the 1860s. The history of Berlin up to that point is illustrated in a series of 36 reliefs on the façade. During communist times, it served as East Berlin's town hall – which made its old nickname, Rotes Rathaus ('Red Town Hall'), after the colour of the façade, doubly fitting. West Berlin's city government workers moved here from their town hall, Rathaus Schöneberg, in 1991.

DDR Museum

Karl Liebknecht Strasse 1 (847 123 731/www.ddr-museum.de). S5, S27, S9, S75 Hackescher Markt. **Open** 10am-8pm Mon-Fri, Sun; 10am-10pm Sat. **Admission** €5.50; €3.50 reductions. **Map** p53 D3 ⓶⓶

This is 'Ostalgia' in action. Touch screens, sound effects and even the 'DDR Game' mean that the more distasteful aspects of East German life are cheerfully glossed over. The museum is essentially a collection of DDR memorabilia, from travel tickets to Palast der Republik serviettes. Climb inside the Trabi or sit on a DDR couch in a DDR living room where you can watch DDR TV. Information on the Stasi gets

the interactive treatment too – you can pretend to be a Stasi officer and listen in on a bugged flat. Take it all with a large pinch of salt.

Fernsehturm

Panoramastrasse 1A (242 3333/ www.berlinerfernsehturm.de). U2, U5, U8, S5, S7, S9, S75 Alexanderplatz. **Open** *Mar-Oct* 9am-midnight daily. *Nov-Feb* 10am-midnight daily. **Admission** €10.50; €6.50 reductions; free under-3s. **Map** p53 E3 ⓶⓼

Built in the late 1960s at a time when relations between East and West Berlin were at their lowest ebb, the 368m (1,207ft) Television Tower – its ball-on-spike shape visible all over the city – was intended as an assertion of communist dynamism and modernity. East Berlin authorities, however, were displeased to note a particular phenomenon: when the sun shines on the tower, reflections on the ball form the shape of a cross. Berliners dubbed this stigmata 'the Pope's revenge'. Nevertheless, the authorities were proud enough of their tower to make it one of the central symbols of the East German capital, and today it is one of Berlin's most popular graphic images. Take an ear-popping trip in the lift to the observation platform at the top. The view is unbeatable by night or day. If heights make you hungry, take a twirl in the revolving restaurant, which offers an even better view.

Hanf Museum

Mühlendamm 5 (242 4827/ www.hanfmuseum.de). U2, U5, U8, S5, S7, S9, S75 Alexanderplatz. **Open** 10am-8pm Tue-Fri; noon-8pm Sat, Sun. **Admission** €3; free under-10s. No credit cards. **Map** p53 E4 ⓶⓽

The world's largest hemp museum aims to teach the visitor about the uses of the plant throughout history, as well as touching on the controversy surrounding it. The café (doubling as a video and reading room) has cakes made with and without hemp.

Fernsehturm

history, intellectual Berlin and the military. There are models of the city at different times, and some good paintings.

Museum Kindheit und Jugend

Wallstrasse 32 (275 0383/www. berlin-kindheitundjugend.de). U2 Märkisches Museum. **Open** 9am-5pm Mon-Fri. **Admission** €2; €1 reductions; €2.50 family. No credit cards. **Map** p53 E5 ⑫

The Museum of Childhood and Youth is the place to come if you want to show kids how lucky they are to be going to school today and not 50 years ago. Apart from old toys, it displays artefacts from classrooms during the Weimar Republic, the Nazi era and under communism.

Nikolaikirche

Nikolaikirchplatz (2472 4529/ www.stadtmuseum.de). U2, U5, U8, S5, S7, S9, S75 Alexanderplatz. **Open** 10am-6pm Tue-Sun. **Admission** €5; €3 reductions. No credit cards. **Map** p53 E4 ⑬

Inside Berlin's oldest congregational church is an interesting historical collection chronicling Berlin's development until 1648. Old tiles, tapestries, stone and wood carvings – even old weapons and punishment devices – are on display. The collection includes fascinating photos of wartime damage, plus examples of how the stones melted together in the heat of bombardment.

Marienkirche

Karl-Liebknecht-Strasse 8 (242 4467/ www.marienkirche-berlin.de). U2, U5, U8, S5, S7, S9, S75 Alexanderplatz. **Open** *Apr-Sept* 10am-9pm daily. *Oct-Mar* 10am-6pm daily. **Admission** free. **Map** p53 E3 ⑫

Begun in 1270, this is one of Berlin's few remaining medieval buildings. Just inside the door is a wonderful Dance of Death fresco dating from 1485, and the 18th-century Walther organ here is considered his masterpiece. Tours are available.

Märkisches Museum

Am Köllnischen Park 5 (3086 6215/ www.stadtmuseum.de). U2 Märkisches Museum. **Open** 10am-6pm Tue, Thur-Sun; noon-8pm Wed. **Admission** €5; €3 reductions. **Map** p53 E5 ⑫

This extensive, curious and somewhat old-fashioned museum traces the history of Berlin through a wide range of historical artefacts. Different sections examine themes such as Berlin as a newspaper city, women in Berlin's

Eating & drinking

Cafehaus am Petriplatz

Kleine Gertraudenstrasse 3 (2065 3730/www.cafehaus-petriplatz.de). U2 Spittelmarkt. **Open** 11am-7pm daily. **€€**. No credit cards. **Café**. **Map** p53 D5 or E4 ⑫

An oasis in its area, this cute, family-run café offers a variety of ice-creams if you just want to cool down, and an impressive menu of traditional German dishes at very reasonable prices if you're

BERLIN BY AREA

Power clubs

Post-Wall Berlin has always been generously endowed with transitional spaces suitable for nightlife. As the unifying city remodelled and rebuilt, old shops, cellars, toilets, offices, bank vaults and bunkers have all served as temporarily autonomous party zones. But as the unified electric grid was gradually brought into the 21st century, Berlin has always had an appetite for transforming obselete power stations into banging, techno havens.

It began with the legendary E-Werk in the early 1990s, and has continued into the present with both the superclub Berghain (p104) and the huge Tresor 3.0 (p85) installed in former generating facilities. Newcomer **Dice Club** (right) is power-station club number four, cleverly taking up residence in a disused DDR transformer station not far from Alexanderplatz. But Dice doesn't aspire to be another pilled-out minimal sanctuary in the manner of Berghain. The feel here is glitzy and upmarket, and a lot of cash has been sunk into both a top-notch sound system and inventive lighting rigs. Also, the music policy stretches beyond the thud of minimal house. Yet it maintains Berlin nightlife's traditional post-industrial vibe with bare concrete walls, utility flooring, iron staircases and original power station signage. 'These power stations possess a distinctive charm; rough, simple and authentic,' muses Dice owner Isan Oral. 'It's basically a mirror image of how Berlin functions as a city.'

seeking more substantial refreshment. The enormous schnitzel with home-pickled apple Rotkohl is outstanding.

Shopping

Kaufhof

Alexanderplatz 9 (0180 517 2517/ www.galeria-kaufhof.de). U2, U5, U8, S5, S7, S9, S75 Alexanderplatz. **Open** 9.30am-10pm Mon-Sat. **Map** p53 E3 **125**
Once the retail showpiece of communist East Berlin, this busy, utilitarian megastore underwent huge renovation and expansion in 2006. Today, it is the most successful branch of the Kaufhof chain.

Nightlife

C-Base

Rungestrasse 20 (2859 9300/www. c-base.org). U8, S5, S9, S7, S75 Jannowitzbrücke. No credit cards. **Map** p53 F5 **126**
This sprawling venue appears to have been constructed by throwing a collection of rooms and industrial rubbish up into the air and seeing where it all lands. It's a quirky mix of tumbledown ceilings, exposed wires, flickering strip lights and retro computer consoles. The spacious upstairs dancefloor opens out on to a riverside drinking area, while the spiral staircase takes you down to the lower deck where there is a smaller club room and chill-out area.

Dice

NEW *Voltairestrasse 5 (0163 436 8524/www.dice-cub.de). U8, S5, S7, S75, S9 Jannowitzbrücke.* **Open** midnight-open end Fri, Sat. No credit cards. **Map** p53 F4 **127**
See box left.

Golden Gate

Dircksenstrasse 77-78 (no phone/ www.goldengate-berlin.de). S5, S7, S75, S9 Hackescher Markt. **Open** from 10pm Wed; from 11pm Thur-Sat. No credit cards. **Map** p53 F4 **128**

Housed in a ramshackle former bike shop beneath the S-Bahn Arches, Golden Gate's popularity is enjoying something of an upswing. Once home to a hit-and-miss music policy, this grimy little club has now settled on a series of all-weekend techno parties. The venue is almost a scaled-down version of Berghain (p104), with a refreshingly intimate atmosphere. People either jam into the small dancefloor room or lounge around the bar or the upstairs toilets. It's an anything-goes location with a chilled-out crowd and nice backyard garden in summer.

Sage Club

Köpenicker Strasse 76 (278 9830/ www.sage-club.de). U8 Heinrich-Heine-Strasse. **Open** 7pm-late Thur, Fri, Sat. No credit cards. **Map** p53 F5 ❿

A labyrinthine complex of half a dozen or so dancefloors accessed via the north-side entrance to Heinrich-Heine-Strasse U-Bahn station make up Sage Club, which caters to a relatively young, rock-oriented crowd. On Thursdays and Fridays it's a chilled-out, unpretentious place where skinny jeans and leather jackets tend to be the uniform of choice. On Saturdays you'll have better luck with some fetish gear, as Sage is the current home of the notoriously decadent mixed/straight sex and techno night, the KitKat Club (www.kitkatclub.de).

Tresor.30

Köpenicker Strasse 70 (no phone/ www.tresorberlin.de). U8 Heinrich-Heine-Strasse or S5, S9, S7, S75 Jannowitzbrücke. **Open** midnight-late Wed, Fri, Sat. **Map** p53 F5 ❿

This new incarnation of the original Berlin techno club is taking a little time to find its feet. Housed in what was formerly the main central-heating power station for East Berlin, the colossal location is breathtaking, and since only a tiny portion of its 28,000sq m (300,000sq ft) is in use, there's plenty of room for future development in what

is intended to be not just a club, but a huge centre of alternative art and culture. The basement floor is an experience you'll not forget; a black hole occasionally punctuated by flashing strobes with some of the loudest, hardest techno you are likely to hear.

Week12End Club

Alexanderplatz 5, 12th floor (2463 1676/www.week-end-berlin.de). U2, U5, U8 or S5, S7, S75, S9 Alexanderplatz. **Open** 11pm-late Thur-Sat. No credit cards. **Map** p53 E3 ❿

Situated right at the focus point of former East Berlin, Week12End's home is way up at the top of one of Alexanderplatz's many communist-era tower blocks. While the interior of the club itself is nothing impressive, the roof terrace is a big draw – a perfect summer location combining often excellent music (2ManyDJs and DFA anyone?) with spectacular cityscape views. It should be awfully pretentious, but somehow it isn't.

WMF CLUB

NEW *Klosterstrasse 44 (no phone/ www.wmf-club.com). U2 Klosterstrasse.* **Open** 11pm-late Fri, Sat. No credit cards. **Map** p53 E4 ❿

A Berlin institution on hiatus the past few years, WMF has been around forever, jumping from location to location and delighting partygoers wherever it went. Now in its eighth incarnation, the newly reopened WMF is housed in a former telecommunications office, boasting a sprawling high-ceilinged space spread across various levels, including three bars, a chilled-out open-air beer garden, a massive main dancefloor and several smaller stages. The aesthetic is minimalist and interiors evoke the original office aesthetic, endowing parties with a fabulously illicit feel. Up-till-dawn parties, in-the-know crowds and big-name electro artists remain WMF staples – recent acts included Modeselektor, CSS, Peaches and Ellen Allien.

Prater p92

Prenzlauer Berg

Prenzlauer Berg spreads up the hill north-east of Mitte. A residential district and the most beautiful borough of east Berlin, it is devoid of landmark sights but has a busy cultural life. The area around Kollwitzplatz and the Wasserturm along Knaackstrasse has a convivial scene of restaurants and cafés. More alternative venues are clustered in the 'LSD' area around Lychener Strasse, Stargarder Strasse and Duncker Strasse. Kastanienallee is the area's most happening main thoroughfare, and blends into the Mitte North nightlife quarter at its southern extremity. At its northern end, Kastanienallee meets Schönhauser Allee, Prenzlauer Berg's main street. This leads north into east Berlin's gay district.

Sights & museums

Prenzlauer Berg Museum

Prenzlauer Allee 227 (902 953 911). U2 Senefelderplatz. **Open** 9am-6pm Mon-Fri. **Admission** free. **Map** p87 B3 ❶

The Prenzlauer Berg Museum is a small but interesting permanent exhibit on the history and culture of the district – lots of old photos – with temporary exhibitions too.

Zeiss-Grossplanetarium

Prenzlauer Allee 80 (4218 4512/ www.astw.de). S4, S8, S85 Prenzlauer Allee. **Open** 9am-noon Tue, Wed, Thur; 7-9pm Fri; 2.30-9pm Sat; 1.30-5pm Sun. **Admission** €5; €4 reductions. No credit cards. **Map** p87 C1 ❷

This vast planetarium was built in the 1980s. Though changing exhibitions are in German only, the shows in the auditorium are entertaining for all.

Eating & drinking

8mm

Schonhauser Allee 177B (4050 0624/ www.8mmbar.com). U2 Senefelderplatz. **Open** 9pm-late daily. No credit cards. **Bar**. **Map** p87 B3 ❸

This purple-walled dive exists to remind travellers that Berlin isn't Stuttgart. The attractive, young and poor go for that fifth nightcap at around 6am, and local scenesters rub shoulders with anglophone expats. There seems to be more hard alcohol consumed here than in your average Berlin hangout and, yes, sometimes films are shown, should anyone still be in a fit enough state to watch.

A Cabana

Hufelandstrasse 15 (4004 8508). Tram M4 Hufelandstrasse. **Open** 4pm-1am Tue-Sun. €€. No credit cards. **Portuguese**. Map p87 C3 ④

A bit further east than the fashionable parts of this borough, but convenient for Magnet (p73) and the Knaack Club,

this family-run place is great for relaxing over a big bowl of fresh soup, fish or tasty paella. Home-style cooking is A Cabana's forte, and its menu changes frequently. There's also occasional live music.

Anna Blume

Kollwitzstrasse 83 (4404 8749/ www.cafe-anna-blume.de). U2 Eberswalder Strasse. **Open** 8am-2am daily. No credit cards. **Café**. Map p87 B2 ⑤

This café and florist rolled into one is named after a poem by Kurt Schwitters. The pastries are quite expensive but high quality, the terrace is a particularly nice spot to sit in summer, and the interior, not surprisingly, smells of flowers.

Becketts Kopf

Pappelallee 64 (0162 2379 418). U2 Eberswalder Strasse. **Open** 8pm-4am Tue-Sun. No credit cards. **Bar**. **Map** p87 B1 ⑥

The head of Samuel Beckett stares at you from the window of this red-walled, intimate spot, which prides itself on expert cocktails and a variety of scotches and whiskies. Prices are about average for mixed drinks in Berlin but quality is several notches above. Occasional DJs play avant-jazz.

The Bird

NEW *Am Falkplatz 5 (5105 3283/ www.thebirdinberlin.com). U2, S8, S41, S42 Schönhauser Allee.* **Open** 6pm-late Mon-Sat; noon-late Sun. €€. No credit cards. **American**. **Map** p87 A1 ⑦

The Bird is the latest US-style eatery set up for those keen to throw their diet to the wall and gorge on a plate of pure, unadulterated calories. The bar resembles the set of *Cheers*: naked brickwork, chunky wooden tables and American tap beers. The menu is crammed with burgers, wings and steaks, all done in gallons of oil. The food is good but the staff tend to be a touch obnoxious.

Café Anita Wronski

Knaackstrasse 26-28 (442 8483). U2 Senefelderplatz. **Open** 9am-2am daily. No credit cards. **Café**. **Map** p87 B2 ⑧

Friendly café on two levels with scrubbed floors, beige walls, hard-working staff and as many tables crammed into the space as the laws of physics allow. Excellent brunches, and plenty of other cafés on this stretch if there's no room here. Quiet in the afternoon and a good spot to sit and read.

Café Galião

Marienburger Strasse 26B (0174 842 2965). M4 Hufelandstrasse. **Open** 10am-5pm Mon-Sat. No credit cards. **Café**. **Map** p87 C2 ⑨

Café Galião is a comfortable low-key daytime café with a friendly atmosphere. Youngish locals stop by for frequently changing specials such as home-made soups and organic stews, as well as big tasty salads and fresh ciabatta sandwiches. Order one of the fruit shakes and finish it off with a custard mini-tart.

Dr Pong

Eberswalder Strasse 21 (no phone/ www.drpong.net). U2 Eberswalder Strasse. **Open** 8pm-late Mon-Sat; 2pm-late Sun. No credit cards. **Bar**. **Map** p87 B1 ⑩

Bring your table tennis bat and prepare for ping-pong madness. The action doesn't start until around midnight, but when it does you can expect 30 or so players – some good, some bad – to surround the table. Beer, soda, tea and juice are available, and sometimes cakes or pastries, but otherwise there's no food. No tables, either. Just a bunch of chairs and two couches in a smoked-out, garage-like room. All in all, it's lots of fun. Note that the opening hours are unreliable.

Entweder Oder

Oderberger Strasse 15 (448 1382). U2 Eberswalder Strasse. **Open** 10am-late daily. €€. No credit cards. **German**. **Map** p87 A2 ⑪

German food with a light touch: roasts, grilled fish and the occasional schnitzel cosy up to fresh salads and simple potato side dishes. The menu changes daily and everything is organic. Connected to the underground art scene back in the days of the Wall, this place still rotates new work by local artists.

Gagarin

Knaackstrasse 22-24 (442 8807). U2 Senefelderplatz. **Open** 10am-2am daily. **Café**. **Map** p87 B2 ⑫

Brought to you by the folks who run Gorki Park and Pasternak, adding a bar to their troika of Russian hospitality.

The Bird

The vogue-ish retro space-age decor (colourful planets and Yuri's likeness adorn the walls) and electronic sounds provide the backdrop for Baltika beer and tasty Russian pub grub.

Gugelhof

Knaackstrasse 37 (442 9229/ www. gugelhof.de). U2 Senefelderplatz. **Open** 4pm-1am Mon-Fri; 10am-1am Sat, Sun. €€€. **German.** **Map** p87 B2 ⑬

A mature Alsatian restaurant that pioneered the Kollwitzplatz scene in the 1990s. The food is refined but filling, the service formal but friendly, and the furnishings are comfortably worn in. The choucroute contains the best charcuterie in town, and the Backöfe – lamb, pork and beef marinated in riesling and stewed and served in an earthware pot with root vegetables and a bread-crust lid – shows the kitchen at its most characterful. There's also a fine selection of Alsatian tartes flambées. Reservations are recommended. Breakfast is served until a leisurely 4pm at weekends.

Hausbar

Rykestrasse 54 (4404 7606). U2 Senefelderplatz. **Open** 7pm-5am daily. No credit cards. **Bar. Map** p87 B2 ⑭

Bright red and gold, with a glorious cherub-filled sky on the ceiling, this small pocket of fabulousness seats about 15 people at a push. Hausbar is much more fun than all the wanky cafés with Russian literary names you'll find around the corner, and it's particularly inviting at three or four in the morning.

I Due Forni

Schönhauser Allee 12 (4401 7333). U2 Senefelderplatz. **Open** noon-midnight daily. €€. No credit cards. **Italian.** **Map** p87 B3 ⑮

The punky staff at I Due Forni look more likely to throw you out of a club than tease your tastebuds. But in a city of cheap pizzas baked by Turks or Palestinians pretending to be Italian, the stone-oven pizza here is authentic and excellent. A bit pricier than elsewhere, a meal can still run under €10, and there are also daily pasta specials and a salad that's essentially a head of lettuce you

BERLIN BY AREA

have to chop up yourself. Its smaller, sister pizzeria is almost as good.

In't Veld Schockoladen

Dunckerstrasse 10 (6391 6497/ www.intveld.de). U2 Eberswalder Strasse. **Open** noon-9pm daily. **Café**. Map p87 C1 ⓰

Kitted in retro orange and brown, floor-lit, and with a muted soundtrack of funk and soul, this café attached to the In't Veld chocolate shop serves a glorious selection of cocoas and other hot drinks. After a mug or two of thick, creamy chocolate (try it with orange, almonds or cinnamon) it's hard not to feel that this is the most relaxing place in Berlin.

Klub der Republik

Pappelallee 81 (no phone). U2 Eberswalder Strasse/bus N42. **Open** 8pm-4am daily. No credit cards. **Bar**. Map p87 B1 ⓱

Above a music school and accessed via a wobbly staircase in the courtyard, this spacious bar manages to mix the best of the retro design craze with the sort of lively revelry associated with the East in the mid 1990s. The beer selection is gratifyingly big – try the Augustiner, one of Munich's best brews. The DJs are top-notch, playing anything from 1960s soul to jazz fusion to electronica.

Konnopke's Imbiss

Under U-Bahn tracks, corner of Danziger Strasse/Schönhauser Allee (442 7765). U2 Eberswalder Strasse. **Open** 5.30am-7pm Mon-Fri; 11.30am-7pm Sat. €. No credit cards. **German**. Map p87 B1 ⓲

The Currywurst is justly famous at this venerable sausage stand, which has been under the same family management since 1930. It serves a variety of other snacks, too, plus the morning papers, and has a rudimentary seating area under the tracks.

Links vom Fischladen

NEW *Schönhauser Allee 129 (4431 9574). U2 Eberswalder Strasse.*

Open 11.30am-9pm Mon-Sat. No credit cards. **Café**. Map p87 B1 ⓳

A trek along Prenzlauer Berg's main drag is going to leave you in need of refreshment and, assuming you have strength enough to resist McDonald's and Starbucks, then head here. Named for its location 'left of the fish shop', this neat little café serves more milkshake concoctions than Willy Wonka could shake a stick at. Alongside the usual suspects are heart attack-inducing treats such as Oreo and Mars milkshakes, all freshly made to the consistency you prefer and priced between €4.40 and €4.90. It also serves cakes and fresh burgers.

La Muse Gueule

Mao Thai

Wörther Strasse 30 (441 9261/
www. maothai.de). U2 Senefelderplatz.
Open noon-midnight daily. €€€.
Thai. **Map** p87 B2 ⓴

Mao Thai's charming service and
excellent food comes with a 'to whom
it may concern' framed testimonial
from the Thai ambassador, on the
stairs down to the lower level. Classics
such as tom kai gai, spring rolls, green
papaya salad with peanuts and sweet
vinegar dressing, and glass noodle
salad with minced pork are all spectacular. Comfortable, well established
and friendly.

Marien Burger

Marienburger Strasse 47 (3034 0515/
www.marienburger-berlin.de). M2
Marienburger Strasse or M4
Hufelandstrasse. **Open** 11am-10pm
daily. €. No credit cards. **American**.
Map p87 C2 ㉑

Berlin burger bars tend to suffer from
some form of pseudo-Americana
theme, so this simple but lively neighbourhood hangout is a welcome relief.
Grease out with the traditional variations (cheese, chilli, barbecue) or go
even further with the deluxe double
Marien Burger. Even the singles are
pretty big. An extra 90 cents gets you
organic beef, and there are also chick-
en, fish and vegetarian varieties.

Massai

Lychenerstrasse 12 (4862 5595/
www.massai-berlin.de). U2 Eberswalder
Strasse. **Open** 4pm-midnight Mon-
Thur; 5pm-midnight Fri-Sun. €€€. No
credit cards. **African**. **Map** p87 B1 ㉒

A warm and friendly restaurant decked
out in traditional Eritrean colours and
serving exquisite East African dishes
using palm nut oil, peanut sauce, paprika, and berbere sauce made from hot
cayenne pepper, sweet paprika and ginger. Highlights include agbisa (West
African aubergines in palm nut sauce
with onions and paprika) and kilwa (ten-
der lamb fried in spicy butter). It's all
pleasantly light and spicy, and you can
also try ostrich and crocodile.

Miro

Raumerstrasse 28-29 (4473 3013/
www.miro-restaurant.de). S8, S41,
S42, S85 Prenzlauer Allee.
Open 3pm-midnight Mon-Fri; 10am-
midnight Sat, Sun. €€. **Turkish**.
Map p87 C1 ㉓

Named, they say, not after the painter
but in honour of a 'Mesopotamian natural philosopher', this cool, roomy
place serves excellent Anatolian specialities and well-priced drinks. The
menu is long and intriguing, with
ample vegetarian possibilities, legions
of starters and a good salad selection –
all of which arrive in hearty, generous
proportions. Friendly service too.

La Muse Gueule

NEW *Sredzkistrasse 14 (4320 6596).*
U2 Eberswalder Strasse. **Open** 5.30pm-
midnight daily. €€. No credit cards.
French. **Map** p87 B2 ㉔

The focus here is on good food and wine
in a refreshingly unpretentious space,
with simple wooden tables and chairs.
With French owners, French chef,
French waiters and French regulars,
you could be forgiven for thinking
you're in Paris, not Berlin. Alongside a
regularly changing menu are standard
dishes including home-made quiche,
and cheese and charcuterie plates. What
the service lacks in speed it makes up
for in charm, and anyway, this is the
kind of place where you want to linger.

November

Husemannstrasse 15 (442 8425/www.
cafe-november.de). U2 Eberswalder
Strasse. **Open** 9am-2am Mon-Sat;
10am-2am Sun. No credit cards.
Café. **Map** p87 B2 ㉕

Friendly place that's especially nice during the day when light floods in through
picture windows, offering views of
beautifully restored Husemannstrasse.
There's a breakfast buffet till 3pm
on Saturdays and 4pm on Sundays.

Pasternak

*Knaackstrasse 22-24 (441 3399/
www.restaurant-pasternak.de). U2
Senefelderplatz or M2 Knaackstrasse.*
Open 9am-1am daily. **€€€. Russian.**
Map p87 B2 ㉖
Small bar and Russian restaurant that's
often crammed, which can be irritating
at some tables – try for one in the small
side room. The atmosphere is friendly
and the food fine and filling. Kick off
with borscht or the ample fish plate,
then broach the hearty beef stroganoff.

Prater

*Kastanienallee 7-9 (448 5688/www.
pratergarten.de). U2 Eberswalder
Strasse.* **Open** 6-11pm Mon-Sat; noon-
11pm Sun. **€€.** No credit cards.
Bar/German. Map p87 B2 ㉗
Almost any evening, this huge and
immaculately restored swing-era bar,
across the courtyard from the theatre of
the same name, attracts a smart, crowd.
The beer-swilling lustiness, big wooden
tables and primeval platefuls of meat
and veg can make you feel like you've
been teleported to Munich. In summer,
the shady beer garden makes for an all-
day buzz. Brunch is served from 10am
to 4pm on Saturdays and Sundays.

Rakete

*Schönhauser Allee 39A (0160 9763
6247/www.rakete-berlin.de). U2
Eberswalder Strasse.* **Open** 8pm-late
Mon-Sat. No credit cards. **Bar.**
Map p87 B2 ㉓
Small, white and bright, with minimalist furnishings and low-key techno in
the background, Rakete has become a
casual hangout for local music and film
scenesters, though it's as likely as not
to have only a handful of people inside.
No draught beer, but the bartenders
know how to mix a drink.

Salsabil

*Wörther Strasse 16 (4404 6073). U2
Senefelderplatz.* **Open** noon-1am daily.
€. No credit cards. **Lebanese.**
Map p87 B2 ㉙

This Arabic/North African Imbiss has
all the usual trappings of tabbouleh,
falafel, houmous and schwarma, plus
lamb sausage, shredded chicken, lots
of fried vegetables and some kind of
balls made of fried egg and courgette
(eiji). It's all very tasty and reasonably
priced to eat here or take out. The
assorted platter for two is mammoth.
Nice choice of desserts too.

Schwalbe

*Stargarder Strasse 10 (4403 6208/
www.schwalbeberlin.de). U2, S8, S41,
S42, S85 Schönhauser Allee.* **Open**
6pm-2am Mon-Fri; 1pm-2am Sat, Sun.
No credit cards. **Bar. Map** p87 B1 ㉚
Schwalbe is about as chi-chi as a football bar gets, offering German and
Italian league games in a fashionable
café environment where you can grab
a coffee and cake instead of a beer.
Downstairs there are three strangely
crowded Kicker (table football) tables
and DJs on a Saturday.

Schwarzsauer

*Kastanienallee 13 (448 5633/www.
schwarzsauer.com). U2 Eberswalder
Strasse.* **Open** 9am-6am daily. No
credit cards. **Bar. Map** p87 B2 ㉛
Possibly the most popular bar on
Kastanienallee and the main meeting
place for those who inhabit the twi-
light zone between Prenzlauer Berg
and Mitte. Odd, then, that its ambience is pretty plain, its staff Berlin
surly, and its food and drink of only
adequate quality. In summer, the outside tables overflow day and night. In
winter, a tolerance for cigarette smoke
is helpful.

Sezarmeze

*Prenzlauer Allee 197 (4403 4280). U2
Eberswalder Strasse.* **Open** 11am-2am
daily. **€.** No credit cards. **Middle**
Eastern. Map p87 C2 ㉜
A welcome alternative to the typical
Turkish Imbiss, featuring home-made
snacks. The prerequisite falafel and
schwarma are prepared with sheep

cheese spreads flavoured with garlic and herbs, as well as freshly grilled vegetables, all wrapped up in durum bread. Meals can be ordered by phone.

Si An

Rykestrasse 36 (4050 5775/www.sian-berlin.de). U2 Senefelder Platz or M2 Marienburger Strasse. **Open** noon-midnight daily. **€€**. No credit cards. **Vietnamese**. Map p87 B2 ㉝

You can tell you're approaching the right address because the Asian decor is literally spilling out into the street, as is the hungry crowd at this popular Vietnamese restaurant. The small but varied menu of tasty noodle-based soups and dishes changes twice weekly. The bad news is that when it's crowded, service can be slow. The good news is that it's slow because dishes are made fresh to order.

Sumo Sushi

Kastanienallee 24 (4435 6130). U2 Eberswalder Strasse. **Open** noon-11pm Mon-Fri; 3-11pm Sat, Sun. **€€**. No credit cards. **Japanese**. Map p87 B2 ㉞

Stands out for its sashimi, made with very fresh-tasting tuna or salmon, and California maki, rice rolls with crabmeat and avocado rolled in red caviar.

Suppen Cult

Prenzlauer Allee 42 (4737 8949/ www.suppen-cult.de). M2 Marienburger Strasse or M4 Hufelandstrasse. **Open** 11am-8pm Mon-Fri; noon-4pm Sat. **€**. No credit cards. **International**. Map p87 C2 ㉟

A healthy alternative to fast food for lunch, snacks or early dinner, this sit-down Imbiss offers a wide and tasty assortment of fresh soups and stews to eat in or take out. The menu changes weekly but features the likes of creamed vegetables with ginger and orange or organic lamb stew with coriander and sour cream. Summer brings out chilled soups and various fruit recipes. Also home-made desserts and fresh juices.

Trattoria Paparazzi

Husemannstrasse 35 (440 7333). U2 Eberswalder Strasse. **Open** 6pm-1am daily. **€€€**. No credit cards. **Italian**. Map p87 B2 ㊱

Behind the daft name and ordinary façade is one of Berlin's best Italian restaurants. Cornerstone dishes are malfatti (pasta rolls seasoned with sage) and strangolapretti ('priest stranglers' of pasta, cheese and spinach with slivers of ham), but it's worth paying attention to the daily specials too. Booking is essential.

Wohnzimmer

Lettestrasse 6 (445 5458/www.wohnzimmer-bar.de). U2 Eberswalder Strasse. **Open** 9am-4am daily. No credit cards. **Café/bar**. Map p87 B1 ㊲

Immediately behind the door of this shabbily elegant 'living room' there's a bar-like structure made from an ensemble of kitchen cabinets. Threadbare divans and artsy bar girls make this the perfect place to discuss Dostoevsky with career students over a tepid borscht. Evening light from candelabra reflects on gold-sprayed walls as students and maudlin poets chase brandies with Hefeweizen. Daytimes can be sluggish.

Shopping

Eisdieler

Kastanienallee 12 (2839 1291/ www.eisdieler.de). U2 Eberswalder Strasse. **Open** noon-8pm Mon-Sat. Map p87 B2 ㊳

A group of young Berlin designers pooled resources to transform this former ice shop into an urban streetwear collective, and each of them manages a label under the Eisdieler banner – club-wear, second-hand gear, casualwear and street style.

Flohmarkt am Arkonaplatz

Arkonaplatz (0171 710 1662). U8 Bernauer Strasse. **Open** 10am-4pm Sun. Map p87 A2 ㊴

Flohmarket am Arkonaplatz has a broad array of retro gear ranging from records to clothing, books to trinkets, bikes to coffee tables – all at moderate prices. Best selection in the morning.

Flohmarkt am Mauerpark

Bernauer Strasse 63-64 (0176 2925 0021). U8 Bernauer Strasse. **Open** 8am-6pm Sat, Sun. **Map** p87 A1 ④⓪
This is one of the biggest and busiest flea markets in Berlin, retailing everything from cheap Third World fashion to cardboard boxes of black market CDs. Students and residents alike sell their things here at great prices, and you might just find a treasure trove of awesome second-hand clothing, books, bags and other goods.

Organic Market at Kollwitzplatz

Kollwitzplatz (4433 9137). U2 Senefelderplatz. **Open** noon-7pm Thur; 9am-4pm Sat. **Map** p87 B2 ④①
Small, open-air organic market. Steaming punch and wholegrain cinnamon waffles make it gemütlich in winter, but it's more lively in summer.

Saint Georges

Wörther Strasse 27 (8179 8333/www. saintgeorgesbookshop.com). Tram M2 Marienburger Strasse. **Open** 11am-8pm Mon-Fri; 11am-7pm Sat. **Map** p87 C2 ④②
Comfortable leather couches are provided for browsing a decent and nicely priced selection of English-language books, old and new. Lots of biographies and contemporary lit, plus a good turnover of dog-eared classics.

Scuderi

Wörther Strasse 32 (4737 4240/ www.scuderi-schmuck.de). U2 Senefelderplatz. **Open** 11am-7pm Mon-Fri; 11am-4pm Sat. **Map** p87 B2 ④③
Bettina Siegmund and Daniela Nagi work magic with gold, silver, pearls, stones and hand-rolled glass, creating lightweight ornaments that make a strong statement.

Skunkfunk

Kastanienallee 19 & 20 (4403 3800/ www.skunkfunk.com). U2 Eberswalder Strasse. **Open** noon-8pm Mon-Fri; noon-7pm Sat. **Map** p87 A2 ④④
Spanish urban label with adjacent stores housing men's and women's wear in lush cotton, fruity to earthy colours and asymmetric styles. Jackets are streamlined, and the men's jeans beautifully tailored. The name is on everything, sometimes too obviously and sometimes within a charming detail.

Nightlife

Duncker

Dunckerstrasse 64 (445 9509/ www.dunckerclub.de). U2 Eberswalder Strasse or S8, S41, S42, S85 Prenzlauer Allee. **Open** 9pm-late Mon; 10pm-late Tue, Thur, Sun; 11pm-late Fri, Sat. No credit cards. **Map** p87 C1 ④⑤
Duncker does have a reasonably varied line-up but definitely operates within a very dark sphere. It's perfectly located in a neo-Gothic church in a non-descript Prenzlauer Berg side street. While the tail end of the week focuses mainly on new wave, dark wave and indie, it's the Monday night goth party that is the club's bread and butter. Surprisingly in a city the size of Berlin, venues catering for our friends in black are few and far between, making this a precious gem for fans of the genre.

Icon

Cantianstrasse 15 (322 970 520/ www.iconberlin.de). U2 Eberswalder Strasse/tram M10. **Open** 11pm-late Tue; 11.30pm-late Fri, Sat. No credit cards. **Map** p87 B1 ④⑥
A tricky-to-locate entrance in the courtyard just north of the junction with Milastrasse leads to an interesting space cascading down the levels into a long stone cellar. It's a well-ventilated little labyrinth, with an intense dancefloor space, imaginative lighting, good sound and a separate bar. Music here takes in

Eats of the East

Osseria

Today, east Berlin is full of decent restaurants, but 20 years ago there was nothing but meat and two veg. Restaurants came in three, state-certified categories, staff were taught to do things in the same grumpily state-certified way, dishes were bland and fresh vegetables scarce. It would be some feat to replicate the true culinary horror of those days, but **Osseria** is having a go.

On a suitably gloomy corner in Weissensee, just north of Prenzlauer Berg, this GDR-themed restaurant is a clutter of products and memorabilia from the communist era – cameras, radios, books, record sleeves, banknotes. The menu also evokes the good old, bad old days, with dishes such as *eisbein* (pork knuckle), fillet of pork 'Hawaii' (with pineapple and nasty cheese) and, the standard communist-era vegetarian option, spinach with fried eggs and boiled potatoes. Most items reflect a traditional Germanness that survived in East Berlin while being displaced in the West by international cuisines. Hungarian goulash provides a rare cosmopolitan touch and you can wash it down with a glass of Vita-Cola, some sweet Rotkäppchen sparkling wine, or a *kaffee 'komplett'* (that is, with milk).

Sadly, Osseria fails the authenticity test on multiple counts. The menu is long and varied and nicely printed rather than fuzzily produced on some antediluvian duplicating machine, most items on it are available when you order them, service is friendly, the cutlery is of normal heft rather than being made from some spookily light aluminium alloy, there's no shortage of fresh vegetables, and the food is still warm when you get it.

For all its blandness, this food is of a quality that would only have been found in the best of GDR restaurants. Still, this is how it exists in the memory of the ageing East Berliners to whose 'ostalgia' this curious establishment exists to cater for. And, hey, there's a delivery service too.

■ Osseria, Langhansstrasse 103 (9606 8525/www.osseria-berlin.de). Open 11am-11pm daily.

BERLIN BY AREA

techno, reggae and hip hop, but mostly this is Berlin's premier drum 'n' bass club. Best when the core crowd of locals is augmented by a wider audience for some special event, but this is not usually a spot for the in-crowd.

Roadrunner's Paradise

Saarbrückerstrasse 24 (4405 6006/ www.roadrunners-paradise.de). U2 Senefelderplatz. **Open** varies. No credit cards. **Map** p87 B3 ㊸

Navigate your way through to the third courtyard of the former Koenigstadt brewery and you'll find Roadrunner's tucked away in the corner next to a motorcycle repair shop, a suitably greasy location for this butch venue. On offer is a tasty but irregular mixture of live shows and DJ sets, primarily focusing on garage, blues-rock, rockabilly and surf. The tiny stage may seem a lost in the wide-open concert room but there's plenty of room to dance and the sound system is surprisingly up to scratch. Alternatively, pull up a bar

Skunkfunk p94

stool and marvel at the array of 1950s American kitsch while sinking a beer.

Arts & leisure

Ballhaus Ost

Pappelallee 15 (4799 7474/www. ballhausost.de). U2 Eberswalder Strasse. **Map** p87 B1 ㊸

This somewhat dilapidated former ballroom offers art, performance art, dance productions and concerts, offering a unique and authentic cultural evening. There's also a lounge and bar populated by a very cool crowd.

Max-Schmeling-Halle

Am Falkplatz (443 045/tickets 4430 4430/www.max-schmeling-halle.de). U2 Eberswalder Strasse or U2, S4, S8 Schönhauser Allee. **Map** p87 A1 ㊹

Named after the German boxer who knocked out the seemingly invincible Joe Louis in 1936 (Louis settled the score two years later in only 124 seconds), this 11,000-capacity indoor arena faces an uncertain future. It was built as part of Berlin's abortive bid for the 2000 Olympics, and its anchor tenants, basketball side ALBA Berlin, have moved to the O2 World. Its main attraction now is the up-and-coming Olympic handball club, Berliner Füchse. With practically no public parking, it's got its back to the wall against the new, bigger kid in town.

Theater unterm Dach

Kulturhaus im Ernst-Thälmann-Park, Danziger Strasse 101 (902 953 817/ www.theateruntermdach-berlin.de). S8, S41, S42, S85 Greifswalder Strasse/ tram M4, M10. No credit cards. **Map** p87 C2 ㊿

In the large attic of a converted factory, situated well off the beaten path, Theater unterm Dach is the place to see new German fringe groups. Productions are always full of energy and can be quite inspiring. Small but distinctly exciting programme.

Karl Marx Alee

Friedrichshain

Stretching eastwards from Mitte along the Stalinist spine of Karl-Marx-Allee, and taking in a post-industrial area by the river, Friedrichshain is the inner-Berlin district that most clearly recalls the old East. **Karl-Marx-Allee** is a grand avenue built in Soviet style – it was the builders working on its construction who started the 1953 East Berlin uprising. Most of the district's life is centred around **Simon-Dach-Strasse**, the hub for a young, anarchic community of bohos and students, while the slowly disappearing former factories near the river have been hosting nightclubs for a decade or so. There's no sightseeing to speak of, save for the **East Side Gallery** – a stretch of former Wall east of the Oberbaumbrücke on Mühlenstrasse, which is bedecked with paintings from international artists.

Eating & drinking

Café 100Wasser
Simon-Dach-Strasse 39 (2900 1356). U5 Frankfurter Tor or U1, S3, S5, S6, S7, S9, S75 Warschauer Strasse. **Open** 9am-late daily. No credit cards. **Café. Map** p99 C2 ●
The all-you-can-eat brunch buffet (€7.90 Saturday, €9.50 Sunday) has a cult following among students and other late risers. Take your time and don't panic as the buffet gets plundered. Just when the food seems to be finished, out comes loads of new stuff.

Chüchliwirtschaft
NEW *Grünberger Strasse 68 (no phone). U1, S5, S7, S9, S75 Warschauer Strasse or U5 Frankfurter Tor.* **Open** 4-11pm Wed-Fri; 6-11pm Sat; 3-10pm Sun. No credit cards. **Café. Map** p99 C2 ●
It's crêpes galore at this artsy café. Swiss couple Klaus Linder and Roswitha Marie first started selling

their sweet and savoury creations from a van on Boxhagener Platz and now they've graduated to a small eaterie around the corner. Crêperie doesn't equate to fast food in this case. Wait and you'll be rewarded with beautifully presented pancakes, from sweet classics such as sugar and lemon to the more experimental Ovomaltine cream.

Cupcake

NEW *Krossener Strasse 12 (2576 8687/www.cupcakeberlin.de). U1, S5, S7, S9, S75 Warschauer Strasse.* **Open** noon-7pm Wed-Sun. No credit cards. **Café**. **Map** p99 C2 **❸**
Dawn Nelson, an American former make-up artist, makes her cupcakes like they're works of art. Swirls of raspberry cream, a cherry perching on the top and Oreo cookie fillings. Some say the cakes are too sweet, others can't get enough. Americanophiles can get their fix of Rice Krispie cakes and New York cheesecake, plus there's root beer, cream soda and Dr Pepper as well as the usual teas and coffees.

Ehrenburg

Karl-Marx-Allee 103A (4210 5810). U5 Weberwiese. **Open** 10am-late daily. No credit cards. **Café**. **Map** p99 B1 **❹**
Named after Russian-Jewish novelist Ilja Ehrenburg, a dedicated socialist, this café, with its sober, geometric decoration, is one of the few stylish places around Weberwiese U-Bahn station. Although the library looks like it's part of the decorative style, you're free to pick up a book and study the works of Ehrenburg, Lenin, Stalin, Engels or Marx as you enjoy a latte macchiato and other capitalist achievements.

Fliegender Tisch

Mainzer Strasse 10 (2977 6489). U5 Samariter Strasse. **Open** noon-midnight Mon-Fri, Sun; 5pm-midnight Sat. **€€**. No credit cards. **Italian**. **Map** p99 D1 **❺**
A small and unassuming restaurant away from the hubbub of Simon-Dach-Strasse, the 'flying table' nevertheless fills up with locals of an evening. Generous helpings of Italian comfort food, including gnocchi, risotto and, of course, the speciality thin-crust pizzas, leave you with a warm, fuzzy feeling and a round belly.

Frittiersalon

Boxhagener Strasse 104 (2593 3906/www.frittiersalon.de). U5 Frankfurter Tor. **Open** 6pm-late Mon; noon-late Tue-Fri; 1pm-late Sat, Sun. **€€**. No credit cards. **International**. **Map** p99 C1 **❻**
Organic burgers, Bratwurst and fries are flipped with attitude and served with delicious home-made ketchup, sauces and dips in this 'multikulti' gourmet chip shop. Burgers of the week involve some curious clashes of culture – a Middle East-influenced 'halloumi burger', for example, where a slab of fried cheese is embellished with yoghurt sauce, sesame dip and salad. For vegetarians there are also soya and camembert burgers, plus a meat-free Currywurst.

Goodies

NEW *Warschauer Strasse 69 (0179 738 0813). U1, S3, S5, S7, S9, S75 Warschauer Strasse.* **Open** 7am-8pm Mon-Fri; 9am-8pm Sat, Sun. No credit cards. **Café**. **Map** p99 C2 **❼**
This small café offers an enormous selection of coffees, teas, shakes and smoothies, as well as an assortment of home-made baked goods, creative sandwiches and New York-style bagels. The organic soup changes daily and there's a small but varied selection of ready-made salads. Though relatively swish for the neighbourhood, Goodies maintains a pleasant community vibe with its fair prices, friendly service, laid-back atmosphere, free Wi-Fi and children's area.

Habermeyer

Gärtnerstrasse 6 (2977 1887/www.habermeyer-bar.de). U1, S3, S5,

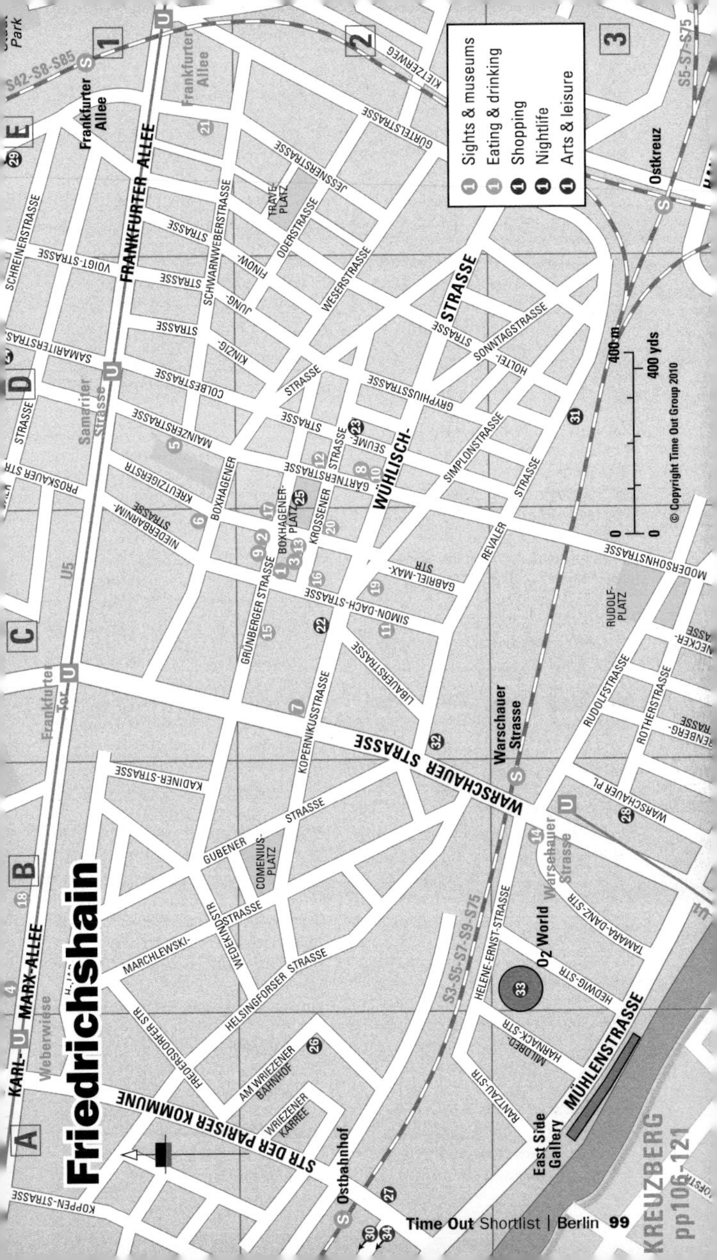

Friedrichshain
Sights & museums
Eating & drinking
Shopping
Nightlife
Arts & leisure
A
B
C
D
E
1
2
3
Frankfurter Allee
FRANKFURTER ALLEE
KARL-MARX-ALLEE
Weberwiese
Frankfurter Tor
Samariter Strasse
U5
S42-S8-S85
S3-S5-S7-S9-S75
S5-S7-S75
Ostkreuz
Ostbahnhof
Warschauer Strasse
WARSCHAUER STRASSE
WÜHLISCH-STRASSE
BOXHAGENER STRASSE
BOXHAGENER PLATZ
GRÜNBERGER STRASSE
KOPERNIKUSSTRASSE
SIMON-DACH-STRASSE
GABRIEL-MAX-STR
LIBAUERSTRASSE
KROSSENER STRASSE
GÄRTNERSTRASSE
SEUME-STRASSE
GRYPHIUSSTRASSE
SIMPLONSTRASSE
REVALER STRASSE
HOLTEI-STRASSE
SONNTAGSTRASSE
MODERSOHNSTRASSE
RUDOLFSTRASSE
RUDOLF-PLATZ
ROTHERSTRASSE
WARSCHAUER PL
TAMARA-DANZ-STR
HEDWIG-STR
MÜHLENSTRASSE
HELENE-ERNST-STRASSE
MILDRED-HARNACK-STR
RANTZAU-STR
O2 World
East Side Gallery
KREUZBERG pp106-121
STR DER PARISER KOMMUNE
KOPPEN-STRASSE
FREDERSDORFER STR
AM WRIEZENER BAHNHOF
WRIEZENER KARREE
HELSINGFORSER STRASSE
MARCHLEWSKI-STRASSE
WEDEKINDSTR
GUBENER STRASSE
COMENIUS-PLATZ
KADINER-STRASSE
NIEDERBARNIM-STRASSE
KREUTZIGERSTR
MAINZERSTRASSE
COLBESTRASSE
KINZIG-STRASSE
JUNG-STRASSE
FINOW-STRASSE
SCHWARNWEBERSTRASSE
WESERSTRASSE
ODERSTRASSE
TRAVE-PLATZ
JESSNERSTRASSE
GÜRTELSTRASSE
KIETZER WEG
PROSKAUER STR
SAMARITERSTRASSE
VOIGT-STRASSE
SCHREINERSTRASSE
400 m
400 yds
© Copyright Time Out Group 2010

Schneeweiss p102

S7, S75, S9 Warschauer Strasse.
Open 7pm-late daily. No credit cards.
Bar. Map p99 D2 ❽
Not a dive, but certainly not fancy,
Habermeyer is where local hipsters go
for low-key drinks, casual conversation,
table football, and a marked absence of
the teenagers and tourists who nightly
flock to Simon-Dach-Strasse. The decor
is unobtrusively 1970s, the lighting is
dim and reddish, and most nights the
music is delivered by a DJ.

Hot Dog Soup

NEW *Grünberger Strasse 67 (no phone/*
www.hot-dog-soup.de). U1, S3, S5, S7,
S9, S75 Warschauer Strasse or U5
Frankfurter Tor. **Open** 11.30am-11pm
Mon-Sat; 11.30am-9pm Sun. **€**. No
credit cards. **German**. Map p99 C2 ❾
Head here for a quick pick-me-up after
scouring the flea market on
Boxhagener Platz. Hot Dog Soup
serves up a daily changing menu of six
tasty soups, including cold ones in
summer, and a wide choice of organic
Neuland hot dogs in variations such as
'Red Hot Chilli' and 'Hawaii' (with
pineapples, chilli sauce and onions).
Sausage and soup also come in vegetarian and vegan varieties.

Kaufbar

NEW *Gärtnerstrasse 4 (2977 8825/*
www.kaufbar-berlin.de). U1, S3, S5,
S7, S9, S75 Warschauer Strasse.

Open 10am-1am daily. No credit cards.
Bar/café. Map p99 D2 ❿
A small, stylish bar and café with a
neighbourly atmosphere and a gim-
mick. You can buy the chairs you're sitting on, the table you're eating from,
that fork you're holding, the artwork
on the walls – just about everything, in
fact – hence the name ('Buy-Bar'). Light
organic snacks such as salads and
soups are served and in summer there
is a pretty garden area.

Künstliche BEATmung

Simon-Dach-Strasse 20 (7022 0472/
www.kuenstlichebeatmung.de). U1, S3,
S5, S6, S7, S9, S75 Warschauer
Strasse. **Open** 7pm-2am daily. No
credit cards. **Bar**. Map p99 C2 ⓫
The low-domed ceiling, plastic furniture
and coloured neon are like a cross
between cocktail bar and space capsule.
Around midnight, the beautiful young
things start dribbling in and any odd-
ness is soon swallowed in the crush.
Main attraction is an elaborate drinks
menu, which provides hundreds of lurid
opportunities for experimental boozing.

Macondo

NEW *Gärtnerstrasse 14 (0151 1073*
8829). U1, S3, S5, S7, S9, S75
Warschauer Strasse or U5 Samariter
Strasse. **Open** 3pm-late Mon-Fri;
10am-late Sat, Sun. No credit cards.
Café/bar. Map p99 D2 ⓬

This café/bar on Boxhagener Platz brands itself a 'Leseplatz' (reading place) and it's perfect for just that. Kitted out, like so many Berlin cafés, with fraying but trendy vintage furniture and offering a good selection of board games, it's a chill-out bar rather than a night-out place. Snacks such as fried yucca and a €5 Latin American brunch on Sundays keep the intellects sated.

Meyman

Krossener Strasse 11A (0163 806 1636/www.meyman-restaurant.de). U1, S3, S5, S7, S9, S75 Warschauer Strasse or U5 Samariterstrasse. **Open** noon-2am Mon-Thur, Sun; noon-3pm Fri, Sat. **€**. No credit cards. **North African**. Map p99 C2 ⑬
Moroccan and Arabic specialities plus good fresh fruit shakes and pizza are served in this warm and comfortable Imbiss, where there are usually plenty of tables. It's a bit pricier than some comparable places, but the super-fresh ingredients and a wide variety of dishes keep the crowds coming back for more – and few others are open this late.

Monster Ronson's Ichiban Karaoke

Warschauer Strasse 34 (8975 1327/ www.karaokemonster.com). U1, S3, S5, S7, S9, S75 Warschauer Strasse. **Open** 7pm-midnight daily. No credit cards. **Bar**. Map p99 B3 ⑭
In 1999, Monster Ronson – aka Ron Rineck – moved to Berlin from Salt Lake City with $7,000. As his savings dwindled, he began sleeping in his car, bought a second-hand karaoke machine, and soon was driving to squat houses all over Europe, throwing karaoke parties and getting paid. Eventually, he saved up enough to open his very own karaoke bar and today Monster Ronson's Ichiban Karaoke is packed most nights with pop star wannabes belting out songs in one of several karaoke booths, some small and intimate, others complete with stage area.

Nil

Grünberger Strasse 52 (2904 7713/ www.nil-imbiss.de). U1, S3, S5, S7, S9, S75 Warschauer Strasse or U5 Frankfurter Tor. **Open** 11am-midnight daily. **€**. No credit cards. **African**. Map p99 C2 ⑮
Sudanese Imbiss offering good-value lamb and chicken dishes and an excellent vegetarian selection, including falafel, halloumi and aubergine salad. Hot peanut sauces are the tasty but sloppy speciality.

Paule's Metal Eck

Krossener Strasse 15 (291 1624/ www.paules-metal-eck.de). U5 Frankfurter Tor or U1, S3, S5, S6, S7, S9, S75 Warschauer Strasse. **Open** *Summer* 5pm-late daily. *Winter* 7pm-late daily. No credit cards. **Bar**. Map p99 C2 ⑯
Neither a typical heavy metal bar nor remotely typical for this area, the Egyptian-themed Eck attracts a young crowd with relentless metal videos, a decent selection of beers and both pool and table football. Inoperative disco balls, mummy overhead lamps and formidable dragon busts deck an interior half designed like a mausoleum, half in gloomy medieval style. A small menu changes weekly and there's live Bundesliga football on weekend afternoons.

Le Petit Laboratoire

NEW *Grünberger Strasse 87 (0151 5905 0323/www.myspace.com/ lepetitlaboratoire). U5 Samariter Strasse.* **Open** 3pm-late Wed-Sat; noon-late Sun. No credit cards. **Bar**. Map p99 C2 ⑰
This French bohemian bar, with lots of sofas, bright colours and a comforting ramshackle feel, is a new Friedrichshain favourite. The highlight is a selection of delicious, self-invented cocktails such as the 'Tiramisu' or the one made with a hot herbal tea. The bar also works as a gallery space and plays host to regular concerts. The Gallic proprietors haven't

got the hang of German yet, so English is the working language, as a big sign behind the bar announces.

Prager Hopfenstube

Karl-Marx-Allee 127 (426 7367). U5 Weberwiese. **Open** 11am-midnight daily. **€€. Czech. Map** p99 B1 ⓭

All the favourites from your last Prague holiday appear here: svickova (roast beef), veprova pecene (roast pork), knedliky (dumplings) and the lone vegetarian prospect: smazeny syr or breaded and deep-fried hermelin cheese served with remoulade and fries. Sluice down this heavy fare with mugs of Staropramen beer; afterwards, a Becherovka herbal digestif helps thwart indigestion. Fast and friendly service is a pleasingly inauthentic touch.

Schneeweiss

Simplonstrasse 16 (2904 9704/ www.schneeweiss-berlin.de). U1, S3, S5, S7, S9, S75 Warschauer Strasse. **Open** 10am-1am daily. **€€€.**
Modern European. Map p99 C2 ⓳

This smart and understated establishment done out in fashionably minimalist white offers modern European dishes it describes as 'Alpine' – essentially, a well-presented fusion of Italian, Austrian and south German ideas. There are daily lunch and dinner menus, plus a breakfast selection and snacks, shakes and schnitzels served throughout the day. Although upmarket for the area, it's great quality for the price and deservedly popular, so make sure you book.

Shisha Alarabi Lounge

Krossener Strasse 19 (2977 1995). U1, S3, S5, S7, S9, S75 Warschauer Strasse or U5 Samariterstrasse. **Open** 10am-late daily. **€€.** No credit cards.
Middle Eastern. Map p99 C2 ⓴

Arabic restaurant/bar serving exotic vegetarian and meat dishes from Lebanon, Syria and Iraq. Hookahs are the real attraction for the twentysomething crowd: repair to the smoking room and take advantage of the ten flavoured tobaccos at €6 per hookah (€4.50 after 8pm).

Supamolly

Jessner Strasse 41 (2900 7294/ www.supamolly.de). U5, S4, S8, S10 Frankfurter Allee/bus N5. **Open** 8pm-late Tue-Sat. No credit cards.
Bar. Map p99 E1 ㉑

Having opened in the early 1990s as a semi-legal bolthole fronting a lively squat, Supamolly (or Supamolli) is a miracle of survival. The frequent live punk and ska shows in the club behind the bar dictate only some of the clientele; a healthy mix of young and ageing punks, unemployed activists and music-lovers of all types gather in this dim, mural-smeared, candlelit watering hole until the early morning. DJs at weekends.

Shopping

Big Brobot

Kopernikusstrasse 19 (7407 8388/ www.bigbrobot.com). U5 Frankfurter Tor. **Open** 11am-8pm Mon-Fri; 11am-6pm Sat. **Map** p99 C2 ㉒

The first German home for British label Fenchurch. Big Brobot also stocks Boxfresh, Stüssy and X-Large, among others. There are all sorts of cultish accessories, as well as comics and small-edition publications. The refreshingly unpretentious staff are friendly and helpful.

Das Blaue Wunder

Seumestrasse 12 (2576 8900). U5 Samariterstrasse. **Open** 4-8pm Mon-Fri; 10am-4pm Sat. No credit cards.
Map p99 D2 ㉓

This neighbourhood treasure stocks organic wines from all over Germany. Owner Klaus Sommer loves to sit you down for a chat and a tasting.

East of Eden

Schreinerstrasse 10 (423 9362/www. east-of-eden.de). U5 Samariterstrasse.

Beach bars

Waterside cocktails, white sand beaches, palm trees? Hardly the first things that come to mind when you hear the words 'Berlin summer'. But, from rooftop oases to poolside playgrounds, this city is a veritable hotbed of urban beach bars.

Badeschiff

On a deserted strip of riverbank behind the East Side Gallery, **YAAM** (Stralauer Platz 35, Friedrichshain, www.yaam.de) is one of the oldest and best loved of these summer hotspots. The Young African Art Market was conceived in 1994 by a group of activist artists and athletes as a space for multicultural and interdisciplinary experimentation. Packed to the brim with local street art, craft stands, and food vendors offering African and Jamaican specialities, YAAM also boasts a half pipe, climbing wall and basketball court available for free use. A chilled-out Caribbean vibe runs throughout the sprawling Spree complex, where the Red Stripe flows freely and the ragga plays all night.

Head just next door to **Wild West Strandmarkt** (Holzmarktstrasse 24, Friedrichshain, www.strand markt.de) for another bit of tropical paradise. Part bar, part beach, part amusement park, the Strandmarkt features everything from rodeo architecture to a 'western wellness' masseuse, a mechanical bull and live country music – all brought to you by the masterminds behind Mitte mainstay White Trash Fast Food. And, if you're in the mood for an actual swim, your best bet is over the river at the **Badeschiff** (p107), a floating public pool adored by locals and tourists.

For something a little less hip and a little more upscale, head to **Beach at the Box** (Englische Strasse 21-23, Tiergarten, www. boxberlin.com). This new kid on the riverbank has been making waves with its pristine sands, swanky daybeds and swaying palms. Measuring 600 square metres, the Box boasts two bars, a restaurant, and a sun deck with Spree views, all of them filled with dark wood, thatched canopies and a young, good-looking clientele. Also worth a visit are **Strandbar Mitte** (Gipsstrasse 11, Mitte, www. strandbar-mitte.de/strandbar/ index.html), **Lunas Strandgarten** (Revaler Strasse 34, Friedrichshain, www.freiluftre bellen.de/lunas-strandgarten) and **Deck 5** (Schönhauser Allee 80, Prenzlauer Berg, www.freiluftrebellen.de/deck-5).

Open noon-7pm Mon-Fri; noon-4pm Sat. No credit cards. **Map** p99 D1  24

The owners of this old-school second-hand shop shuttle frequently to London in search of paperback staples and rare editions. Books are also available to borrow at a small fee. Readings and concerts too.

Flohmarkt am Boxhagener Platz

Boxhagener Platz (0178 476 2242). U1, S3, S5, S7, S9, S75 Warschauer Strasse or U5 Samariterstrasse. **Open** 10am-6pm Sun. **Map** p99 D2 25

Many local young artists and T-shirt designers set up stalls at this overflowing market, while punky types and bohemian mothers shop for vintage sunglasses and unusual crockery. Depending on the day, you could snatch some great second-hand finds from students selling their old stuff. This place can be very cheap if you bargain hard enough.

Nightlife

Berghain/Panorama Bar

Wriezener Karree (no phone/www. berghain.de). S3, S5, S7, S75, S9 Ostbahnhof. **Open** 11pm-late Thur; midnight-late Fri, Sat. No credit cards. **Map** p99 A2 26

A strong contender for best club in the city, if not Europe. In basic terms, it's a techno club in a former power station, but it has to be experienced to be fully understood. Even non-fans of the genre fall head over heels in love with the relaxed atmosphere, interesting mix of eccentrics, well-thought-out design details, fantastic sound system and sexually liberal attitude.

Tip for newbies: Berghain's anything-goes approach extends only as far as what they don't see you doing. If you're searched at the door, an amnesty box gives you the opportunity to surrender anything illegal you may have before being cleared for entry. The club's reputation for a difficult and random door policy is not entirely undeserved. Panorama, with its smaller dancefloor and Wolfgang Tillmans artwork, is open all weekend; the more intense Berghain part of the venue, complete with darkrooms, is only open on Saturdays.

Fritzclub im Postbahnhof

Strasse der Pariser Kommune 8 (698 1280/www.fritzclub.com). S3, S5, S7, S9, S75 Ostbahnhof. No credit cards. **Map** p99 A2 27

This restored industrial building is relatively young in comparison to other venues, but its association with Radio Fritz gives it the clout to stage the likes of Arcade Fire, Stereophonics, Luka Bloom and Fun Lovin' Criminals.

Haus B

Warschauer Platz 18 (296 0800/www. dashausb.de). U1, S3, S5, S9, S75 Warschauer Strasse. **Open** 10pm-5am Wed; 10pm-7am Fri, Sat. No credit cards. **Map** p99 B3 28

Haus B is an East German gay relic, formerly known as Die Busche: loud, tacky, mixed and packed, this is one of east Berlin's oldest discos and is full of loutish lesbians, gay teens and their

Suicide Circus

girlfriends. A must for kitsch addicts and mainstream pop/dance fans; definitely a no-go area for guys who like a masculine atmosphere.

K17

Pettenkofer Strasse 17 (4208 9300/ www.k17.de). U5, S8, S9, S41, S42, S85 Frankfurter Allee. **Open** 10pm-late Tue-Fri. No credit cards. **Map** p99 E1 ㉙

Goth, EBM, industrial and metal are undead and well in this three-floor club. Parties have names such as Dark Friday and Schwarzer Donnerstag and the occasional live earaches feature hardcore, nü-metal and crossover bands. There's also a Dark Hostel within the same complex, offering goth-friendly accommodation.

Maria am Ostbahnhof

Stralauer Platz 34-35 (2123 8190/ www.clubmaria.de). S3, S5, S7, S9, S75 Ostbahnhof. No credit cards. **Map** p99 A2 ㉚

The premier venue for hipper live acts not quite ready for Columbiahalle also hosts dance nights that, although drawing top-notch DJs, don't come off very glam in Maria's concrete bunker environs. Yet its stylish post-industrial design is one of its attractions, along with the labyrinth of lounges that swells or shrinks according to the organisers' whim.

Rosi's

Revalerstrasse 29 (no phone/www.rosis-berlin.de). S3, S5, S7, S8, S9, S41, S42, S75, S85 Ostkreuz. **Open** 11pm-late Thur-Sat. No credit cards. **Map** p99 D3 ㉛

If you were asked to think of the typical Berlin club then something like Rosi's would no doubt spring to mind. It's a tumbledown, DIY affair; all bare bricks and mismatched flea market furniture. The atmosphere is very relaxed and the club tends to attract a young, studenty crowd. Live acts are a regular feature, DJs mainly spin electro and rock, and Karrera Klub hosts parties

from time to time. The beer garden is a popular hangout on summer nights.

Suicide Circus

NEW *Revaler Strasse 99 (no phone/ www.suicide-berlin.com). U1, S3, S5, S7, S75, S9 Warschauer Strasse.* **Open** midnight-open end Fri, Sat; 6pm-late Sun. No credit cards. **Map** p99 C2 ㉜

The desolate area around Warschauer Strasse S-Bahn station has had a shot in the arm – and not the kind it's normally known for. Suicide Circus opened on land owned by the Berlin transport authority, the BVG, and has been hosting crazy electro all-nighters, new wave discos and techno parties to provide a bright spot in a part of town not known for great clubs. Around the corner within the same compound is the new Astra concert venue, which has hosted gigs by Peaches and the Gossip.

Arts & leisure

O2 World

Muhlenstrasse 12-30 (2060 7080/ www.o2world.de). S3, S5, S7, S9, S75 Ostbahnhof. No credit cards. **Map** p99 B3 ㉝

The city's glitzy new multi-purpose arena has a 17,000 capacity and can be converted from rock venue to sports venue in a few hours flat. It's now home to both the Eisbären ice hockey team and the ALBA basketball team, as well as hosting a variety of one-off sport and music events. There are extensive conference facilities too.

Radialsystem V

Holzmarktstrasse 33 (6889 0777/ www.radialsystem.de). S3, S5, S7, S9, S75 Ostbahnhof. No credit cards. **Map** p99 A2 ㉞

This 'new space for the arts' and base for Sasha Waltz's dance company is also home to early music ensemble Akamus (www.akamus.de). A former pumping station by the river, it promotes a variety of one-off performance events and attracts a well-heeled crowd.

Badeschiff

Kreuzberg

Though it's now administratively joined to Friedrichstrasse across the River Spree, Kreuzberg has not only managed to maintain some of the independence of spirit that characterised its role as the centre of alternative politics and lifestyle during the Wall years, but it is also acquiring new life in the backwash from the last decade's drive to the east. Kreuzberg is fashionable once again. It's also the capital of Turkish Berlin, has a big gay community and, in the northern area that borders Mitte, possesses a clump of important museums and landmarks.

Eastern Kreuzberg

The Oberbaumbrücke was once a border crossing for Berliners, mostly used by eastern pensioners. Now, renovated by Santiago Calatrava in the 1990s, it's the only road connection to Friedrichshain.

The area around its eastern foot, radiating out from Schlesisches Tor station and spilling eastwards over the border into Treptow, has been on the up for the last few years and is solidifying as a new centre for nightlife. A little to the west, Kottbusser Tor is the centre of Turkish Berlin and Oranienstrasse is the district's main drag. Though there's plenty of entertainment around here, there's little in the way of formal sightseeing.

Sights & museums

Museum der Dinge
NEW *Oranienstrasse 25 (9210 6311/www.museumderdinge.de). U1, U8 Kottbusser Tor.* **Open** noon-7pm Mon, Fri-Sun. **Admission** €4; €2 reductions. No credit cards. **Map** p108 A1 (or B2) ❶
On the top floor of a typical Kreuzberg apartment block, the 'Museum of

Things' contains every kind of small object you could imagine in modern design from the 19th century onwards – from hairbrushes and fondue sets to beach souvenirs and Nazi memorabilia. It's not a musty collection, but a sleek, minimalist room organised by themes such as 'yellow and black' or 'functional vs kitsch', rather than by era or type, so that the 'things' – around 20,000 of them – appear in new contexts. Great shop too.

Eating & drinking

Ankerklause

Kottbusser Brücke, corner of Maybachufer (693 5649/www. ankerklause.de). U8 Schönleinstrasse. **Open** 4pm-late Mon; 10am-late Tue-Sun. No credit cards. **Bar**. **Map** p108 A2 ❷

Although it looks over Kreuzberg's Landwehr Canal, the only thing nautical about this 'anchor den' is the midriff-tattooed, punk-meets-portside swank of the bar staff. A slamming jukebox (rock, sleaze, beat), a weathery terrace and good sandwich melts offer ample excuse to dock here from afternoon until whenever the staff decide to close. Convivial during the week, packed at weekends.

Badeschiff

Eichenstrasse 4 (533 2030/www. arena-berlin.de/badeschiff.aspx). U1 Schlesisches Tor or S8, S9, S41, S42, S85 Treptower Park. **Open** *Summer* 8am-late daily. No credit cards. **Bar**. **Map** p108 E2 ❸

Moored on a post-industrial stretch of the River Spree, the 'bathing ship' is a cargo container turned public pool, with floating wooden lounge deck, open-air bar, onshore beach, sun chairs and hammocks. In summer, DJs spin minimal techno while young locals sip cocktails and soak up the sun; in winter, the whole thing is turned into a covered wellness retreat complete with two saunas, heated pool, bar, lounge and outdoor cooling platform. Whether channelling Ibiza or Helsinki, it's always good for a chilled-out taste of local flair. At press time it had yet to sort out its winter 2009-10 opening hours.

Baraka

Lausitzer Platz 6 (612 6330/ www.baraka-berlin.de). U1 Görlitzer Bahnhof. **Open** noon-midnight Mon-Thur, Sun; noon-1am Fri, Sat. €. No credit cards. **North African**. **Map** p108 C1 or C2 ❹

North African and Egyptian specialities such as couscous and foul (red beans and chickpeas in sesame sauce) enhance a menu that also includes lots of well-executed standards such as falafel, schwarma and kofte. You can take away your meal or eat in the cavernous restaurant with its cosy seating on embroidered cushions.

Barbie Deinhoff's

Schlesische Strasse 16 (no phone/ www.barbiedeinhoff.de). U1 Schlesisches Tor. **Open** 6pm-6am daily. No credit cards. **Bar**. **Map** p108 D2 ❺

Run by celebrity drag queen Lena Braun, this lively and unusual bar attracts both the more bourgeois members of Berlin's cross-dressing community and the loucher denizens of the Kreuzberg mainstream. The look is pitched somewhere between tacky kitsch and futuristic chic. There are often lectures and art events in the early evening, before the debauchery kicks off.

Bistro Yilmaz Kardesler

Kottbusser Damm 6 (no phone). U8 Schönleinstrasse. **Open** 10am-1am daily. €. No credit cards. **Turkish**. **Map** p108 B3 ❻

It's crowded, it's nondescript, but this humble Imbiss sells one of the best doner kebabs in Berlin. Crammed full of salad and seasoned with a startling array of spices, this is the Turkish fast food icon at its addictive best. And

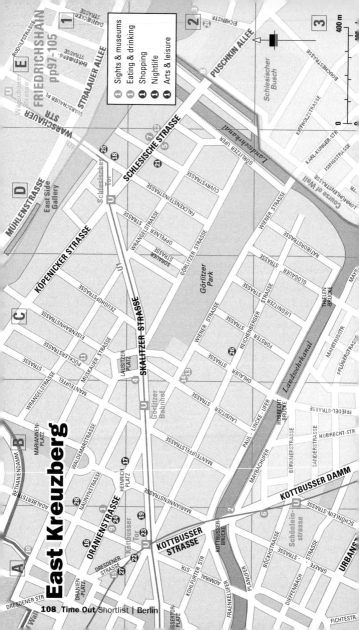

East Kreuzberg

FRIEDRICHSHAIN pp97-105

	Sights & museums
	Eating & drinking
	Shopping
	Nightlife
	Arts & leisure

Görlitzer Park

East Side Gallery

Schlesisches Tor

Görlitzer Bahnhof

Kottbusser Tor

Course of Wall

Schlesischer Busch

400 m

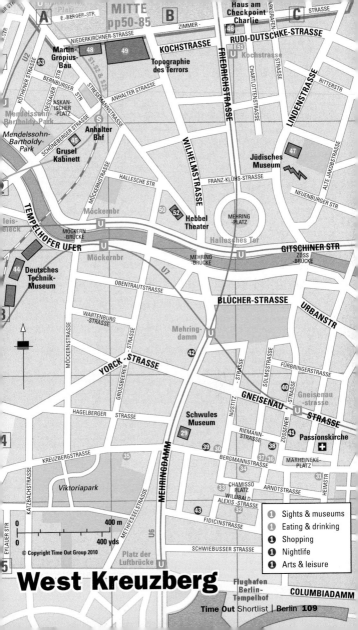

West Kreuzberg

A E.-BERGER-STR.
N 4. STR.
U2

Haus am
Checkpoint
Charlie

MARKGRAFEN STR.
ZIMMER-
STRASSE
NIEDERKIRCHNER-STRASSE
48 **49**
KOCHSTRASSE
RUDI-DUTSCHKE-STRASSE
46
51
Kochstrasse
Martin-
Gropius-
Bau
53
Topographie
des Terrors

CHARLOTTENSTRASSE
FRIEDRICHSTRASSE
LINDENSTRASSE
RITTERSTR.

KÖTHENER STRASSE
BERNBURGER
STR.
DESSAUER
STR.
ASKAN-
ISCHER-
PLATZ
STRESEMANNSTRASSE
ANHALTER STRASSE

J
Mendelssohn-
Bartholdy-
Park

SCHÖNEBERGER STRASSE
MÖCKERNSTRASSE
S
Anhalter
Bhf

Mendelssohn-
Bartholdy-
Park
45
Grusel
Kabinett

HALLESCHE STR

WILHELMSTRASSE
FRANZ-KLÜHS-STRASSE

Jüdisches
Museum
47

ALTE JAKOBSTRASSE
NEUENBURGER STR

Möckernbr
U
50 **52**
Hebbel
Theater
MEHRING
-PLATZ
Halleisches Tor
GITSCHINER STR
ZOSS-
BRÜCKE

leise-
eleck

TEMPELHOFER UFER
MÖCKERN-
BRÜCKE
U
Möckernbr
U
MEHRING-
BRÜCKE
U

44
Deutsches
Technik-
Museum
OBENTRAUTSTRASSE
U7

MÖCKERNSTRASSE
WARTENBURG-
STRASSE
BLÜCHER-STRASSE
URBANSTR

Mehring-
damm
U
42

GROSSBEEREN - STRASSE
YORCK - STRASSE
NOSTITZ - STRASSE
SOLMSSTRASSE
FÜRBRINGERSTRASSE
GNEISENAU -
40
Gneisenau
-strasse
STRASSE

HAGELBERGER STRASSE
ZOSSENER STR
Schwules
Museum
29
39 **30**
RIEMANN-
STRASSE
38
41
Passionskirche

KREUZBERGSTRASSE
MEHRINGDAMM
35
BERGMANNSTRASSE
37 36
34
MARHEINEKE-
PLATZ
HEIMSTR.
31

Viktoriapark
KATZBACHSTRASSE
METHFESSELSTRASSE
33
CHAMISSO
PLATZ
ARNDTSTRASSE
WILLIBALD-
ALEXIS -STRASSE
32
43
FIDICINSTRASSE

EYLAUER STR
0   400 m
0   400 yds
U6
SCHWIEBUSSER STRASSE

© Copyright Time Out Group 2010

Platz der
Luftbrücke
U6

Flughafen
Berlin-
Tempelhof
COLUMBIADAMM

1 Sights & museums
2 Eating & drinking
3 Shopping
4 Nightlife
5 Arts & leisure

if you're turned off by that great slab of meat slowly sweltering on the spit, there's also a good selection of grilled kebab.

Cake
Schlesische Strasse 32 (6162 4610/ www.cake-bar.de). U1 Schlesisches Tor. **Open** 6pm-late daily. No credit cards. **Bar**. Map p108 D2 **7**

A diverse crowd in both age and nationality – the hostel across the street lends a youthful international air – mills about in this lounge that comes with old easy chairs, sofas, art-covered walls and a dark red, musty interior. Music gently hums overhead, providing a great atmosphere for relaxing and chatting. It's even got a vintage jukebox equipped with a variety of oldies. DJs mostly weekends for free. Happy hour 7-9pm daily.

Club der Visionäre
Am Flutgraben 1 (6951 8942/ www.clubdervisionaere.com). U1 Schlesisches Tor or S8, S9, S41, S42, S85 Treptower Park. **Open** 2pm-late Mon-Fri; noon-late Sat, Sun. *Food served* 6pm-1am daily. No credit cards. **Bar**. Map p108 E2 **8**

On an inlet off the Spree just over the border into Treptow, this popular timbered bar occupies an old boathouse, several floating docks and a decommissioned boat. The vibe is warm and welcoming with haphazard, DIY decor. DJs spin minimal techno for the small dancefloor but most people prefer just to sit under the tree canopy enjoying a casual waterside drink. Later at night, things get more lively.

Hasir
Adalbertstrasse 10 (614 2373/www. hasir.de). U1, U8 Kottbusser Tor. **Open** 24hrs daily (often closes 2-3hrs early morning). €€€. No credit cards. **Turkish**. Map p108 A1 **9**

You thought the Turks had been chewing doner since time immemorial? Sorry, it was invented in Germany in 1971 by Mehmet Aygun, who eventually opened the highly successful chain of Turkish restaurants of which this is the flagship branch. While you'll get one of the best doners in Berlin, you owe it to yourself to check out the rest of the menu, which involves various other skewered meats in sauce, and some morish bread rolls.

Henne
Leuschnerdamm 25 (614 7730/www. henne-berlin.de). U1, U8 Kottbusser Tor. **Open** 7pm-1am Tue-Sat; 5pm-1am Sun. €€. No credit cards. **German**. Map p108 A1 **10**

Only one thing on the menu – half a roast chicken – but Henne's birds are organically raised and milk-roasted. The only decisions required here are whether you want to have cabbage or potato salad, and which beer you fancy washing it all down with (try the Monchshof). Check the letter over the bar from JFK, regretting missing dinner here.

Markthalle
Pücklerstrasse 34 (617 5502/ www.weltrestaurant-markthalle.de). U1 Görlitzer Bahnhof. **Open** 10am-1am daily. €€. **German**. Map p108 C1 **11**

This unpretentious schnitzel restaurant and bar, with chunky tables and wood-panelled walls, has become something of a Kreuzberg institution. Breakfast is served up until 5pm, salads from noon, and, in the evening, a selection of filling and reasonably priced meals. It's also fun just to sit at the long bar and sample its selection of grappas. After dinner, see what's on downstairs at the Privat Club.

Mysliwska
Schlesische Strasse 35 (611 4860). U1 Schlesisches Tor. **Open** 7pm-late daily. No credit cards. **Bar**. Map p108 D2 **12**

This small, dark bar draws a mixed local crowd and doesn't get going until late. The spartan interior boasts old, small, poker-like tables and stiff wooden chairs. Except for a pistachio dispenser and a frequently unpopulated, disco-balled side room, frills are kept to a minimum. There's live music once or twice a month and DJs play most weekends (no entrance fee).

Travolta

Wiener Strasse 14B (0176 2841 8879). U1 Görlitzer Bahnhof. **Open** 7pm-3am daily. No credit cards. **Bar**. Map p108 C2 🔞
This is old-school Kreuzberg: scruffy, congenial and cheap. Try a shot of Mexicaner – vodka, tequila, tomato and tabasco for just €1.50. Beer, meanwhile, is philanthropically priced at €2.80 for the half-litre. Music runs from punk to funk to Zappa, and the table football is popular.

Wiener Blut

Wiener Strasse 14 (618 9023). U1 Görlitzer Bahnhof. **Open** 6pm-late Mon-Fri, Sun; 3.30pm-late Sat. No credit cards. **Bar**. Map p108 C2 🔞
A narrow, darkish bar equipped with booths and a well-abused table football table, Wiener Blut sometimes features DJs who fill the place with wild beats and wild friends. Otherwise, it's just another red bar. The tables out front are perfect in summer.

Würgeengel

Dresdener Strasse 122 (615 5560/ www.wuergeengel.de). U1, U8 Kottbusser Tor. **Open** 7pm-late daily. No credit cards. **Bar**. Map p108 A1 🔞
Red walls and velvet upholstery convey an atmosphere aching for sin, while well-mixed cocktails and a fine wine list served by smartly dressed waiting staff make this a place for the more discerning drinker. The glass-latticed ceiling and a 1920s chandelier elegantly belie the fairly priced drinks and tapas on offer. It's a particularly nice place to be in summer, when a canopy of greenery curtains the outdoor picnic tables.

Berlin, uncooked

Berlin's culinary reputation might revolve around the Currywurst, but not everything on offer here is heavy, or even cooked. Since March 2009, chef Boris Lauser has served gourmet raw-food meals out of his apartment at Dresdener Strasse 114 in Kreuzberg.

He's also been building a following of hipsters, business people and curious Berliners who want to taste something new. 'I loved having people over for dinner when I lived in Italy, so when I came to Berlin, I decided to continue at home,' says Lauser, whose interest in food began during a stint working for the UN in Rome. His first training in raw-food preparation was in Asia; he then continued in a more formal setting in Arizona.

Now, from an upper-storey perch in a glass building just steps from the former Wall, the softly spoken 34-year-old serves dishes like 'spaghetti Bolognese' (the 'pasta' isn't pasta at all, but sliced courgette). A 'cheesecake' is so delicious that diners would never guess it's sugar-free and non-dairy.

Guests can book these 'rawsome' dinners in advance (dinner for two is €60 per person with wine pairings), but Lauser also hosts brunches and caters events for up to 50 people; all from his home kitchen with organic ingredients. 'I'm happy to bring something like this to Berlin,' says Lauser. The feeling seems to be mutual.
■ www.balive.org

BERLIN BY AREA

Shopping

Cherrybomb

Oranienstrasse 32 (614 6151). U1, U8 Kottbusser Tor. **Open** 11am-8pm Mon-Fri; 11am-6pm Sat. **Map** p108 A1 ⓰

German labels like Blutsgeschwister, Boogaloo and Berlin's own Volksmarke, plus the Netherland's King Louis and Colcci from Brazil, rub shoulders in this low-lit storefront. Although popular with women, there's plenty of streetwear for men too. The aesthetic is classic and functional.

Depot 2

Oranienstrasse 9 (611 4655/ www.depotzwei.de). U1 Görlitzer Bahnhof. **Open** 11am-8pm Mon-Sat. No credit cards. **Map** p108 B2 ⓱

Eastern earthiness combined with a skater/hip hop aesthetic has made IrieDaily one of the most popular local brands. This is the company's flagship. Girls' tops and trousers are flattering and edgy, the hoodies slinky and cosy; men's cargo pants are classy and velvety. Innovative accessories include belts and bags.

Nightlife

Dot Club

NEW *Falckensteinstrasse 47 (7676 6267/www.liveatdot.com). U1 Schlesisches Tor.* **Map** p108 D1 ⓲

In the former 103 Club, Dot is Berlin's new hub for live hip hop and old-school rap. In its first six months, its stage was graced by the likes of Grandmaster Flash, Ghostface Killah and De La Soul as well as more underground acts such as Dilated Peoples and Dead Prez. A beacon of hip hop in an electro town, this two-storey club has an authentic vibe, an enthusiastic crowd and impressive acoustics. It's not all beats and rhymes, though. Indie favourites such as the Go! Team, Circlesquare and Glass Candy also make frequent appearances, and there are DJ nights too.

Festsaal Kreuzberg

Skalitzer Strasse 130 (6165 6003/ www.festsaal-kreuzberg.de). U1, U8 Kottbusser Tor. No credit cards. **Map** p108 A2 ⓳

Festsaal means 'ballroom' and this venue near Kottbusser Tor has quite a refined edge despite the shabbiness of the interior, reinforced by a regular programme of literary and cultural events such as readings and poetry slams. The big hall and good sound system are often put to use for gigs or DJ sets. A special highlight is provided by the two tiny cellar rooms – a great location for small but intense electro parties such as DJ Emma Eclectic's You're My Disco.

Glashaus

Eichenstrasse 4 (5332 0340/ www.arena-berlin.de). U1 Schlesisches Tor or S8, S9, S41, S42, S85 Treptower Park. **Open** 10pm-late Sat. No credit cards. **Map** p108 E2 ⓴

The bare brick walls and sparse lighting of this dingy and intimate location make it look more like a dungeon than a club. It has an adequate sound system for its size, but does tend to get a bit sleazy towards the early hours. It is part of the riverside complex that includes the Badeschiff (p107).

Lido

Cuvrystrasse 7 (6956 6840/www.lido-berlin.de). U1 Schlesisches Tor. **Open** 10pm-late Fri, Sat. No credit cards. **Map** p108 D2 ㉑

Lido is the HQ of famed Berlin indie-rocksters Karrera Klub, who have been champions of new music in the city for over ten years now. This former theatre is a suitably spacious location to present a mixture of upcoming new live acts and hardy perennials. Lido has one of the best sound systems in the city and it has been put to superb use by MSTRKRFT. What was once a rear courtyard now has a canopy, so even in inclement weather you can take a break from the heat of the dancefloor.

Möbel-Olfe

Möbel-Olfe

Reichenberger Strasse 177, corner of Dresdner Strasse (2327 4690/ www.moebel-olfe.de). U1, U8 Kottbusser Tor. **Open** 6pm-late Tue-Sun. No credit cards. **Map** p108 A2 ㉒
It's an odd location for a gay bar, wedged among Turkish snack bars in a down-at-heel 1960s development at Kottbusser Tor and visible to the world through picture windows on two sides, but this place has been packed since the day it opened, mainly with gay and lesbian beer-lovers thanks to a good range on offer. Unpretentious, crowded, mixed and fun, with regular DJ nights too.

Paloma Bar

NEW *Skalitzer Strasse 135 (no phone). U1, U8 Kottbusser Tor.* **Open** 9am-open end Thur-Sat. No credit cards. **Map** p108 A2 ㉓
This hidden gem overlooking the scruffy urban spectacle that is Kottbusser Tor is a bookend kind of hangout; you either start here before hitting the clubs or stumble in at 7am for a final beer. It's tricky to find; take the concrete steps next to the Kaiser's

supermarket in Skalitzer Strasse and at the top turn left. That nondescript metal door is the entrance. It's a tiny, welcoming place, usually with standing-room only and a DJ spinning electro in the corner. Try to grab a window seat and enjoy the entertainment of 'Kotti' at night.

Roses

Oranienstrasse 187 (615 6570). U1, U8 Kottbusser Tor. **Open** 10pm-5am daily. No credit cards. **Map** p108 B1 ㉔
Whatever state you're in (the more of a state, the better), you'll fit in just fine at this boisterous den of glitter. It draws customers from right across the sexual spectrum, who mix and mingle and indulge in excessive drinking amid the plush, kitsch decor. No place for uptights, always full, very Kreuzbergish.

Watergate

Falckensteinstrasse 49 (6128 0396/ www.water-gate.de). U1 Schlesisches Tor. **Open** 11pm-late Wed, Fri, Sat; check website for occasional Tue, Thur events. No credit cards. **Map** p108 D1 ㉕

BERLIN BY AREA

This two-floor riverside club has a slick feel, a great view of the Spree and a better-than-average sound system. The two best features here are the panorama windows above the river and the flash, ceiling-mounted lighting display. Both floors are open on weekends and usually host two different sets of acts. Music policy is in the electro, house and minimal techno area – Ricardo Villalobos and Richie Hawtin often play – although artists such as Booka Shade and Digitalism occasionally appear.

Zpyz

NEW *Reichenberger Strasse 125 (no phone/www.myspace.com/zpyzclub). U1, U8 Kottbusser Tor.* No credit cards. **Map** p108 C2

Opening hours vary at this fashionably under-the-radar club, which only puts on parties when it feels like it – check its page before setting out. The place is just one large room on the first floor in the Hinterhof, with a bar and compact dancefloor. It has an illicit vibe but is very relaxed with reasonably cheap beer and mostly electronic sounds. It's pronounced 'spice', by the way.

Arts & leisure

Babylon Kreuzberg (A&B)

Dresdener Strasse 126 (6160 9693/www.yorck.de/kinos/detail/10000 8). U1, U8 Kottbusser Tor. No credit cards. **Map** p108 A1 ⊕

Another Berlin perennial, this twin-screen theatre runs a varied programme featuring indie crossover and UK films. Formerly a neighbourhood Turkish cinema, its programme is now almost all English-language and this place offers a homey respite from the multiplex experience.

Ballhaus Naunynstrasse

Naunynstrasse 27 (347 459 845/ tickets 347 459 844/www.ballhaus naunynstrasse.de). U1, U8 Kottbusser Tor. **Map** p108 B1 ⊕

Don't expect to hear anything ordinary at this Kreuzberg cultural centre. A varied assortment of western and oriental music is on the menu, with drinks and snacks in the café out front. The long, rectangular hall, which seats 150, plays host to the excellent Berlin Chamber Opera, among others.

Western Kreuzberg

The neighbourhood around busy Bergmannstrasse – bustling with cafés, second-hand stores, fashion retailers, delis, book and music shops – has long bucked the general trend for everything to drift eastwards and today is livelier than ever. By day, anyway; there's less of a scene by night. Some of Berlin's most beautiful streets are hereabouts – check the restored area around Chamissoplatz – and, on the other side of Mehringdamm, Viktoriapark, with its artificial hill and waterfall, is one of the city's most characterful green spaces.

Mehringdamm

Kreuzberg

Sights & museums

Schwules Museum

*Mehringdamm 61 (6959 9050/
www.schwulesmuseum.de). U6, U7
Mehringdamm.* **Open** 2-6pm Mon,
Wed-Fri, Sun; 2-7pm Sat. **Admission**
€5; €3 reductions. No credit cards.
Map p109 B4 ㉙

The Gay Museum, opened in 1985,
is still the only one in the world dedicated to homosexual life in all its forms.
The museum, its library and archives
are staffed by volunteers and function
thanks to private donations and
bequests (such as the archive of DDR
sex scientist Rudolf Klimmer). On the
ground floor is the actual museum,
housing permanent and temporary
exhibitions. On the third floor, the
library and archives house around
8,000 books (around 500 in English),
3,000 international periodicals, photos,
posters, plus TV, film and audio
footage, all available for lending.

Eating & drinking

Atlantic

*Bergmannstrasse 100 (691 9292). U6,
U7 Mehringdamm.* **Open** 9am-1am
Mon-Thur, Sun; 9am-2am Fri, Sat. No
credit cards. **Café. Map** p109 B4 ㉚

Atlantic's sunny pavement café thrives
in the summer, and a beer as late as
8pm will still have you sitting in a ray
of light, if you're lucky enough to get a
table. Breakfast, including 11 different
ways to have your eggs scrambled, is
served until 5pm. There are also daily
lunch specials, and dinner is a cheap
but decent affair. The staff change
every two days, as does the music.

Austria

*Bergmannstrasse 30, on Marheineke
Platz (694 4440). U7 Gneisenaustrasse.*
Open 6pm-1am daily. €€€. **Austrian.**
Map p109 C4 ㉛

With a collection of antlers, this place
does its best to look like a hunting
lodge. The meat is organic, and there

are also organic wines, Kapsreiter and
Zipfer beer on tap, and a famously
over-the-top schnitzel. Outdoor seating
on a tree-lined square makes it a pleasant warm-weather venue too. Book at
weekends and in summer.

Grünfisch

*Willibald-Alexis-Strasse 27 (6162
1252/www.gruenfisch.de). U7
Gneisenaustrasse.* **Open** 6pm-midnight
Tue-Sun. €€. No credit cards.
Italian. Map p109 C5 ㉜

A mix of modern and traditional
Sicilian dishes including some excellent seafood – monkfish wrapped in
parma ham, grouper in an almond
crust on rocket with fried oyster
mushroom strips – are served at this
tasteful place on leafy Chamissoplatz.
Tables outside in summer offer one of
central Berlin's most picturesque and
peaceable dining spots, but the
Sicilian organic wine from the
Azienda Agricola G Milazzo, exclusive to Grünfisch, is worth sipping
any time of year.

Haifischbar

*Arndtstrasse 25 (691 1352/
www.haifischbar-berlin.de). U6, U7
Mehringdamm.* **Open** 7pm-late daily.
No credit cards. **Bar. Map** p109 C4 ㉝

A well-run and friendly bar where the
staff are expert cocktail-shakers, the
music's hip and tasteful in a trancey
kind of way, and the back room,
equipped with a sushi bar, is a good
place to relax at the end of an evening.
Certainly the most happening bar in the
Bergmannstrasse Kiez, and with some
kind of crowd any night of the week.

Knofi

*Bergmannstrasse 11 (6956 4359
/www.knofi.de). U7 Gneisenaustrasse.*
Open 24hrs daily. €. No credit cards.
International. Map p109 C4 ㉞

Connected to the Mediterranean speciality store across the street, Knofi
is cosy and not much larger than an
Imbiss, but it boasts a cheap and

BERLIN BY AREA

delicious speciality in the form of crêpe-like gosses – both vegetarian or filled with schwarma – and generous portions of soup. It's also a top-notch bakery.

Osteria No.1

Kreuzbergstrasse 71 (786 9162/ www.osteria-uno.de). U6, U7 Mehringdamm. **Open** noon-2am daily. **€€€**. **Italian**. **Map** p109 B4 ③⑤

Most of Berlin's best Italian chefs paid their dues at this 1977-founded estab-lishment, learning their lessons from a family of restaurateurs from Lecce. Osteria is run by Fabio Angilè, nephew of the owner of Sale e Tabacchi (p121). Excellent three-course lunch menu and, in summer, one of Berlin's loveliest garden courtyards. Staff are super-friendly too. Booking is recommended.

Pagode

Bergmannstrasse 88 (691 2640/ www.pagode-thaifood.de). U7 Gneisenaustrasse. **Open** noon-midnight daily. **€€**. No credit cards. **Map** p109 C4 ③⑥

At Pagode you can watch the gaggle of Thai ladies whipping up your meal behind the counter and ensure that everything is fresh and authentic. Red and green curries here are sensational and the pad thai is heavenly. If the place looks crowded, don't worry: there's extra seating in the basement where you can watch the residents of a huge fish tank.

Sumo

Bergmannstrasse 89 (6900 4963/www.s-u-m-o.com). U7 Gneisenaustrasse. **Open** noon-midnight daily. **€€**. No credit cards. **Japanese**. **Map** p109 C4 ③⑦

Fresh Japanese food and intense flavours in a well-lit modern interior spread over two floors. The sushi is masterful but you can also enjoy standards such as tempura udon soup, warm bean salad, chicken yakitori and grilled tuna on rice. The feeling is modern Japanese toned down for German tastes.

Shopping

Another Country

Riemannstrasse 7 (6940 1160/ www.anothercountry.de). U7 Gneisenaustrasse. **Open** 11am-8pm Mon-Fri; 11am-4pm Sat. No credit cards. **Map** p109 C4 ③⑧

An impressive second-hand bookshop mostly used as a library, Another Country is stocked with about 20,000 English-language titles that can be bor-rowed or bought. The spacious, wel-coming premises abound with comfortable nooks and crannies for curling up with a book, and the store plays host to a weekly film night, TV night and dinner night.

Colours

Bergmannstrasse 102 (694 3348). U7 Gneisenaustrasse. **Open** 11am-7pm Mon-Fri; 11am-6pm Sat. **Map** p109 C4 ③⑨

Rows of jeans, leather jackets and dresses, including party stunners and fetching Bavarian dirndls, plus the odd gem from the 1950s or '60s.

Paul Knopf

Zossener Strasse 10 (692 1212/ www.paulknopf.de). U7 Gneisenaustrasse. **Open** 9am-6pm Tue, Fri; 2-6pm Wed, Thur. No credit cards. **Map** p109 C4 ④⓿

A Kreuzberg institution stocking thousands of buttons in every shape, colour and style you can think of. Whatever you're seeking, Paul Knopf ('button') will help you find it. His patient and amiable service is remark-able considering most transactions are for tiny sums.

Space Hall

Zossener Strasse 33 (694 7664/www.space-hall.de). U7 Gneisenaustrasse. **Open** 11am-8pm Mon, Tue, Wed, Sat; 11am-10pm Thur, Fri. **Map** p109 C4 ④①

Space Hall holds a huge range of new and second-hand CDs. Techno, house

Bergmannstrasse

and electronica are the emphasis, but there's also lots of hip hop, indie and rock. Vinyl of every kind from new releases to rarities can be found in sister shop Space Honda at no.35. Prices are competitive, and the employees know their stuff.

Nightlife

BKA Theater

Mehringdamm 34 (202 2007/www.bka-theater.de). U6, U7 Mehringdamm. **Performances** 8pm daily. No credit cards. **Map** p109 B3

With a long tradition of taboo-breaking acts, BKA still features some of the weirdest and most progressive cabaret performers in town: intelligent drag stand-up, freaky chanteuses and power-packin' divas. The theatre is filled with private tables and arena seats overlooking the stage. Fresh performances and good theme parties.

Arts & leisure

F40

Fidicinstrasse 40 (box office 691 1211/ information 693 5692/www.etberlin.de).

U6 Platz der Luftbrücke. No credit cards. **Map** p109 B5 ⓸⓷

Under directors Günther Grosser and Bernd Hoffmeister, F40 (formerly known as Friends of Italian Opera) offers a high-quality programme. Expect house productions, international guest shows and co-productions with performers from Berlin's lively international theatre scene. Theater Thikwa, one of Europe's most renowned companies working with disabled actors, is also based here.

Northern Kreuzberg

The area between the Landwehr Canal and the border with Mitte suffered greatly in World War II and today is a disjointed part of town with a few wastelands still punctuating patches of new buildings. Some of the city's major cultural institutions and historical memorials are scattered around here, though, especially along the line of the former Wall and in the area left blank by the disappearance of Anhalter Bahnhof, once the city's biggest station.

Deutsches Technikmuseum Berlin

Trebbiner Strasse 9 (902 540/ www.sdtb.de). U1, U7 Möckernbrücke. **Open** 9am-5.30pm Tue-Fri; 10am-6pm Sat, Sun. **Admission** €4.50; €2.50 reductions. **Map** p109 A2/A3 ㊹

Opened in 1982 in the former goods depot of the Anhalter Bahnhof, the German Museum of Technology is an eclectic, eccentric collection of new and antique industrial artefacts. The rail exhibits have pride of place, with the station sheds providing an ideal setting for locomotives and rolling stock from 1835 to the present. Other exhibitions focus on the industrial revolution; street, rail, water and air traffic; computer technology; and printing technology. Behind the main complex is an open-air section with two functioning windmills and a smithy. The nautical wing has vessels and displays on inland waterways and international shipping, while another wing covers aviation and space travel. There are models and original designs and electronic information points offering commentaries in English on subjects from the international slave trade to the mechanics of a space station. The Spectrum annex, at Möckernstrasse 26, houses over 200 interactive devices and experiments.

Gruselkabinett

Schöneberger Strasse 23A (2655 5546/ www.gruselkabinett-berlin.de). S1, S2 Anhalter Bahnhof. **Open** 10am-3pm Mon; 10am-7pm Tue, Thur, Sun; 10am-8pm Fri; noon-8pm Sat. **Admission** €8.50; €5.50-€6.50 reductions. No credit cards. **Map** p109 A2 ㊺

This chamber of horrors is housed in a World War II air-raid shelter. Built in 1943, the five-level bunker was part of an underground network connecting various similar concrete structures throughout Berlin, and today houses both the Gruselkabinett and an exhibit on the bunker itself. The 'horrors' begin at ground level with an exhibit on medieval medicine (mechanical figures amputate a leg to the sound of canned screaming). Elsewhere, there's a patented coffin designed to advertise your predicament should you happen to be buried alive. Upstairs is scarier: a musty labyrinth with a simulated cemetery, strange cloaked figures, lots of spooky sounds and a few surprises. Kids love it, but not those under ten.

Haus am Checkpoint Charlie

Friedrichstrasse 43-45 (253 7250/ www.mauermuseum.de). U6 Kochstrasse. **Open** 9am-10pm daily. **Admission** €9.50; €5.50 reductions. No credit cards. **Map** p109 B1 ㊽

A little tacky, but essential for anyone interested in the Wall and the Cold War. This private museum opened not long after the DDR erected the Berlin Wall in 1961 with the purpose of documenting the events that were taking place. The exhibition charts the history of the Wall, and gives details of the ingenious and hair-raising ways people escaped from the DDR – as well as exhibiting some of the actual contraptions that were used, such as a homemade hot-air balloon.

Jüdisches Museum

Lindenstrasse 9-14 (2599 3300/guided tours 2599 3305/www.juedisches-museum-berlin.de). U1, U6 Hallesches Tor. **Open** 10am-10pm Mon; 10am-8pm Tue-Sun. **Admission** €5; €2.50 reductions. **Map** p109 C2 ㊼

The ground plan of Libeskind's remarkable building, completed in 1998, is in part based on an exploded Star of David, in part on lines drawn between the site and former addresses of figures in Berlin's Jewish history, such as Mies van der Rohe, Arnold Schönberg and Walter Benjamin. The entrance is via a tunnel from the Kollegienhaus next door. The underground geometry is startlingly independent of the above-ground building. One passage leads to the exhibition halls, two others intersect en route to the Holocaust Tower and the ETA Hoffmann Garden, a grid of 49 columns, tilted to disorientate. Throughout, diagonals and parallels carve out surprising spaces, while windows slash through the structure and its zinc cladding like the knife-wounds of history. And then there are the 'voids' cutting through the layout, negative spaces that stand for the emptiness left by the destruction of German Jewish culture.

The permanent exhibition, which opened in 2001, struggles in places with such powerful surroundings. What makes the exhibit engaging is its focus on the personal: it tells the stories of prominent Jews, what they contributed to their community and to the cultural and economic life of Berlin and Germany. After centuries of prejudice and pogroms, the outlook for German Jews seemed to be brightening.

Then came the Holocaust. This part of the exhibit is the most harrowing. The emotional impact of countless stories of the eminent and ordinary, and the fate that almost all shared, is hard to convey adequately in print. The museum is a must-see, but expect long queues and big crowds. Last entrance is one hour before closing time. There are also some excellent temporary exhibitions to visit.

Martin-Gropius-Bau

Niederkirchnerstrasse 7 (254 860/ www.gropiusbau.de). S1, S2, S26 Anhalter Bahnhof. **Open** 10am-8pm Mon, Wed-Sun. **Map** p109 A1 ㊽
Cosying up to where the Wall once stood (there is still a short, pitted stretch running along the south side of nearby Niederkirchnerstrasse), the Martin-Gropius-Bau is named after its architect, uncle of the more famous Walter. Built in 1881, it has been renovated and serves as a venue for an assortment of large-scale art exhibitions and themed

Jüdisches Museum

Tempelhof Airport RIP

In October 2008, after years of political wrangling, Berlin's **Flughafen Tempelhof**, one of the world's oldest airports, which lies at Kreuzberg's southern border, was closed. For those who had pushed for closure, including mayor Klaus Wowereit, it was a huge drain on the city's budget. But for its supporters, including Angela Merkel, it was an architectural landmark and monument to over 100 years of aviation history. In 1909 flight pioneer Orville Wright landed on the airfield, which became a commercial airport in the 1920s. In the 1930s the monumental arc-shaped terminal, still one of the world's largest buildings, was constructed for Hitler as a symbolic entryway into the planned new city of Germania. After the war it became a US Air Force base and stage for the late 1940s Berlin Airlift. For decades it was West Berlin's only airport, but with the opening of Flughafen Tegel in 1975, the decline of Tempelhof began.

A huge campaign to save Tempelhof showed up some of the city's remaining faultlines – those for it were mostly westerners and conservatives; east Berliners didn't even care enough to vote in the non-binding referendum – but the decision lay with the Berlin Senate, whose mind was made up. Plans for Tempelhof were being mooted long before closure, including an offer by American billionaire Ronald S Lauder to turn the listed terminal into a giant health centre, with its airport intended to serve wealthy patients.

Tempelhof's long-term future remains undecided, but the 900-acre site in the heart of the city is a potential goldmine, and many Berliners fear that it will simply become yet more shopping malls and exclusive housing developments. Lobby groups like be4tempelhof are still fighting to save Tempelhof as a working airport and UNESCO World Heritage Site, but don't stand much chance. In 2008 the Bread & Butter fashion trade fair signed a ten-year lease on part of the terminal building, controversially beating off less commercial bids from Babelsberg film studios and the Deutsches Technik Museum. The 'mother of all airports', as Sir Norman Foster dubbed Tempelhof, appears to have had its day.

shows. Summer 2010 features a Frida Kahlo retrospective, an exhibition about 300 years of science in Berlin, and 'Teotihuacan: The Mystery of the Pyramids'. It's also a venue for the Berlin Biennale.

Topographie des Terrors

Niederkirchnerstrasse 8 (2548 6703/ www.topographie.de). S1, S2, S26 Anhalter Bahnhof. **Open** *Oct-Apr* 10am-6pm daily. *May-Sept* 10am-8pm daily. **Admission** free. **Map** p109 A1 ㊾

Essentially a piece of waste ground that was once the site of the Prinz Albrecht Palais, headquarters of the Gestapo, and the Hotel Prinz Albrecht, which housed offices of the Reich SS leadership. This was the centre of the Nazi police state apparatus and it was from here that the Holocaust was directed, and the Germanisation of the east dreamt up. Until a documentation centre opens in May 2010, there's not much here except an open-air exhibition about the history of the site and a temporary building where you can buy a catalogue and pick up a free audio guide. A surviving segment of the Wall runs along the site's northern boundary. The main entrance is where that meets the north-east corner of the Martin-Gropius-Bau.

Eating & drinking

Grossbeerenkeller

Grossbeerenstrasse 90 (251 3064). U1, U7 Möckernbrücke. **Open** 4pm-1am Mon-Fri; 6pm-1am Sat. **€€**. No credit cards. **German**. **Map** p109 B2 ㊿

In business since 1862, with walls adorned by fading photos of faded theatre stars, Grossbeerenkeller serves good home cooking of a solid Berlinisch bent. It offers a true taste of Alt-Berlin.

Sale e Tabacchi

Rudi-Dutschke-Strasse 23 (252 1155). U6 Kochstrasse. **Open** 9am-2am Mon-Fri; 10am-2am Sat, Sun. **€€€**. **Italian**. **Map** p109 C1 (51)

Well known for fish dishes (tuna and swordfish carpaccio or loup de mer) and for the pretty courgette flowers filled with ricotta and mint, not to mention its large, impressive selection of Italian wines. The interior design is meant to reflect a time when salt (sale) and tobacco (tabacchi) were sold exclusively by the state. In summer, enjoy lunch or dinner in the garden under lemon, orange and pomegranate trees.

Arts & leisure

HAU

Main office: HAU2, Hallesches Ufer 32 (box office 2590 0427/information 259 0040/www.hebbel-am-ufer.de). U1, U7 Möckernbrücke or U1, U6 Hallesches Tor. **Map** p109 B2 (52)

The most exciting stage programming in the city is currently coming from the amalgamation of the century-old former Hebbel Theater (HAU1), Theater am Hallesches Ufer (HAU2) and Theater am Ufer (HAU3). Under intendant Matthias Lilienthal this tripartite theatre has become a hotbed of new international work and is one of the leading venues for young, international, experimental and innovative performing arts.

Other locations: HAU1, Stresemannstrasse 29; HAU3, Tempelhofer Ufer 10.

Meistersaal

Köthener Strasse 38 (325 999 710/ www.meistersaal-berlin.de). U2, S1, S2, S25, S26 Potsdamer Platz. **Map** p109 A1 (53)

What was once the Hansa recording studio now hosts solo instrumentalists and chamber groups that can't afford to book the Kammermusiksaal of the Philharmonie. But don't let that fool you. Music-making of the highest rank occurs here in this warm and welcoming little salon, which is notable for its superb acoustics. Back when this was a studio, David Bowie and Iggy Pop were among the many who recorded here.

Winterfeldt Markt p126

Schöneberg

The largely residential district of Schöneberg is both culturally and geographically halfway between Kreuzberg and Charlottenburg. The area around Winterfeldtplatz, with its twice weekly market, is lively with cafés and shops. The scene continues south down Goltzstrasse. Motzstrasse has been a gay area since the 1920s (gay and lesbian victims of the Holocaust are commemorated on a plaque outside Nollendorfplatz station) and remains the boys' main drag. Wittenbergplatz, at Schöneberg's north-west corner, is home to **KaDeWe**, continental Europe's biggest department store, famous for its sixth-floor food hall. From here, Tauentzienstrasse runs west into the Ku-damm, marking the beginning of west Berlin's main shopping mile.

Eating & drinking

La Cocotte

Vorbergstrasse 10 (7895 7658/ www.lacocotte.de). U7 Eisenacher Strasse. **Open** 6pm-1am daily. **€€€**. No credit cards. **French**. **Map** p123 B4 ❶
Friendly, gay-owned place where good cooking is enhanced by a sense of fun and occasional themed events – such as the Beaujolais nouveau being welcomed by a 'rustic chic' buffet and a programme of accordion music and 1980s French pop. Vegetarians aren't forgotten, there's a nice terrace, and the toilets are absolutely beautiful.

Green Door

Winterfeldtstrasse 50 (215 2515/ www.greendoor.de). U1, U2, U3, U4 Nollendorfplatz. **Open** 6pm-3am Mon-Thur, Sun; 6pm-4am Fri, Sat. No credit cards. **Bar**. **Map** p123 B2 ❷

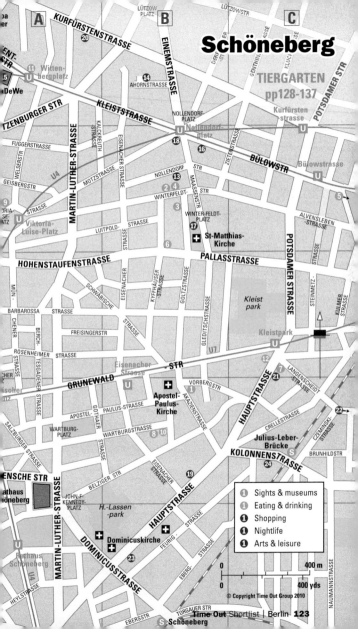

Schöneberg

TIERGARTEN
pp128-137

Kurfürstenstrasse

Kleist park

Eisenacher Strasse

Apostel-Paulus-Kirche

St-Matthias-Kirche

Kleistpark

Julius-Leber-Brücke

Rathaus Schöneberg

Rathaus Schöneberg

Dominicuskirche

H.-Lassen-park

Viktoria-Luise-Platz

①	Sights & museums
①	Eating & drinking
①	Shopping
①	Nightlife
①	Arts & leisure

0   400 m

0   400 yds

© Copyright Time Out Group 2010

It really does have a green door, and behind it there's a whole lotta cocktail shaking going on. The drinks menu is impressively long, as is the curvy bar, and it's in a good location just off lively Winterfeldtplatz.

Habibi

Goltzstrasse 24, on Winterfeldtplatz (215 3332). U1, U2, U3, U4 Nollendorfplatz. **Open** 11am-3am Mon-Thur, Sun; 11am-5am Fri, Sat. €. No credit cards. **Middle Eastern**. **Map** p123 B2 ❸
Best branch of a small chain serving Middle Eastern specialities including falafel, kibbeh, tabbouleh and various combination plates. Wash it down with freshly squeezed juice, and finish up with a complimentary tea and one of the wonderful pastries. Light, bright, well run and deservedly popular.
Other locations: Akazienstrasse 9 (787 4428).

Honeypenny

NEW *Winterfeldtstrasse 44 (01578 361 9203). U1, U2, U3, U4 Nollendorfplatz.* **Open** 8pm-1am Mon-Sat; 10am-1am Sun. No credit cards. **Café. Map** p123 B2 ❹
With its comfortable, vaguely retro interior and summer tables overlooking the square, this is currently our café of choice in the busy Winterfeldt neighbourhood. Breakfast is served until 3pm for a mix of Schöneberg stalwarts and the flotsam that drifts in for the market on Wednesdays and Saturdays. You can get a toasted sandwich any time of day, and cocktails kick in from around 6pm.

Munch's Hus

Bülowstrasse 66 (2101 4086/www. munchshus.de). U2 Bülowstrasse. **Open** 10am-1am daily. €€. **Norwegian. Map** p123 C2 ❺
In a corner of town bereft of good places to eat, Berlin's only Norwegian restaurant is frequented by businessmen and artists from the neighbourhood.

Daily specials are reminiscent of the rounded German meal – potatoes and well-dressed greens accompany most dishes – but with a twist that usually involves dill. Creamy, fresh soups and delicious fish dishes are the specialities, but light sandwiches and salads are also available.

Mutter

Hohenstaufenstrasse 4 (2191 5100). U1, U2, U3, U4 Nollendorfplatz. **Open** 10am-4am daily. **Café. Map** p123 B2 ❻
'Mother' (or 'nut', as in bolt) tries to do everything at once: two bars; an enormous selection of wines, beers and cocktails; breakfasts until 6pm; a sushi bar from 6pm, plus other snacks throughout the day. It's a big place, but it can be difficult to find a seat on weekend nights, when trancey sounds pulse in the front bar (there is more sedate music in the café area at the back). It's roomy, the decor is heavy on gold paint and the spectacular corridor to the toilets is worth a visit in itself.

KaDeWe p126

Petite Europe

*Langenscheidtstrasse 1 (781 2964). U7
Kleistpark.* **Open** 5pm-1am daily. €€.
Italian. Map p123 C3 **7**

You may have to wait for a table in this
popular place, but the turnover's fast.
Weekly specials are good, as are the pizzas, and although none of it is haute cuisine, it's all well made and inexpensive.
Free bruschette arrive when you've
ordered and a complimentary grappa
is offered when you ask for the bill.

Pinguin Club

*Wartburgstrasse 54 (781 3005/
www.pinguin-club.de). U7 Eisenacher
Strasse.* **Open** 9pm-4am daily. No
credit cards. **Bar. Map** p123 B4 **8**

Though somewhat past its heyday, this
speakeasy-style bar remains one of
Berlin's finest and friendliest institutions. It's decorated with original 1950s
Americana and rock 'n' roll memorabilia, the owners all have punk roots and
good sounds are a feature. Take your
pick from 156 spirits, and don't be surprised if everyone starts singing along
to Nick Cave or Dean Martin.

Potemkin

*Viktoria-Luise-Platz 5 (2196 8181).
U4 Viktoria-Luise-Platz.* **Open** 8am-
1am Tue-Sun. No credit cards. **Café.
Map** p123 A2 **9**

Film stills and the likeness of *Battleship
Potemkin* director Sergei Eisenstein
adorn the wall, and the red and
black decor has a constructivist feel.
Breakfasts also sport titles of Eisenstein
films, from the basic 'Ivan the Terrible'
to 'Viva Mexico', with marinated chicken breast served with pineapple and
cheese on toast. There's also a daily
lunch special and snacks such as moz-
zarella rolls stuffed with serrano ham.

Renger-Patzsch

NEW *Wartburgstrasse 54 (784 2059/
www.renger-patzsch.com). U7
Eisenacher Strasse.* **Open** 6pm-1am
daily. €€€. No credit cards.
German. Map p123 B4 **10**

The pan-German menu – soup and
salad starters, a sausage and sauerkraut platter, plus daily varying meat
and fish dishes – is finely prepared by
chef Hannes Behrmann. House speciality is Alsatian Pflammkuchen or tarte
flambée: a crisp pastry base baked and
served with toppings in several mouth-
watering variations. Long wooden
tables are shared by different parties
and in summer there's a nice garden on
this quiet and beautiful corner.

Witty's

*Wittenbergplatz (no phone). U1, U2,
U3 Wittenbergplatz.* **Open** 11am-1am
daily. €. No credit cards. **German.
Map** p123 A1 **11**

There are Imbiss stands on every corner of Wittenbergplatz, but this one –
on the north-west corner opposite
KaDeWe – is one of the best in the city.
A courteous operation, it serves only
Neuland organic meat, has stunning
thick-cut chips served with a choice of
seven sauces, and there's usually a
queue of well-heeled folk eager to
snack on a sausage that's as good as
anything served in the gourmet food
hall over the road.

Zoulou Bar

*Hauptstrasse 4 (7009 4737/
www.zouloubar.de). U7 Kleistpark.*
Open 7pm-6am daily. No credit cards.
Bar. Map p123 C3 **12**

Small, dark bar with a funky vibe and
occasional DJs. It can get packed
between 10pm and 2am; visit later,
when the crowd has thinned.

Shopping

Fingers

*Nollendorfstrasse 35 (215 3441). U1,
U2, U3, U4 Nollendorfplatz.* **Open**
3-6.30pm Tue-Fri; 11.30am-3pm Sat.
No credit cards. **Map** p123 B2 **13**

Down the road from Christopher
Isherwood's old gaff (that's at no.17),
here are splendid finds from the 1940s,
'50s and '60s, including lipstick-shaped

cigarette lighters, vintage toasters, weird lighting and eccentric glassware.

Garage

Ahornstrasse 2, off Einemstrasse (211 2760). U1, U2, U3, U4 Nollendorfplatz. **Open** 11am-7pm Mon-Fri; 11am-6pm Sat. **Map** p123 B1 ⑭
Garage sells cheap second-hand clothing priced by the kilo. The large selection at this barn-like emporium is well organised, making it easy to root out last-minute party gear.

KaDeWe

Tauentzienstrasse 21-24 (212 10/ www.kadewe.de). U1, U2, U3 Wittenbergplatz. **Open** 10am-8pm Mon-Thur; 10am-9pm Fri; 9.30am-10pm Sat. **Map** p123 A1 ⑮
The largest department store in continental Europe carries name brands in every well-stocked department. Though the range of actual merchandise can be somewhat predictable, if you know what you're looking for you'll find it here. The undoubted highlight is the extraordinary food hall.

Mr Dead & Mrs Free

Bülowstrasse 5 (215 1449/www. deadandfree.com). U1, U2, U3, U4 Nollendorfplatz. **Open** noon-7pm Mon-Fri; 11am-4pm Sat. **Map** p123 B2 ⑯
Long Berlin's leading address for independent and underground rock, Mr Dead & Mrs Free has bucketloads of British, US and Australian imports, a large vinyl section and staff that know their music. Small but choice selection of books and magazines as well.

Winterfeldt Markt

Winterfeldtplatz (no phone). U1, U2, U3, U4 Nollendorfplatz. **Open** 8am-1pm Wed; 8am-3.30pm Sat. **Map** p123 B2 ⑰
On Saturdays, it seems like all of west Berlin is visiting this market, full to the brim with vegetables, cheese, wholegrain breads, Wurst, meats, flowers, clothes, soaps, candles and toys. Many are there for their weekly shopping; others, to meet a friend at one of the many cafés off the square. A Berlin institution worth experiencing first-hand.

Nightlife

Goya

NEW *Nollendorfplatz 5 (844 1550/ www.goya-berlin.de). U1, U2, U3, U4 Nollendorfplatz.* **Open** 11pm-6am Fri-Sat. **Map** p123 B2 ⑱
Newly relaunched club in a historic venue that adds a much needed dash of glitz and glamour to the area. The heart of the club is a grand 300sq m (3,225sq ft) hall with a stage, soaring columns, Murano chandeliers and two gorgeous circular galleries. Each of these features their own bar, lounge area and majestic balustrade that's perfect for admiring the chic crowd shaking it to electro, hip hop and pop hits down below. Club at weekends, event space during the week.

Havanna Club

Hauptstrasse 30 (784 8565/www. havanna-berlin.de). U7 Eisenacher Strasse. **Open** 9pm-late Wed; 10pm-late Fri, Sat. No credit cards. **Map** p123 B4 ⑲
Three dancefloors with salsa, merengue and R&B. It's a popular place with expatriate South Americans and Cubans. An hour before opening you can pick up a few steps at a salsa class for €4, which is also reckoned to be a good way to meet people.

Kleine Nachtrevue

Kurfürstenstrasse 116 (218 8950/ www.kleine-nachtrevue.de). U1, U2, U3 Wittenbergplatz. **Open** 8pm-3am Tue-Sat. **Performances** 10.45pm Tue-Sat. **Map** p123 A1 ⑳
Used as a location for many films, this is as close as it gets to real nostalgic German cabaret – intimate, dark, decadent but very friendly. Nightly shows consist of short song or dance numbers sprinkled with playful nudity and

Goya

whimsical costumes. Special weekend performances at 9pm vary from erotic opera or a four-course meal to songs sung by the male 'reincarnation' of Marlene Dietrich.

Neues Ufer

Hauptstrasse 157 (7895 7900). U7 Kleistpark. **Open** 11am-2am daily. No credit cards. **Map** p123 C4 ㉑
Established in the early 1970s as Café Nemesis, later renamed Anderes Ufer and more recently recast as its current self, this is actually the city's oldest gay café and was David Bowie's local during his Berlin days. Relaxed daytime scene, convivial at night.

Scheinbar Varieté

Monumentenstrasse 9 (784 5539/ www.scheinbar.de). U7 Kleistpark. **Open** from 7.30pm. No credit cards. **Map** p123 C4 ㉒
Experimental, fun-loving cabaret in a tiny club that explodes with fresh talent. If you like surprises, try the open-stage nights, where great performers mix with terrible ones, creating a surreal night for all.

Arts & leisure

Odeon

Hauptstrasse 116 (7870 4019/www. yorck.de/yck/yorck_ie/yorck_kinos/odeon .php). U4, S45, S46 Innsbrucker Platz or S1, S4 Schöneberg. No credit cards. **Map** p123 B5 ㉓
The Odeon is a last hold-out of the big, old, single-screen neighbourhood cinema. Deep in the heart of Schöneberg, programming is exclusively English-language, providing a reasonably intelligent, though increasingly mainstream, selection of Hollywood and UK fare.

Xenon

Kolonnenstrasse 5/6 (7800 1530/ www.xenon-kino.de). U7 Kleistpark or S1 Julius-Leber-Brücke. No credit cards. **Map** p123 C4 ㉔
Only in Berlin would a dedicated gay cinema simultaneously be a multiple award-winner for children's programming. Those who have come of age can find gay and lesbian programming, largely but not exclusively from the US and UK.

Potsdamer Platz

Tiergarten

Tiergarten takes its name from the huge, wooded park that is the district's central feature. A former hunting ground for the Prussian electors, it was severely damaged during World War II, had all its trees chopped down for firewood in the desperate winter of 1945-46, and was slowly restored thereafter. During the Cold War, the Wall ran down its eastern side. Now the Tiergarten is once again the link between Mitte and Charlottenburg, a beautiful park that, even when full of joggers, cyclists and sunbathers, rarely feels very crowded.

At the park's north-eastern end is the **Reichstag**, the new government quarter and Berlin's futuristic new **Hauptbahnhof**. t its south-west corner is Berlin's zoo. East of that along the south side of the park lies the diplomatic district, replete with gleaming new embassies. The big art galleries and concert venues of the 1970s **Kulturforum** and the postmodern towers and arcades of **Potsdamer Platz** lie at the park's south-eastern corner.

Sights & museums

Bauhaus Archiv – Museum für Gestaltung

Klingelhöferstrasse 13-14 (254 0020/ www.bauhaus.de). Bus 100, 106, 187, M29 Lützowplatz. **Open** 10am-5pm Mon, Wed-Sun. **Admission** Mon, Sat, Sun €7; €4 reductions; Wed-Fri €6; €3 reductions. No credit cards.
Map p130 C4 ❶
Walter Gropius, founder of the Bauhaus school, designed the elegant white building that now houses this absorbing design museum. The permanent exhibition presents furniture, ceramics, prints, sculptures, photographs and sketches created in the Bauhaus workshop between 1919 and 1933, when the school was closed down by the Nazis. There are also first-rate temporary exhibitions and an interesting gift shop offering 250 designer items.

Daimler Contemporary

Alte Potsdamer Strasse 5 (2594 1420/www.sammlung.daimler.com). U2, S1, S2, S26 Potsdamer Platz. **Open** 11am-6pm daily. **Admission** free. **Map** p131 F4 ❷

Daimler's art collection is serious stuff, sticking to the 20th century, and covering abstract, conceptual and minimal art; its collection includes around 1,300 works from artists such as Josef Albers, Max Bill, Walter de Maria, Jeff Koons and Andy Warhol. The gallery rotates themed portions of the collection, typically 30-80 works at a time, and often stages joint shows in a spirit of dialogue with other private collections.

Filmmuseum Berlin

Potsdamer Strasse 2 (300 9030/ www.filmmuseum-berlin.de). U2, S1, S2, S26 Potsdamer Platz. **Open** 10am-6pm Tue, Wed, Fri-Sun; 10am-8pm Thur. **Admission** €6; €4 reductions. No credit cards. **Map** p131 E3 ❸

Since 1963, the Deutsche Kinemathek has been amassing a collection of films, memorabilia, documentation and antique film apparatus. In 2000, all this stuff found a home in this roomy, well-designed exhibition space on two floors of the Filmhaus in the Sony Center, chronicling the history of German cinema. Striking exhibits include the two-storey-high video wall of disasters from Fritz Lang's adventure films and a morgue-like space devoted to films from the Third Reich. But the main attraction is the Marlene Dietrich collection – personal effects, home movies and designer clothes. Exhibitions are often linked with film programming at the Arsenal cinema (p137) downstairs.

Gedenkstätte Deutscher Widerstand

Stauffenbergstrasse 13-14 (2699 5000/ www.gdw-berlin.de). U2, S1, S2, S26 Potsdamer Platz. **Open** 9am-6pm Mon-Wed, Fri; 9am-8pm Thur; 10am-6pm Sat, Sun. *Guided tours* Sat, Sun 3pm. **Admission** free. **Map** p131 D4 ❹

The Memorial to the German Resistance chronicles the German resistance to National Socialism. The building is part of a complex known as the Bendlerblock, owned by the German military from its construction in 1911 until 1945. At the back is a memorial to the conspirators killed during their attempt to assassinate Hitler at this site on 20 July 1944. Regular guided tours are in German only, but you can book an English tour four weeks in advance.

Gemäldegalerie

Kulturforum, Matthäikirchplatz (266 423 040/www.smb.museum/gg). U2, S1, S2, S26 Potsdamer Platz. **Open** 10am-6pm Tue, Wed, Fri-Sun; 10am-10pm Thur. **Admission** €8; €4 reductions. No credit cards. **Map** p131 E4 ❺

The Picture Gallery's first-rate early European collection features a healthy selection of the biggest names in Western art. There are around 20 Rembrandts, the best of which include a portrait of preacher and merchant Cornelis Claesz Anslo and his wife, and an electric Samson confronting his father-in-law. Two of Franz Hals's finest works are here – the wild, fluid, almost impressionistic *Malle Babbe* ('Mad Babette') and the detailed portrait of the one-year-old Catharina Hooft and her nurse. Other highlights include a version of Botticelli's *Venus Rising*, and Correggio's brilliant *Leda with the Swan*.

Haus der Kulturen der Welt

John-Foster-Dulles-Allee 10 (397 870/ www.hkw.de). Bus 100. **Open** 10am-7pm daily. **Admission** varies. **Map** p131 E2 ❻

With a mission to promote art from developing countries, the 'House of World Cultures' mounts spectacular large-scale exhibitions on subjects such as contemporary Indian art, Bedouin culture and the Chinese avant-garde. The programme also involves readings,

BERLIN BY AREA

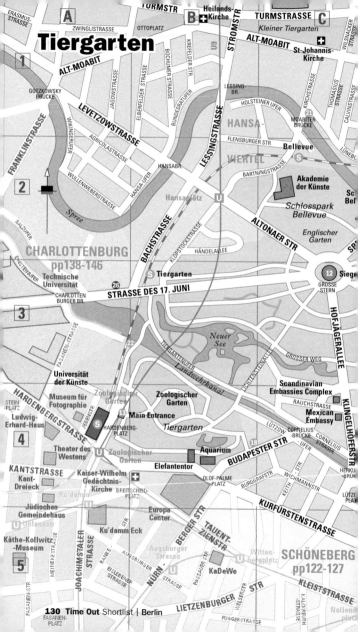

Tiergarten

Map labels:

A **B** **C**

1 **2** **3** **4** **5**

ERASMUS-STRASSE
ZWINGLISTRASSE
Heilands-
Kirche
TURMSTRASSE
Kleiner Tiergarten
OTTOPLATZ
ALT-MOABIT
St-Johannis-
Kirche

ALT-MOABIT
GÖTZKOWSKY BRÜCKE
JAGOWSTRASSE
KREFELDER STR
BOCHUMER STRASSE
ELBERFELDER STRASSE
BUNDESRATUFER
STROMSTR
U9
LESSING-
BR.
HOLSTEINER UFER
MOABITER BRÜCKE
KIRCHSTRASSE
THOMASIUS STRASSE
CALVINSTR
WILSNACKER STR

LEVETZOWSTRASSE
WIKINGERUFER
AGRICOLASTRASSE
HANSAUFER
HANSABR.
LESSINGSTRASSE
HANSA-
VIERTEL
FLENSBURGER STR
Bellevue
LÜNEBU

FRANKLINSTRASSE
WULLENWEBERSTRASSE
Spree
HANSAPLATZ
BARTNINGSTRASSE
Akademie
der Künste
Sc
Bel

SALZUFER
SIEMENSUFER
Technische
Universität
CHARLOTTENBURG
pp138-146
CHARLOTTENBURGER BR.
26
STRASSE DES 17. JUNI
BACHSTRASSE
KLOPSTOCKSTRASSE
HÄNDELALLEE
Schlosspark
Bellevue
Englischer
Garten
ALTONAER STR
SPR
12
Siege
GROSSE
STERN
HOFJÄGERALLEE

FASANENSTRASSE
Tiergarten
22
TIERGARTENUFER
Landwehrkanal
Neuer
See
GROSSER WEG
Scandinavian
Embassies Complex
RAUCHSTRASSE
Mexican
Embassy
KLINGELHÖFERSTR
HERKU
GRÜ

Universität
der Künste
HARDENBERGSTRASSE
STEIN-
PLATZ
Museum für
Fotografie
Zoologischer
Garten
Zoologischer
Garten
JEBENSTR
HARDENBERG-
PLATZ
13
Main Entrance
Tiergarten
LICHTENSTEINALLEE
LÜTZOW
CORNELIUS-
BRÜCKE
CORNELIUS
STRASSE
UFER
LÜTZO
PLA

Ludwig-
Erhard-Haus
Theater des
Westens
Zoologischer
Garten
Elefantentor
Aquarium
48
BUDAPESTER STR
OLOF-PALME-
PLATZ
BURGGRAFSTR
WICHMANNSTR
KEITH
STR

KANTSTRASSE
Kant-
Dreieck
Kaiser-Wilhelm
Gedächtnis-
Kirche
BREITSCHEID-
PLATZ
Ku'damm
Europa
Center
KURFÜRSTENSTRASSE

Jüdisches
Gemeindehaus
Uhlandstr
Ku'damm Eck
BERGER STR
TAUENT-
ZIENSTR
SCHÖNEBERG
pp122-127

Käthe-Kollwitz
-Museum
JOACHIMSTALER
STRASSE
MEINEKESTRASSE
RANKE
STR
AUGSBURGER
Augsburger
Strasse
EISLEBENER
STRASSE
NÜRN-
BERGER
STRASSE
PASSAUER STR
KaDeWe
Witten-
bergplatz
KLEISTSTRASSE
KALCKREUTH
STRASSE
Nollen

FASANENSTR
FASANEN-
PLATZ
EISLEBENER STRASSE
LIETZENBURGER STRASSE
WELSERSTR
FUGGERSTRASSE

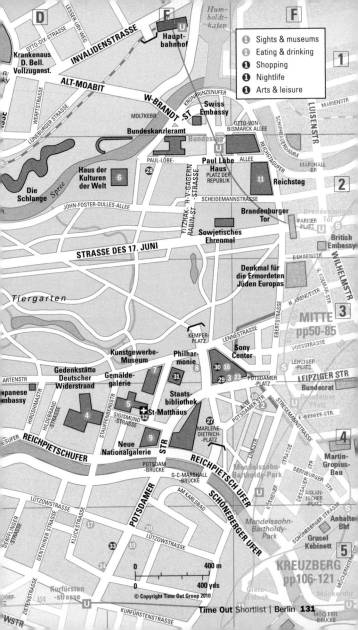

lectures, discussions, concerts and dance. Housed in Hugh Stubbins's oyster-like building, erected in 1957 as America's contribution to the Interbau Exhibition, this is a unique Berlin cultural institution. Decent café too. The Haus is open every day, but exhibitions close on Tuesday.

Kunstgewerbemuseum

Kulturforum, Matthäikirchplatz (266 424 301/www.smb.museum). U2, S1, S2, S26 Potsdamer Platz. **Open** 10am-6pm Tue-Fri; 11am-6pm Sat, Sun. **Admission** €8; €4 reductions. **Map** p131 E3 ❼
The Museum of Decorative Art contains a frustrating collection of European arts and crafts, stretching from the Middle Ages through Renaissance, baroque and rococo to Jugendstil and art deco. There are some lovely pieces on display, particularly furniture and porcelain, but labelling is only in German and the layout is confusing.

Musikinstrumentenmuseum

Ben-Gurion-Strasse 1 (254 810/www.sim.spk-berlin.de). U2, S1, S2, S26 Potsdamer Platz. **Open** 9am-5pm Tue, Wed, Fri; 9am-10pm Thur; 10am-6pm Sat, Sun. **Admission** €4; €2 reductions; free under-16s; free 1st Sun of mth. No credit cards. **Map** p131 E3 ❽
More than 2,200 musical instruments dating to the 1500s are crammed into this small museum next to the Philharmonie. Among them are rococo musical clocks, for which 18th-century princes commissioned jingles from Mozart, Haydn and Beethoven. Museum guides play obsolete instruments such as the Kammerflugel; on Saturdays at 11am, the wonderful Wurlitzer organ – salvaged from an American silent movie house – is cranked into action.

Neue Nationalgalerie

Potsdamer Strasse 50 (266 2651/www.neue-nationalgalerie.de). U2, S1, S2, *S26 Potsdamer Platz.* **Open** 10am-6pm Tue, Wed, Fri; 10am-10pm Thur; 11am-6pm Sat, Sun. **Admission** €8; €4 reductions. *Special exhibitions* varies. **Map** p131 E4 ❾
Designed in the 1960s by Mies van der Rohe, the New National Gallery houses German and international paintings from the 20th century. It's strong on Expressionism: there are key works by Kirchner, Heckel and Schmidt-Rottluff, as well as pieces by lesser-known Expressionist painters such as Ludwig Meidner. Cubist pieces cover the likes of Picasso, Gris and Léger. The Neue Sachlichkeit is well represented by paintings from George Grosz and Otto Dix, while the Bauhaus contributes work from Paul Klee and Wassily Kandinsky. Another focus is American ColorField painting, with pieces by Barnett Newman, Morris Louis and Frank Badur. The permanent collection is often put into storage to allow for big shows and temporary exhibitions.

Panoramapunkt

Kollhoff Tower, Potsdamer Platz 1, entrance on Alte Potsdamer Strasse (2529 4372/www.panoramapunkt.de). U2, S1, S2, S26 Potsdamer Platz. **Open** 11am-8pm daily. **Admission** €5; €4 reductions. No credit cards. **Map** p131 F4 ❿
'The fastest elevator in Europe' shoots up to the 100m (328ft) viewing platform in the Kollhoff Tower. The building's north-east corner is at the point where the borders of Tiergarten, Mitte and Kreuzberg all meet. You can peer through railings and the neighbouring postmodern high-rises at the landmarks of new Berlin. There are good views to the south and west; looking north, the DB Tower gets in the way. But it's closed for renovation until spring 2010.

Reichstag

Platz der Republik (2270/www.bundestag.de). S1, S2 Unter den Linden/bus 100. **Open** *Dome* 8am-

Polar star

Meet Knut, Berlin Zoo's most famous resident.

Berlin doesn't have much of a celebrity culture. For the last few years its biggest star has been, not an actor or a musician, but a bear. Knut the no-longer-so-cuddly polar bear was born at **Berlin Zoo** (p134) in December 2006, and melted hearts worldwide when he was abandoned by his mother. An animal rights activist declared he should be left to die rather than raised 'as a domestic pet', children protested that 'Knut Must Live!', and Knut's fame and fortune were in the bag.

He's been the subject of books, songs, blogs, DVDs and TV shows. He's inspired ringtones, keyrings and a range of cuddly toys. *Vanity Fair* put him on its cover. And Berlin Zoo reported record profits in 2007, with visitor numbers up by 30 per cent. Berlin became used to the phenomenon of 'Knut tourists', but life in the limelight has not always been kind. In September 2008, Knut's trainer, Thomas Dörflein, who had been his constant companion, died of a heart attack. Knut was distraught.

Keeper Markus Röbke reported that not only was Knut missing Dörflein, but that the bear had become addicted to attention. He waves back when waved to, but howls when there are no visitors. 'Knut needs an audience,' said Röbke. 'That has to change.' Perhaps also addicted to the attention – or at least to the extra millions in Knut-related revenue – the zoo ignored Röbke's suggestion that Knut be moved to an animal park, and in July 2009 forked out €430,000 to settle a custody dispute with Neumünster Zoo. Knut ain't going nowhere.

At press time, the zoo was attempting to wean Knut off his dependence on humans by introducing him to a playmate, the three-year-old female polar bear Gianna from Munich's Hellebrunn Zoo. Knut was 'surprised and astounded' to find another bear in his enclosure – all the more so when Gianna cuffed him about the head on their first encounter – but zookeepers are hoping that love will find a way.

midnight daily; last entry 10pm.
Admission free. **Map** p131 F2 ⓫

Infamously gutted by fire on 17 February 1933 – an event the Nazis used as an excuse to suspend basic freedoms – the Reichstag is today home to the Bundestag, the Federal German Parliament. The celebrated renovation by Lord Foster was conceived as a 'dialogue between old and new' and resulted in a cupola that is open to the general public. A trip to the top is a must, but expect airport-style security and long queues. At the centre of the dome is a funnel of mirrors, angled so as to shed light on the workings of democracy below but also lending an almost funhouse effect to it all.

Siegessäule

Strasse des 17. Juni (391 2961). S5, S7, S9, S75 Bellevue/bus 100. **Open** *Summer* 9.30am-6.30pm Mon-Fri; 9.30am-7pm, Sat, Sun. *Winter* 9.30am-5pm Mon-Fri; 9.30am-5.30pm Sat, Sun. **Admission** €2.50; €1.50 reductions. No credit cards. **Map** p130 C3 ⓬

Tiergarten's biggest monument was built in 1871-73 to commemorate Prussian campaigns against Denmark (1864), Austria (1866) and France (1870-71). Originally planted in front of the Reichstag, the Victory Column was then moved by Hitler to form a centrepiece for the East–West axis connecting western Berlin with the palaces and ministries of Mitte. On top of the column is a gilded Goddess of Victory by Friedrich Drake; captured French cannons and cannonballs, sawn in half and gilded, decorate the column itself. It's 285 steps to the viewing platform.

Zoologischer Garten & Aquarium

Hardenbergplatz 8 (254 010/www.zoo-berlin.de). U2, U9, S5, S7, S9, S75 Zoologischer Garten. **Open** *Zoo* Summer 9am-6.30pm daily. Winter 9am-5pm daily. *Aquarium* 9am-6pm daily. **Admission** *Zoo* €12; €6-€9 reductions. *Aquarium* €12; €6-€9

reductions. *Combined admission* €18; €9-€14 reductions. **Map** p130 A4/B4 ⓭

Germany's oldest zoo was opened in 1841 to designs by Martin Lichtenstein and Peter Joseph Lenné. With almost 14,000 creatures, it's one of the world's most important zoos, with more endangered species in its collection than any in Europe except Antwerp's. It's beautifully landscaped, with lots of architectural oddities, and there are plenty of places for a coffee, beer or snack.

Enter the aquarium from within the zoo or through its own entrance at Budapester Strasse 32 by the Elephant Gate. More than 500 species are arranged over three floors, and it's a good option for a rainy day. On the ground floor are the fish (including some impressive sharks); on the first you'll find reptiles (the crocodile hall is the highlight); while insects and amphibians occupy the second. The dark corridors and liquid ambience, with tanks lit from within and curious aquarian creatures floating by, are as absorbing as an art exhibit. Elsewhere, the baby polar bear Knut has become one of Berlin's major tourist attractions. See box p133.

Reichstag p132

Eating & drinking

Bar am Lützowplatz

*Lützowplatz 7 (262 6807/www.
baramluetzowplatz.com). U1, U2, U3,
U4 Nollendorfplatz.* **Open** 4pm-4am
daily. **Bar**. Map p130 C4 ⑭
Long bar with a long drinks list and
classy customers in Chanel suits sipping expensive, well-made cocktails as
they compare bank balances.

Café Einstein Stammhaus

*Kurfürstenstrasse 58 (261 5096/www.
cafeeinstein.com). U1, U2, U3, U4
Nollendorfplatz.* **Open** 8am-2am daily.
Café. Map p130 C5 ⑮
Red leather banquettes, parquet flooring and the crack of wooden chairs all
contribute to the old Viennese café
experience at Einstein. Fine Austrian
cooking is produced for lunch and dinner. Alternatively, order Apfelstrudel
and coffee and soak up the atmosphere
of this elegant 1878 villa, or take a
leisurely brunch in the leafy garden.

Corroboree

*Sony Center, Bellevuestrasse 5 (2610
1705/www.corroboree.info). U2, S1,
S2, S26 Potsdamer Platz.* **Open**
9am-1am daily. €€€. **Australian**.
Map p131 E3 ⑯
Big, noisy and one of the only decent
places to eat in the Sony Center. It's
hearty stuff, including kangaroo steak
as well as burgers and noodle dishes, a
small list of Aussie wines, and
macadamia nuts with everything. Not
too exciting for vegetarians, though.

Edd's

*Lützowstrasse 81 (215 5294). U1
Kurfürstenstrasse.* **Open** 11.30am-3pm,
6pm-midnight Mon-Fri; 5pm-midnight
Sat; 2pm-midnight Sun. €€€. No credit
cards. **Thai**. Map p131 D5 ⑰
Known and loved by many, so bookings are pretty much essential for this
comfortable, elegant Thai, where a husband and wife team please their guests
with well-balanced if spicy creations.

Hugo's

*Hotel InterContinental, Budapester
Strasse 2 (2602 1263/www.hugos-
restaurant.de). U2, U9, S5, S7, S9,
S75 Zoologischer Garten.* **Open** 6-
10.30pm Mon-Sat. €€€€. **Modern
European**. Map p130 B4 ⑱
Probably Berlin's best restaurant right
now, and with the awards to prove it.
Chef Thomas Kammeier juxtaposes
classic haute cuisine with an avant-
garde new German style. Dishes such
as cheek of ox with beluga lentils and
filled calamares bring out the best of a
mature kitchen. The beautiful room
occupies the entire top floor of the Hotel
InterContinental (p172).

Joseph Roth Diele

*Potsdamer Strasse 75 (2636 9884/
www.joseph-roth-diele.de). U1
Kurfürstenstrasse.* **Open** 10am-
midnight Mon-Fri; 6pm-midnight Sat.
No credit cards. **Café**. Map p131 E5 ⑲
A traditional Berlin book café, just a
short stroll south of Potsdamer Platz,
which pays homage to the life and
work of inter-war Jewish writer Joseph
Roth. It's an amiable place offering
teas, coffees, wines, beers, snacks and
stunning value light meals.

Kumpelnest 3000

*Lützowstrasse 23 (261 6918/
www.kumpelnest3000.com). U1
Kurfürstenstrasse.* **Open** 5pm-5am
Mon-Thur, Sun; 5pm-late Fri, Sat. No
credit cards. **Bar**. Map p131 E5 ⑳
This perennially popular and studiedly
tacky establishment is at its best at the
end of a long Saturday night, when it's
crowded and people will insist on
drunkenly attempting to dance to disco.

Patio

NEW *Helgolander Ufer, at Kirchstrasse
(4030 1700/www.patio-berlin.de). S5,
S7, S9, S75 Bellevue.* **Open** 10am-1am
Mon-Fri; 9am-1am Sat, Sun. €€€.
International. Map p130 C1 ㉑
On the banks of the Spree just above
the leafy Hansaviertel, this designer

BERLIN BY AREA

barge has a sunny terrace and light-filled lounge, both with views of the willows and grand houses on the bank opposite. The menu features decent Italian classics including stone-oven pizza (from 6pm) and, unexpectedly, sushi. A well-stocked bar fuels an extensive cocktail menu too.

Schleusenkrug

Müller-Breslau-Strasse, corner of Unterschleuse (313 9909/www. schleusenkrug.de). S5, S7, S9, S75 Tiergarten. **Open** *Summer* 10am-1am daily. *Winter* 10am-6pm daily. No credit cards. **Bar/beer garden**. Map p130 B3 ㉒

There are occasional bar and beer garden by the Landwehr Canal, but it's really at its best on a summer afternoon when all sorts gather to sink large glasses of Pils, tuck into a sausage, chat over coffee, or watch the tourists on the canal boats negotiating the adjacent lock.

Sushi Express

Potsdamer Platz 2, Sony Center Passerelle (2575 1863). U2, S1, S2, S26 Potsdamer Platz. **Open** 11.30am-10pm Mon-Fri; noon-10pm Sat; 2-10pm Sun. **€€**. **Japanese**. Map p131 F3 ㉓

Not easy to find, Sushi Express is under the Sony Center courtyard in a passage to the S-Bahn. But the hunt is worth it for tasty sushi, sashimi and assorted delicacies to be plucked off the conveyor belt. The temptation is to keep grabbing, but don't worry, from noon to 6pm Monday to Friday all sushi and rolls are half price. Hot dishes and lunchboxes are also available.

Victoria Bar

Potsdamer Strasse 102 (2575 9977/www.victoriabar.de). U1 Kurfürstenstrasse. **Open** 6.30pm-3am Mon-Thur, Sun; 6.30pm-4am Fri, Sat. No credit cards. **Bar**. Map p131 D5 ㉔

Funky, grown-up cocktail bar for a relaxed, mixed crowd. The low-key concept – long bar, subdued lighting, muffled funk and staff who work well together and know what they're mixing – keeps this place buzzing all week long.

Weitzmann

S-Bahnbogen 390, Lüneburger Strasse (394 2057). S5, S7, S9, S75 Bellevue. **Open** *Imbiss* noon-3pm Mon-Fri. *Restaurant* 6pm-midnight Mon-Fri. **€€**. No credit cards. **German**. Map p131 D2 ㉕

A lovely little place serving the pastas of Swabia, including Spätzle (a dish with Bratwurst, lentils or meatballs), Käsespätzle (with cheese), Maultaschen (like giant ravioli) and Schupfnudeln (a cross between pasta and chips)? A Berg beer makes the perfect accompaniment.

Shopping

Kunst und Trödel Markt

Strasse des 17 Juni (2555 0096/www.berliner-troedelmarkt.de). U2 Ernst-Reuter-Platz or S5, S7, S9, S75 Tiergarten. **Open** 11am-5pm Sat, Sun. Map p130 A3 ㉖

On the stretch west of the S-Bahn station, you'll find good quality, early 20th-century objects with prices to match, alongside a jumble of vintage and alternative clothing, old furniture, second-hand records and books. Interesting stuff, but cramped aisles.

Nightlife

Adagio

Marlene-Dietrich-Platz 1 (258 9890/www.adagio.de). U2, S1, S2, S26 Potsdamer Platz. **Open** 10pm-1am Thur-Sat. Map p131 E4 ㉗

Spin-off of a swanky Zurich disco, its 'medieval' decor and Renaissance-style frescos are jarringly at odds with the Renzo Piano-designed theatre whose basement it occupies. Pricey drinks and a music policy of disco, polite house and oldies cater to fortysomething tourists and afterwork crowds chasing an illusion of exclusivity. No jeans or sports shoes.

Schleusenkrug

Tipi Das Zelt

Grosse Querallee, between the Bundeskanzleramt & Haus der Kulturen der Welt (0180 327 9358/www.tipi-das-zelt.de). Bus 100, 248 Platz der Republik. **Performances** *8pm Tue-Sat; 7pm Sun.* **Map** p131 E2 ㉓
A circus tent in the Tiergarten, near the Federal Chancellery, with cool international performers presenting various comedy, dance, theatre and cabaret shows.

Arts & leisure

Arsenal

Potsdamer Strasse 2 (2695 5100/www.fdk-berlin.de). U2, S1, S2, S25, S26 Potsdamer Platz. No credit cards. **Map** p131 F3 ㉙
Berlin's own cinematheque offers eclectic programming, ranging from classic Hollywood to contemporary Middle Eastern cinema and from Third World documentaries to silent films with live accompaniment. It also shows plenty of English-language films and some foreign films with English subtitles, while its two state-of-the-art screening rooms in the Sony Center make it a welcome corrective to the great Hollywood beasts of its multiplex neighbours.

CineStar Sony Center

Potsdamer Strasse 4 (2606 6400/www.cinestar.de). U2, S1, S2, S25, S26 Potsdamer Platz. No credit cards. **Map** p131 F3 ㉚
Eight screens showing films in their original language, mostly English. Despite a few random sparks of creativity, it is mainstream fare and all major releases tend to show up here.

Philharmonie

Herbert-von-Karajan Strasse 1 (254 880/tickets 2548 8999/www.berlin-philharmoniker.de/en). U2, S1, S2, S25 Potsdamer Platz. **Map** p131 E3 ㉛
Berlin's most famous concert hall, home to the world-renowned Berlin Philharmonic Orchestra, was designed by Hans Scharoun and opened in 1963. Its reputation for superb acoustics is accurate, but it does depend on where you sit. The Berliner Philharmoniker (www.berliner-philharmoniker.de) was founded in 1882 and has been led by some of the world's finest conductors. Since 2002 it has been under the leadership of Sir Simon Rattle. The Berlin Phil gives about 100 performances in the city during its August to June season.

St Matthäus Kirche am Kulturforum

Matthaeikirchplatz (2035 5311/www.stiftung-stmatthaeus.de). U2, S1, S2, S25 Potsdamer Platz. No credit cards. **Map** p131 E4 ㉜
Concerts here might be anything from an organ recital to a chorus of Russian Orthodox monks. Exquisite acoustics.

Wintergarten Varieté

Potsdamer Strasse 96 (no phone/www.wintergarten-variete.de). U1 Kurfürstenstrasse. **Performances** *8pm Mon, Tue, Thur, Fri; 4pm, 8pm Wed; 5pm, 9pm Sat; 3pm, 6pm Sun.* **Map** p131 E5 ㉝
Prussia meets Disney with shows that are slick and professional. Excellent acrobats and magicians, but some questionable comedy acts.

BERLIN BY AREA

Christmas in Charlottenburg

Central Charlottenburg

The focal points of Berlin's well-heeled west end are the tacky commercial cauldron around Zoologischer Garten (known as Zoo Station or Bahnhof Zoo), and the grand avenue of international brands and upmarket shopping that is the **Kurfürstendamm**. Most of the life of this district is to be found on the streets between the **Ku-damm** and almost-parallel **Kantstrasse** to the north, especially on and around **Savignyplatz**.

Sights & museums

Beate-Uhse Erotik-Museum
Joachimstaler Strasse 4 (886 0666/ www.beate-uhse-filialen.de). U2, U9, S5, S7, S9, S75 Zoologischer Garten. **Open** 9am-midnight Mon-Sat; 1pm-midnight Sun. **Map** p139 D2 ●

The three floors of this collection (above a flagship Beate-Uhse retail outlet offering videos and sex toys) contain oriental prints, showroom-dummy tableaux, and glass cases containing such delights as early Japanese dildos, Andean penis flutes, 17th-century chastity belts and a giant coconut that looks like an arse. There's a small, drab exhibit on pioneering sex researcher Magnus Hirschfeld and a corner documenting the career of Frau Uhse herself, who went from Luftwaffe pilot to annual sex-aid sales of €50 million.

Kaiser-Wilhelm-Gedächtniskirche
Breitscheidplatz (218 5023/www. gedaechtniskirche.com). U2, U9, S5, S7, S9, S75 Zoologischer Garten. **Open** 9am-7pm daily. *Guided tours* 1.15pm, 2pm, 3pm Mon-Sat. **Admission** free. **Map** p139 D2 ●

Central Charlottenburg

MITTE
pp50-85

© Copyright Time Out Group 2010

400 m
400 yds

Neuer See

Tiergarten

Aquarium

Elefantentor

Zoologischer Garten
Main Entrance

Europa Center

Zoologischer Garten

Kaiser-Wilhelm Gedächtnis-Kirche

Museum für Fotographie

Universität der Künste

Ludwig-Erhard-Haus

Theater des Westens

Jüdisches Gemeindehaus

Kant-Dreieck

Käthe-Kollwitz-Museum

Ku-damm Eck

KaDeWe

SCHÖNEBERG
pp122-127

Deutsche Oper

Trinitatis-Kirche

Savignyplatz

HARDENBERGSTRASSE

KANTSTRASSE

KURFÜRSTENDAMM

LEIBNIZSTRASSE

LIETZENBURGER STRASSE

UHLANDSTRASSE

JOACHIMSTALER STRASSE

Ludwigskirche

KANTSTRASSE

LEWISHAMSTRASSE

Legend	
1	Sights & museums
2	Eating & drinking
3	Shopping
4	Nightlife
5	Arts & leisure

Time Out Shortlist | Berlin **139**

This neo-Romanesque structure, built in 1891-95 by Franz Schwechten, is one of Berlin's best-known sights. Much of it was destroyed in 1943, and it's been left half-ruined as a reminder of the damage done by the war. Inside the rump of the church is a glittering art nouveau ceiling mosaic depicting members of the House of Hohenzollern on a pilgrimage, plus a cross made of nails from the destroyed Coventry cathedral. The tower is flanked by drab post-war concrete extensions, but inside the wrap-around blue stained glass is stunning.

Käthe-Kollwitz-Museum

Fasanenstrasse 24 (882 5210/ www.kaethe-kollwitz.de). U1, U9 Kurfürstendamm. **Open** 11am-6pm daily. **Admission** €6; €3 reductions. No credit cards. **Map** p139 C3 ❸
Käthe Kollwitz's powerful, deeply empathetic work embraces the full spectrum of life, from the joy of motherhood to the pain of death (with rather more emphasis on the latter than the former). The collection includes her famous lithograph *Brot!*, as well as charcoal sketches, woodcuts and sculptures, all displayed to good effect in this grand villa off the Ku'damm.

Museum für Fotografie

Jebenstrasse 2 (266 2188/www. smb.museum/mf). U2, U9, S5, S7, S9, S75 Zoologischer Garten. **Open** 10am-6pm Tue-Sun. **Admission** €6; €3 reductions. **Map** p139 D1 ❹
Shortly before his death in 2004, Berlin-born Helmut Newton donated over 1,000 of his nude and fashion photographs to the city and provided funds towards the creation of a new gallery. The Museum of Photography, doubling as home for the Helmut Newton Foundation (www.helmutnewton. com), was the result. In a former casino, it's now the largest photographic gallery in the city. The first two floors are given over to Newton's work, parcelled up in a series of alternating exhibitions.

Further space is devoted to temporary shows by other photographers.

Story of Berlin

Kurfürstendamm 207-208 (8872 0100/www.story-of-berlin.de). U1 Uhlandstrasse. **Open** 10am-8pm daily; last entry 6pm. **Admission** €9.80; €8 reductions. **Map** p139 C3 ❺
The huge floorspace is filled with installations and multimedia exhibits created by authors, designers and film and stage specialists, telling Berlin's story from its founding in 1237 to the present day. The 20 themed displays are labelled in both German and English. Underneath all this is a massive nuclear shelter. Built by the Allies in the 1970s, the low-ceilinged, oppressive bunker is still fully functional and can hold up to 3,500 people. Guided tours are included in the price of the ticket.

Eating & drinking

Ashoka

Grolmanstrasse 51 (3101 5806/ www.myashoka.de). S5, S7, S9, S75 Savignyplatz. **Open** 11am-midnight daily. No credit cards. **Indian**. **Map** p139 C2 ❻
Most Indian restaurants in Berlin seem to offer more or less the same menu. This one can be forgiven, as it was the first to open. More than 20 years later, it's still one of the best, offering well-priced, well-prepared dishes in small but quiet and tasteful premises. The branch on Goethestrasse offers vegetarian south Indian cuisine.
Other locations: Satyam, Goethestrasse 5 (3180 6111).

Café Hardenberg

Hardenbergstrasse 10 (312 2644/ www.cafe-hardenberg.de). U2 Ernst-Reuter-Platz. **Open** 9am-1am daily. **Café**. **Map** p139 C1 ❼
Across from the Technical University and usually packed with students drinking coffee. Simple, decent pasta, salads and sandwiches at reasonable prices.

Café im Literaturhaus

Fasanenstrasse 23 (882 5414/www.
literaturhaus-berlin.de). U15
Uhlandstrasse/bus N10, N19, N21,
N27. **Open** 9.30am-1am daily. No
credit cards. **Café**. Map p139 C3 ❽
The café of the Literaturhaus, which
has lectures, readings and a bookshop.
The greenhouse-like winter garden
or salon rooms are great for ducking
into a book over breakfast or a hot pot
of Darjeeling.

Diener

Grolmanstrasse 47 (881 5329). S3,
S5, S7, S9, S75 Savignyplatz. **Open**
6pm-2am daily. No credit cards. **Bar**.
Map p139 C2 ❾
An authentically old-style Berlin bar,
named after famous local boxer Franz
Diener. The walls are adorned with
faded hunting murals and photos of
well-known Germans you won't recognise. You could almost be in 1920s
Berlin. Almost.

First Floor

Hotel Palace, Budapester Strasse 45
(2502 1020/www.firstfloor.palace.de).
U2, U9, S5, S7, S9, S75 Zoologischer
Garten. **Open** noon-3pm, 6.30-11pm
Mon-Fri; 6.30-11pm Sat, Sun. €€€€.
French/European. Map p139 E2 ❿
The dominion of hot young chef
Mathias Buchholz, this is the place for
refined French/European cuisine such
as Bresse pigeon served with
chanterelles and potato ragout, venison
stuffed with foie gras, or loup de mer
and Breton lobster served with saffron
and tomato confit. Three set menus are
offered daily. One of Berlin's top tables.

Florian

Grolmanstrasse 52 (313 9184/www.
restaurant-florian.de). S5, S7, S9, S75
Savignyplatz. **Open** 6pm-3am daily.
€€€. **German**. Map p139 C2 ⓫
Florian has been serving fine south
German food on this quietly posh street
for a couple of decades now, and the
standard never seems to slip. The

Kaiser-Wilhelm-Gedächtniskirche p138

cooking is hearty and inventive, the
service impeccable, the interior sooth-
ingly plain. Cramped summer tables
are the only drawback.

Galerie Bremer

Fasanenstrasse 37 (881 4908/
www.galerie-bremer.de). U1, U9
Spichernstrasse. **Open** 8pm-late
Mon-Sat. No credit cards. **Bar**.
Map p139 C3 ⓬
In the back room of a tiny gallery, this
cocktail bar has the air of a well-kept
secret – you certainly wouldn't find it
if you weren't looking. The relaxing
room is painted in deep, rich colours
with a beautiful ship-like bar designed
by Hans Scharoun, architect of the
Philharmonie and Staatsbibliothek.

Julep's

Giesebrechtstrasse 3 (881 8823/
www.juleps.de). U7 Adenauerplatz.
Open 5pm-1am Mon-Thur, Sun;
5pm-2am Fri, Sat. €€€. **American**.
Map p139 A3 ⓭
Julep's gets the fusion flavours of contemporary American cuisine just right

BERLIN BY AREA

with an array of imaginative dishes such as duck prosciutto or quesadillas with rhubarb and apple chutney, teriyaki chicken with lemongrass and basmati rice or Cajun-style red snapper. The caesar salad is a classic, and indulgent desserts include chocolate brownies made with Jack Daniels. Happy hour is between 5pm and 8pm and all night Sunday.

Marjellchen

Mommsenstrasse 9 (883 2676/www. marjellchen-berlin.de). S5, S7, S9, S75 Savignyplatz. **Open** 5pm-midnight daily. **€€€. German. Map** p139 B2 ⑭
There aren't many places like Marjellchen around any more. It serves specialities from East Prussia, Pomerania and Silesia in an atmosphere of old-fashioned Gemütlichkeit. The beautiful bar and great service are further draws, and the larger-than-life owner recites poetry and sometimes sings.

Paris Bar

Kantstrasse 152 (313 8052). S5, S7, S9, S75 Savignyplatz. **Open** noon-2am daily. **€€€. French. Map** p139 C2 ⑮
With its old-salon appeal – art covers every available inch of wall – this is one of Berlin's tried and true spots. It attracts a crowd of rowdy regulars, and newcomers can feel left out when seated in the rear. The pricey food, it has to be said, isn't nearly as good as the staff pretend. To experience that and the often rude service, you'll need to book.

Restaurant 44

Swissôtel, Augsburger Strasse 44 (220 102 288/www.restaurant44.de). U1, U9 Kurfürstendamm. **Open** noon-2.30pm, 6-10.30pm Mon-Sat. **€€€€.**
French/German. Map p139 D2 ⑯
Chef Danijel Kresovic offers an international menu that fuses European ideas with more exotic flavours in dishes such as monkfish with curry spices, prawn chiboust and chanterelle ragout, or halibut with pata negra,

pistachios and sweet potatoes. A fine selection of wines by the glass too.

Restaurant Gabriel's

Jüdisches Gemeindehaus, Fasanenstrasse 79-80 (882 6138/www.itsgabriel.de). U1, U9 Kurfürstendamm. **Open** 11.30am-3.30pm, 6.30-11pm daily. **€€€.** No credit cards. **Jewish. Map** p139 D2 ⑰
Enter the Jewish Community Centre through airport-style security and head one floor up to this excellent kosher restaurant. Expect a full range of Jewish central and east European specialities, including some of the best pierogi in Berlin.

Sachiko Sushi

Jeanne-Mammen-Bogen 584 (313 2282/www.sachikosushi.com). S5, S7, S9, S75 Savignyplatz. **Open** noon-midnight Mon-Sat; 4pm-midnight Sun. **€€€. Japanese. Map** p139 C2 ⑱
Sachiko Sushi was Berlin's first kaiten (conveyor belt) sushi joint. It's usually packed with upmarket thirtysomethings, plucking the scrummy

Café im Literaturhaus p141

morsels as they circumnavigate a chrome and black stone bar.

Schwarzes Café

Kantstrasse 148 (313 8038/www. schwarzescafe-berlin.de). S5, S7, S9, S75 Savignyplatz. **Open** 24hrs daily (closed 6-10am Tue). No credit cards. **Café. Map** p139 C2 ⑲
Open all hours, Schwarzes Café was once, as the name suggests, all black and anarchistically inclined, but the political crowd moved on decades ago and the decor has been brightened. Service can get overstretched when it's crowded, such as early on weekend mornings, when clubbers stop for breakfast on their way home.

Tai Ji

Uhlandstrasse 194 (313 2881). U2, U9, S5, S7, S9, S75 Zoologischer Garten. **Open** noon-11pm daily. €€€. **Chinese. Map** p139 C2 ⑳
The room – a peaceful, semicircular pavilion overlooking a garden courtyard – is showing its age, but starters such as daugoo and button mushrooms and onion, or wun tun in a red chilli sauce, are sensational. Main courses have bizarre names like Meeting on a Magic Bridge or Eight Drunken Immortals Cross the Sea, but don't let that put you off. Note: half the Beijing-Sichuan dishes are vegetarian.

XII Apostoli

Savigny Passage, Bleibtreustrasse 49 (312 1433). S5, S7, S9, S75 Savignyplatz. **Open** 24hrs daily. €€€. No credit cards. **Italian. Map** p139 C2 ㉑
It's overcrowded, cramped and pricey, the service varies from rushed to rude, the music is irritating – but the pizzas are excellent and it's always open.

Shopping

Bücherbogen

Savignyplatz Stadtbahnbogen 593 (3186 9511/www.buecherbogen.com).

S5, S7, S9, S75 Savignyplatz. **Open** 10am-8pm Mon-Fri; 10am-6pm Sat. **Map** p139 C2 ㉒
This excellent store for all manner of art books fills several of the S-Bahn arches at Savignyplatz with international books and periodicals on painting, sculpture, photography, design and architecture. Many of the books are in English, and most of the staff can speak it.

Budapester Schuhe

Kurfürstendamm 43 (8862 4206/ www.budapester-schuhe.net). U1 Uhlandstrasse. **Open** 10am-7pm Mon-Fri; 10am-6pm Sat. **Map** p139 C3 ㉓
The largest of four Berlin branches offers the latest by the likes of Prada, D&G, Sergio Rossi and Miu Miu. At Kurfürstendamm 199, across the street, you'll find a conservative range for men, and at the Bleibtreustrasse branch, prices are slashed by up to 50% for last year's models, remainders and hard-to-sell sizes.
Other locations: Bleibtreustrasse 24 (881 7001); Kurfürstendamm 199 (881 1707).

Dopo_domani

Kantstrasse 148 (882 2242/www. dopo-domani.com). S5, S7, S9, S75 Savignyplatz. **Open** 10.30am-7pm Mon-Fri; 10am-6pm Sat. **Map** p139 C2 ㉔
Dopo_domani is a veritable temple for design aficionados. Combining an interior design practice with a well-stocked shop, the focus is on Italian outfitters, and the presentation creates an environment you'll dream of calling your own.

Gadget-Gadget

Meineckestrasse 22 (8872 4582/ www.gadget-gadget.com). U1, U9 Kurfürstendamm. **Open** 10am-8pm Mon-Sat. **Map** p139 D3 ㉕
German has no real equivalent for the word 'gadget' and English owner Piers Headley's fun selection of tech toys,

games, tools and computer and iPod accessories is the only store of its kind in Berlin. Useful for an assortment of travel items, including every imaginable kind of adaptor and charger.

Gelbe Musik
Schaperstrasse 11 (211 3962). U3 Augsburger Strasse. **Open** 1-6pm Tue-Fri; 11am-2pm Sat. **Map** p139 D3 ㉖
One of Europe's most important avant-garde outlets has racks of minimalist, electronic, world, industrial and extreme noise. Rare vinyl and import CDs, music press and sound objects make for absorbing browsing.

Harvey's
Kurfürstendamm 55-56 (883 3803/www.harveys-berlin.de). U7 Adenauerplatz. **Open** 11am-8pm Mon-Fri; 11am-7pm Sat. **Map** p139 B3 ㉗
Sigfried Böhnisch has been selling cutting-edge men's labels for over 20 years. He stocks Japanese powerhouses such as Yohji Yamamoto, Issey Miyake and Comme des Garçons, as well as Belgian labels like Martin Margiela and footwear from Canadian shoemaker Paul Harnden.

Leysieffer
Kurfürstendamm 218 (885 7480/www. leysieffer.de). U1 Uhlandstrasse. **Open** 9am-7pm Mon-Sat; 10am-5pm Sun. **Map** p139 ㉘
The beautifully packaged confitures, teas and handmade chocolates from this German fine food company make perfect gifts.

Marga Schoeller Bücherstube
Knesebeckstrasse 33 (881 1112). S5, S7, S9, S75 Savignyplatz. **Open** 9.30am-7pm Mon-Wed; 9.30am-8pm Thur, Fri; 9.30am-6pm Sat. **Map** p139 C2 ㉙
Rated among Europe's best independent literary bookshops by *Bookseller* magazine, this excellent establishment,

founded in 1930, includes one of Berlin's best English-language sections.

Mientus
Wilmersdorfer Strasse 73 (323 9077/ www.mientus.com). U7 Wilmersdorfer Strasse or S5, S7, S9, S75 Charlottenburg. **Open** 10am-7pm Mon-Sat. **Map** p139 A2 ㉚
Clean cuts for sharp men from a range of well-known collections including Dsquared, D&G, K Lagerfeld, Miu Miu and Paul Smith.
Other locations: Kurfürstendamm 52 (323 9077).

Planet Berlin
Schlüterstrasse 35 (885 2717/www. planetwear.com). U1 Uhlandstrasse. **Open** 11.30am-7.30pm Mon-Fri; 11.30am-6pm Sat. **Map** p139 B3 ㉛
Owners Wera Wonder and Mik Moon have been kitting out Berlin's club scene since 1985. Their DJ friends pump out deafening music to put you in the right mood, and the shop brims with sparkling spandex shirts, fluffy vests and dance-durable footwear.

Stilwerk
Kantstrasse 17 (315 150/ www.stilwerk.de). S5, S7, S9, S75 Savignyplatz. **Open** 10am-8pm Mon-Sat. **Map** p139 C2 ㉜
This huge, glassy, design marketplace offers high-end products from an array of retailers, purveying modern furnishings and kitchens, high-tech lighting and bathroom fittings, as well as an assortment of interior items by everyone from Alessi to Zanussi. There's also a fourth-floor showcase for the work of local craftspeople and designers.

Zeha
NEW *Kurfürstendamm 188, entrance on Schlüterstrasse (4737 8646/www. zeha-berlin.de). U7 Adenauer Platz or S5, S7, S9, S75 Savigny Platz.* **Open** 11am-7pm Mon-Fri; noon-6pm Sat. **Map** p139 B3 ㉝
See box right.

Zeha steps west

The East German brand moves into the other side of town.

Zeha

Zeha sports shoes have come a long way from equipping the feet of the East German Olympic team in the 1960s to being sold as an exclusive fashion brand on west Berlin's main shopping drag, Kurfürstendamm. The new **Zeha Berlin** store in Charlottenburg (p144), which opened in September 2009, is the third in the city, and the first in the west. 'It was the logical next step,' says Torsten Heine, who, with his friend Alexander Barré, revived the Zeha brand six years ago. 'Berliners tend not to stray far from their neighbourhoods, least of all to go shopping. People from the west tend not to shop in the east, so instead we've taken Zeha west.'

The idea of reviving the East German professional sports shoe brand, which went out of business in the early 1990s, came about by accident. In 2002, Heine and Barré were working for an event management company when a friend dropped by the office wearing a pair of old Zeha trainers.

For the two men it was a blast from the past: as aspiring professional athletes in their youth, Heine and Barré had both worn Zehas. With no knowledge of the footwear business, they sought out the help of a former Zeha production manager to get their business off the ground, and by 2007 had opened stores in Prenzlauer Berg and Mitte.

The collection still hinges on sports shoes, but has expanded over the years to include non-sports shoes and women's collections.

Where next for Zeha? Although Zeha shoes are already sold through affiliates in other parts of Germany, Heine and Barré have so far been reluctant to open another Zeha store outside Berlin. For now, branching out to the other side of town is a big enough step. It remains to be seen whether the well-heeled 'Wessis' of Charlottenburg are going to warm to an 'Ossi' brand with which they have no nostalgic connection.

BERLIN BY AREA

Nightlife

Abraxas

Kantstrasse 134 (312 9493/www. abraxas-berlin.com). U7 Wilmersdorfer Strasse or S5, S7, S9, S75 Savignyplatz. **Open** 10pm-late Thur-Sat. No credit cards. **Map** p139 B2 ③④

A defiantly unfashionable disco where you don't have to dress up to get in and where academics, social workers, bank clerks and midwives populate the dancefloor. Dance to funk, soul, Latino and jazz in a scene from times gone by.

A-Trane

Bleibtreustrasse 1 (313 2550/www.a-trane.de). S5, S7, S9, S75 Savignyplatz. **Open** 9pm-2am Mon-Thur, Sun; 9pm-late Fri, Sat. *Performances* 10pm daily. **Map** p139 C2 ③⑤

A bit ostentatious, but this jazz club manages to land some decent acts for nightly concerts. Admission free for Saturday night jam sessions.

Café Theater Schalotte

Behaimstrasse 22 (341 1485/www. schalotte.de). U7 Richard-Wagner-Platz. **Performances** usually 8.30pm Thur-Sat. No credit cards. **Map** p139 A1 ③⑥

Nice café, dedicated staff and some excellent cabaret. The O-Tonpiraten, a clever drag theatre troupe, often plays here, and the Schalotte hosts some brilliant acts in November during its annual international a cappella festival.

Quasimodo

Kantstrasse 12A (312 8086/www. quasimodo.de). U2, U9, S5, S7, S9, S75 Zoologischer Garten. **Performances** 10pm Tue-Sun (doors open 9pm). No credit cards. **Map** p139 D2 ③⑦

Privileging the 'jazzy' over jazz, this basement spot appears close to irrevocably severing connections to the music for which it was once noted. Yet it still promotes some good home-grown or international acts, such as heroic singer Terry Callier.

Arts & leisure

Deutsche Oper

Bismarckstrasse 35 (343 8401/ freephone 0800 248 9842/www. deutscheoperberlin.de). U2 Deutsche Oper. **Map** p139 A1 ③⑧

With roots dating back to 1912, the Deutsche Oper built its present 1,900-seat hall in 1961, just in time to carry the operatic torch for West Berlin during the Wall years. Since Reunification it has lost out in profile to the more elegant Staatsoper, but retains a reputation for productions of the classics. Discount tickets available half an hour before performances.

Renaissance

Hardenbergstrasse 6 (312 4202/www. renaissance-theater.de). U2 Ernst-Reuter-Platz. **Map** p139 C1 ③⑨

This classy location hosts some of Germany's best-known performers. The building is one of only two remaining examples of work by Oskar Kaufmann, premier Berlin theatre architect of the early 20th century, and it claims to be Europe's only art deco theatre. It all makes for a great backdrop to the chansons evenings that are served up with a full dinner in the upstairs salon.

Schaubühne am Lehniner Platz

Kurfürstendamm 153 (890 023/ www.schaubuehne.de). U7 Adenauerplatz or S5, S7, S9, S75 Charlottenburg. **Map** p139 A3 ④⓪

One of the most important venues for avant-garde theatre and dance in Berlin. The aim of its three resident directors, Thomas Ostermeier, Luk Perceval and Falk Richter, is to highlight dance, experimental contemporary writers and adaptations of classics. The programme also includes some English-language works – plays by Sarah Kane, Nicky Silver, Mark Ravenhill and Caryl Churchill have all been featured – and English subtitles are sometimes offered.

Max Liebermann Villa p152

Other Districts

North of Mitte, the working-class industrial district of Wedding, formerly on the western side of the Wall, is now politically part of Mitte. The main thing to see here is on the border – the **Gedenkstätte Berliner Mauer**, a memorial incorporating one of the last stretches of the Wall.

Much of the eastern part of the city remains a depressing wasteland of decaying communist blocks, but there are a few things to see and do in Lichtenberg and Treptow, including the latter's Treptower Park, with its giant Sowjetisches Ehrenmal (Soviet War Memorial) built over a mass grave of Russian soldiers who perished in the 1945 assault on Berlin.

Further out east, the charming town of Köpenick, older than Berlin proper, has retained much of its 18th-century character. Schloss Köpenick, with its medieval drawbridge, Renaissance gateway and baroque chapel, stands on an island at the confluence of the rivers Spree and Dahme.

To the south-west, the smart district of Dahlem contains the Freie Universität and a clutch of important museums. Deeper into affluent suburbia, Zehlendorf shades into the Grunewald and a district of forest and lakes.

West of central Charlottenburg, that district stretches a long way into more well-heeled residential suburbia, with a bunch of sights and museums around Schloss Charlottenburg, the enormous Messe-Gelände trade fair grounds near the Funkturm, and the recently renovated **Olympia-Stadion**.

Still further west is the town of Spandau, which, like Köpenick to the east, is older than the rest of the city. The Juliusturm in the **Zitadelle** is Berlin's oldest secular structure and there's a well-preserved Altstadt.

Sights & museums

Alliierten Museum

*Clayallee 135, corner of Huttenweg,
Zehlendorf (818 1990/www.alliierten
museum.de). U3 Oskar-Helene-
Heim/bus 115.* **Open** 10am-6pm Mon,
Tue, Thur-Sun. **Admission** free.

The Allies arrived as conquerors, kept
West Berlin alive during the 1948 Airlift
and finally left in 1994. In what used to
be a US Forces cinema, the Allied
Museum is mostly about the period of
the Blockade and Airlift, documented
with photos, tanks, jeeps, planes,
weapons and uniforms. Outside is the
former guardhouse from Checkpoint
Charlie and an RAF Hastings TG 503.

Anti-Kriegs-Museum

*Brüsseler Strasse 21, Wedding (4549
0110/tours 402 8691/www.anti-kriegs-
museum.de). U9 Amrumer Strasse.*
Open 4-8pm daily. **Admission** free.

The original Anti-War Museum was
founded in 1925 by Ernst Friedrich. In
1933, it was destroyed by the Nazis,
and Friedrich fled to Brussels. There
he had another museum until 1940,
when the Nazis again destroyed his
work. In 1982, a group of teachers
re-established this museum in Berlin.
It now hosts a permanent display
including World War I photos and artefacts from the original museum, children's war toys, and anti-Semitic
material from the Nazi era.

Botanischer Garten & Botanisches Museum

*Königin-Luise-Strasse 6-8, Zehlendorf
(8385 0100/www.bgbm.fu-berlin.
de/BGBM). S1 Botanischer Garten, then
15min walk.* **Open** *Botanischer Garten*
Jan, Nov, Dec 9am-4pm daily; Feb 9am-
5pm daily; Mar, Oct 9am-6pm daily; Apr
9am-8pm daily; May, June 9am-9pm
daily; Aug 9am-8pm daily; Sept 9am-
7pm daily. *Botanisches Museum* 10am-
6pm daily. **Admission** *Combined* €5;
€2.50 reductions. *Museum only* €2;
€1 reductions. No credit cards.

The Botanical Garden was landscaped
at the beginning of the 20th century.
Today, it is home to 18,000 plant
species, 16 greenhouses and a museum.
The botanical gardens make for a
pleasant stroll. The botanical museum
is a bit dilapidated but it's the place to
come for advice on whether those
mushrooms you found in the
Grunewald are delectable or deadly.

Bröhan-Museum

*Schlossstrasse 1A, Charlottenburg
(3269 0600/www.broehan-museum.de).
U2 Sophie-Charlotte-Platz or U7
Richard-Wagner-Platz.* **Open** 10am-
6pm Tue-Sun. **Admission** €5; €4
reductions. Free 1st Wed of mth.

This quiet, private museum is made up
of three well-laid-out levels of international art nouveau and art deco pieces
that businessman Karl Bröhan began
collecting in the 1960s and donated to
the city of Berlin on his 60th birthday.
The wide array of paintings, furniture,
porcelain, glass, silver and sculptures
dates from 1890 to 1939.

Brücke-Museum

*Bussardsteig 9, Grunewald (831
2029/www.bruecke-museum.de).*

Alliierten Museum

Surreal worlds

Museum reshuffle makes space for new collection.

The protracted reorganisation of Berlin's museums, their collections formerly scattered by war and division, is almost complete. The consolidation of the most important collections on Museumsinsel has created a cultural centre of renewed international significance, but left a few gaps elsewhere. In particular, the removal of the Egyptian Museum (at press time the bust of Nefertiti was about to be unveiled at the newly renovated Neues Museum) left some vacant premises among the museums around Schloss Charlottenburg.

After extensive renovations, the buildings originally constructed in 1851 for the horses and coaches of Wilhelm IV are now home to the artworks of the **Sammlung Scharf-Gerstenberg** (p153). Otto Gerstenberg (1848-1935) amassed a huge body of work in the early 20th century; his grandson Dieter Scharf (1926-2001) inherited both his passion for collecting and various work by Goya, Piranesi and others. Scharf used these as the basis for his own collection, focusing on the surreal and fantastic. Before his death, he put these artworks in the care of a foundation to arrange their exhibition in Berlin. They were first exhibited in 2000 at the Neue Nationalgalerie (p132) under the name 'Surreale Welten' ('Surreal Worlds'), which remains the subtitle in their new setting.

Gerstenberg's drawings and etchings by Goya, Piranesi and Méryon, the precursors of Surrealism, are the most focused

Sammlung Scharf-Gerstenberg

part of the collection. In the main hall are works by Dalí, Magritte, Ernst, Picabia, Schwitters and Miró, but there doesn't seem enough of any one thing. It's a great private collection, but perhaps an inadequate public one. Most impressive are the 20 works by Paul Klee, though quite what he has to do with Surrealism remains open to conjecture.

If Klee is your thing, there are more over the road at the Museum Berggruen (p152), along with works by Picasso, Matisse and Giacometti. The conjunction of the two collections is leading the city to bill the Charlottenburg museums as a centre for 'classic modern art'. Meanwhile, if you want more Dalí, try Dalí – Die Ausstellung (p61) at Leipziger Platz in Mitte.

BERLIN BY AREA

U3 Oskar-Helene-Heim, then bus 115 to Pücklerstrasse. **Open** 11am-5pm Mon, Wed-Sun. **Admission** €4; €2 reductions. *Temporary exhibitions* €5. No credit cards.

This small museum is dedicated to the work of Die Brücke ('The Bridge'), a group of Expressionist painters that was founded in Dresden in 1905 before later moving to Berlin. A large collection of oils, watercolours, drawings and sculptures by the main members of the group (Schmidt-Rottluff, Heckel, Kirchner, Mueller and Pechstein) is rotated in temporary exhibitions.

Domäne Dahlem

Königin-Luise-Strasse 49, Dahlem (666 3000/www.domaene-dahlem.de). U3 Dahlem-Dorf. **Open** 10am-6pm Mon, Wed-Sun. **Admission** *Museum* €3; €1.50 reductions; free under-18s. Free to all Wed. No credit cards.

On this organic working farm, children can see how life was lived in the 17th century. Craftspeople preserve and teach their skills. It's best to visit during one of several festivals held during the year, when kids can ride ponies, tractors and hay wagons.

Ethnologisches Museum

Lansstrasse 8, Dahlem (830 1438/ www.smb.spk-berlin.de). U3 Dahlem-Dorf. **Open** 10am-6pm Tue-Fri; 11am-6pm Sat, Sun. **Admission** €6; €3 reductions.

Extensive, authoritative, beautifully laid out, the Ethnological Museum encompasses cultures from Oceania to Central America to Africa to the Far East. Highlights include the Südsee (South Sea) room with New Guinean masks and effigies, and a remarkable collection of original canoes and boats, and the African rooms with superb carvings from Benin and the Congo, and beaded artefacts from Cameroon. There are two other museums in the same building: the Museum für Asiatische Kunst (Museum of Asian Art) with archaeological objects and works of fine art from India, Japan, China and Korea from the early Stone Age to the present; and the Museum Europäischer Kulturen (Museum of European Cultures) with exhibits about European everyday culture from the 18th century to the present.

Funkturm

Messedamm, Charlottenburg (3038 1905). U2 Theodor-Heuss-Platz or Kaiserdamm. **Open** *Aug-June* 10am-8pm Mon; 10am-11pm Tue-Sun. **Admission** €4; €2 reductions. No credit cards.

The 138m (453ft) Radio Tower was built in 1926 and looks a bit like a smaller version of the Eiffel Tower. The observation deck stands at 126m (413ft); vertigo sufferers can seek solace in the restaurant, only 55m (180ft) from the ground.

Gedenkstätte Berliner Mauer

Bernauer Strasse 111, Wedding (464 1030/www.berliner-mauer-dokumentationszentrum.de). U8 Bernauer Strasse or S1, S2 Nordbahnhof. **Open** *Documentation centre* Nov-Mar 10am-5pm Tue-Sun. Apr-Oct 9.30am-7pm Tue-Sun. **Admission** free.

This impeccably restored stretch of the Wall is as sterile a monument as any in Berlin – with a touch of total inauthenticity, the western side is kept clear of graffiti – but does communicate the scale and sheer weirdness of the thing. The documentation centre, featuring displays on the Wall and a database of escapees, is across the street, and from its roof you can view the Wall and the nearby Kapelle der Versöhnung (Chapel of Reconciliation) in former no-man's land.

Gedenkstätte Berlin-Hohenschönhausen

Gensler Strasse 66, Lichtenberg (9860 8230/www.stiftung-hsh.de). M5 Freienwalder Strasse or M6

Gensler Strasse. **Open** *Guided tours* (German) 11am, 1pm Mon-Fri; every hr 10am-4pm Sat, Sun. *Guided tours* (English) 2.30pm Wed, 2pm Sat or by request; group tours book in advance. **Admission** €4; free-€2 reductions. Free to all Mon. No credit cards.

This sprawling former remand prison run by the Stasi was used to incarcerate political prisoners – anyone from the leaders of the 1953 workers' uprising to critical students. You can visit only as part of a guided tour by ex-prisoners; these take 90 minutes. The experience is gut-wrenchingly bleak, but a potent insight into how the Stasi really operated.

Gedenkstätte Haus der Wannsee-Konferenz

Am Grossen Wannsee 56-58, Wannsee (805 0010/www.ghwk.de). S1, S7 Wannsee, then bus 114. **Open** 10am-6pm daily. **Admission** free.

On 20 January 1942, a collection of prominent Nazis, chaired by Heydrich, gathered here to draw up plans for the Final Solution, making jokes and sipping brandy as they sorted out the practicalities of genocide. Today, this infamous villa has been converted into the Wannsee Conference Memorial House, a place of remembrance, with an interesting exhibition on the conference and its consequences.

Gedenkstätte Plötzensee

Hüttigpfad, Charlottenburg (344 3226/ www.gedenkstaette-ploetzensee.de). U9 Beusselstrasse, then bus 123. **Open** Mar-Oct 9am-5pm daily. Nov-Feb 9am-4pm daily. **Admission** free.

This memorial stands on the site where the Nazis executed over 2,500 (largely political) prisoners. In a single night in 1943, 186 people were hanged. In 1952, it was declared a memorial to the victims of fascism and a commemorative wall was built. There is little to see, apart from the execution area with its meat hooks from which victims were hanged, and a small room with an exhibition. The stone urn near the entrance is filled with earth from concentration camps.

Georg-Kolbe-Museum

Sensburger Allee 25, Charlottenburg (304 2144/www.georg-kolbe-museum.de). S5, S75 Heerstrasse/ bus X34, X49, M49. **Open** 10am-6pm Tue-Sun. **Admission** €5; €3 reductions. No credit cards.

Georg Kolbe's former studio has been transformed into a showcase for his work. The Berlin sculptor, regarded as Germany's best in the 1920s, mainly focused on naturalistic human figures. The museum features examples of his earlier, graceful pieces, as well as his later sombre and larger-than-life works

Olympiastadion p153

BERLIN BY AREA

Schloss Charlottenburg

that were created in accordance with the ideals of the Nazi regime. One of his most famous pieces, *Figure for Fountain*, is in the sculpture garden.

Max Liebermann Villa

NEW *Colomierstrasse 3, Wannsee (8058 5900/www.liebermann-villa.de). S1, S7 Wannsee, then bus 114.* **Open** *Apr-Sept* 10am-6pm Mon, Wed, Fri-Sun; 10am-8pm Thur. *Oct-Mar* 11am-5pm Mon, Wed-Sun. **Admission** €6; €4 reductions. No credit cards.
Max Liebermann, perhaps the most famous German Impressionist painter, spent his summers in this beautiful house on the shore of Lake Wannsee from 1910 until the premises were confiscated by the Nazis. You can now wander the sumptuous gardens, subject of many Liebermann paintings, view an exhibition of his canvases in the house, or take coffee and cakes in the extremely decent café.

Museum Berggruen

Westlicher Stülerbau, Schlossstrasse 1, Charlottenburg (3269 5815/ www.smb.museum/mb). U2 Sophie-Charlotte-Platz or U7 Richard-Wagner-Platz. **Open** 10am-6pm Tue-Sun. **Admission** €8; €4 reductions.
Heinz Berggruen was an early dealer in Picassos in Paris, and the subtitle of this museum, Picasso und seine Zeit (Picasso and his Time), sums up this satisfying collection. Over an easily digestible three circular floors, Picasso's astonishingly prolific and diverse output is well represented. There are also works by Braque, Giacometti, Cézanne and Matisse, and most of the second floor is given over to wonderful paintings by Paul Klee.

Museum Berlin-Karlshorst

Zwieseler Strasse 4, corner of Rheinsteinstrasse, south of Lichtenberg (5015 0810/www.museum-karlshorst.de). S3 Karlshorst. **Open** 10am-6pm Tue-Sun. **Admission** free.
After the Soviets took Berlin, they commandeered this former German officers' club as HQ for the military administration and it was here, on the night of 8-9 May 1945, that German commanders signed the unconditional surrender, ending the war in Europe. The museum looks at the German-Soviet relationship over 70 years. Divided into 16 rooms, including the one where the Nazis surrendered, it takes us through two world wars and one cold one, plus assorted pacts, victories and capitulations.

Museumsdorf Düppel

Clauertstrasse 11, Wannsee (802 6671/www.dueppel.de). S1 Mexikoplatz, then bus 118, 629. **Open** 3-7pm Thur; 10am-5pm Sun. Last entry 1hr before closing. Closed Nov-Feb. **Admission** €2; €1 reductions. No credit cards.
At this 14th-century village, reconstructed around archaeological excavations, workers demonstrate handicrafts, medieval technology and farming techniques. Ox-cart rides for kids. Small snack bar.

Olympiastadion

*Olympischer Platz 3, Charlottenburg
(3068 8100/www.olympiastadion-
berlin.de). U2 Olympia-Stadion or
S5 Olympiastadion.* **Open** varies.
Admission varies. No credit cards.
Originally designed by Werner March
and opened in 1936 for the Olympics,
the 74,000-seat stadium underwent a
major and long overdue refitting for
the 2006 World Cup, including better
seats and a roof over the whole lot.
Home of Hertha BSC, it also hosts the
German Cup Final, plus other sporting
events and concerts.

Sammlung Scharf-Gerstenberg

NEW *Schlossstrasse 70, Charlottenburg
(3435 7315/www.smb.museum/ssg).
U2 Sophie-Charlotte-Platz or U7
Richard-Wagner-Platz.* **Open** 10am-
6pm Tue-Sat. **Admission** €8; €4
reductions. No credit cards.
The Scharf-Gerstenberg Collection,
currently on a ten-year loan to the city,
occupies the building used by the
Egyptian Museum before it moved
back to Museumsinsel (the Kalabscha
Gate and the columns of the Temple of
Sahure remain pending their removal
to the Pergamon). Presented as an exhibition called 'Surreal Worlds', it con-
cerns the history of Surrealism and its
forerunners, traced through artists
such as Piranesi, Goya, Dali, Magritte
and Ernst. See also box p149.

Schloss Charlottenburg

*Luisenplatz & Spandauer Damm,
Charlottenburg (320 911/www.spsg.de).
U2 Sophie-Charlotte-Platz or U7
Richard-Wagner-Platz.* **Open** *Old
Palace* 10am-6pm Tue- Sun. Last tour
4pm. *New Wing* (Apr-Oct) 10am-6pm
Mon, Wed-Sun; (Nov-Mar) 10am-5pm
Wed-Sun. **Admission** *Day tickets* €14;
€9 reductions.
Queen Sophie-Charlotte was the impe-
tus behind this sprawling palace and
garden complex (and gave her name to
both building and district) – her hus-

band Friedrich III (later King Friedrich
I) built in 1695-99 as a summer home
for his queen. Later kings also sum-
mered here, tinkering with and adding
to the buildings. It was severely damaged during World War II, but has now
been restored, and stands as the largest
surviving Hohenzollern palace. There
are various parts to which the public
are admitted; easiest option is to go for
the combination ticket that allows
entrance to nearly all of them. The one
must-see is the Neue Flügel (New Wing),
containing the State Apartments of
Frederick the Great. The Neue Pavillon
(New Pavilion) was built by Schinkel in
1824 for Friedrich Wilhelm III, who
liked it so much that he chose to live
here in preference to the main palace.
Within the huge gardens is the 18th-
century Belvedere, containing a collection of Berlin porcelain, and the sombre
Mausoleum, with the tombs of
Friedrich Wilhelm III, his wife Queen
Luise, Kaiser Wilhelm I and his wife.

Schloss Köpenick

*Muggelheimer Strasse 1, Köpenick
(6566 1749/www.smb.museum). S47
Spindlersfeld.* **Open** 10am-6pm Tue-
Sun. **Admission** €4; €2 reductions.
Overspill from the Kunstgewerbe
Museum is presented as 'RoomArt',
with furniture and decorative art from
the Renaissance, baroque and rococo
eras arranged according to period
beneath carefully restored ceiling paintings. There's also an exhibition on the
history of the site, plus a riverside café.

Stasi Museum (Forschungs- und Gedenkstätte Normannenstrasse)

*Ruschestrasse 103, Lichtenberg (553
6854/www.stasimuseum.de). S41, S42,
S8, S85 Frankfurter Allee or U5
Magdalenenstrasse.* **Open** 11am-6pm
Mon-Fri; 2-6pm Sat, Sun. **Admission**
€4; €3.50 reductions. No credit cards.
In what used to be part of the head-
quarters of the Stasi, you can look

around the old offices of feared secret police chief Erich Mielke, preserved as they were right down to his old uniform still hanging in the wardrobe. There are also displays of bugging devices and spy cameras concealed in books, plant pots and car doors, and a variety of communist kitsch, such as banners and busts of Lenin.

Tierpark Berlin-Friedrichsfelde

Am Tierpark 125, Lichtenburg (515 310/www.tierpark-berlin.de). U5 Tierpark. **Open** *Jan-late Mar, late Oct-Dec 9am-4pm daily. Late Mar-mid Sept 9am-6pm daily. Mid Sept-late Oct 9am-5pm daily.* **Admission** €11; €8 reductions; family €18-€29. No credit cards.

One of Europe's largest zoos, with lots of roaming space for herd animals, although others are kept in small cages. Residents include bears, elephants, big cats and penguins. In the zoo's north-west corner is the baroque Schloss Friedrichsfelde. One of the Continent's biggest snake farms is also here.

Zitadelle

Am Juliusturm, Spandau (354 9440/ tours 334 6270/www.zitadelle-spandau.net). U7 Zitadelle. **Open** 10am-5pm daily. **Admission** €4.50; €2.50 reductions. No credit cards.

The oldest structure inside the citadel (and the oldest secular building in Berlin) is the Juliusturm, dating back to about 1160. The bulk of the Zitadelle was designed in 1560-94, in the style of an Italian fort, to dominate the confluence of the Spree and Havel rivers. There are two museums. One tells the story of the citadel; the other is about local history.

Zucker-Museum

Amrumer Strasse 32, Wedding (3142 7574/www.sdtb.de/zucker-museum). U9 Amrumer Strasse. **Open** 9am-4.30pm Mon-Thur; 11am-6pm Sun. **Admission** free. No credit cards.

A museum that is devoted to the chemistry, history and politics of sugar may not sound like the most entertaining venue for a rainy afternoon, but this place, originally opened in 1904, contains a fascinating collection of paraphernalia. Don't miss the slide show on the slave trade.

Nightlife

Insel

Alt-Treptow 6, Treptow (5360 8020/ www.insel-berlin.net). S8, S9, S85 Plänterwald/bus N65. **Open** 7pm-1am Wed; 10pm-late Fri, Sat. No credit cards.

Out of the way, but a great venue – like a miniature castle on a tiny Spree island, with several levels and a top-floor balcony. Once a communist youth club, now a live venue/colourful club – with lots of neon and ultraviolet, crusties and hippies, techno and hip hop, punk and metal. Great in summer.

Villa

Landsberger Allee 54, northern Friedrichshain (www.myspace.com/ fucnetwork). M10 Landsberger Allee/ Petersburger Strasse. **Open** midnight Sat-noon Sun. No credit cards.

A throwback to the days of illegal clubs and underground parties, Villa is a grand and cheerfully decrepit former brewery with multiple dancefloors, several bars, a booming sound system, and a line-up of international DJs. Door policy is strict, but you'll be fine if you know what party you're going to. Since it's technically a registered society (Verein), you must become a 'member' to get in; drop the name of whatever DJ is spinning, and this easy process is handled at the door.

Werkstatt der Kulturen

Wissmannstrasse 32, Neukölln (609 7700/www.werkstatt-der-kulturen.de). U7, U8 Hermannplatz. No credit cards.

This intimate venue usually presents traditional ethnic music or local fusions blending jazz, trance or folk elements.

Sanssouci

Day Trips

Potsdam & Babelsberg

Just south-west of the city limits,
Potsdam is Berlin's Versailles.
Tourists cram into the town in
summer, attracted by its parks,
palaces and baroque architecture,
so make a day trip of it and avoid
peak times if possible.

Potsdam was the summer
residence of the Hohenzollerns
and, despite the damage wrought
during World War II and by East
Germany's socialist planners,
much remains of the legacy of
these Prussian kings. In 1990,
Potsdam was assigned UNESCO
World Heritage status and some
80 per cent of its historic buildings
have since been restored. The best-
known landmark is **Sanssouci**,
the huge landscaped park created
by Frederick the Great.

Cross over the bridge from the
station to reach the Old Town,
starting at the **Nikolaikirche**
and the **Altes Rathaus**. The
Stadtschloss marks the centre of
the town. The baroque quarter is
bounded by Schopenhauerstrasse,
Hegelallee, Hebbelstrasse and
Charlottenstrasse. Some of the
best houses can be found in
Gutenbergstrasse and
Brandenburger Strasse, Potsdam's
pedestrianised shopping drag.
Three baroque town gates – the
Nauener Tor, Jäger Tor and
Brandenburger Tor – stand on
the northern and western edges
of the quarter. North-east of the
Nikolaikirche is the Holländisches
Viertel (Dutch quarter).

The vast Park Sanssouci
stretches away on the west side
of town. North-east of the centre
is another large park complex,
the **Neuer Garten**, with the
Schloss Cecilienhof at its northern
end. Potsdam's third royal park,
Park Babelsberg, to the east,
also makes for a good walk.

The nearby town of Babelsberg is home to the Babelsberg film studio.

Potsdam is too spread out to do everything on foot. A Potsdam Card from the tourist office (p157) costs €9.80 and provides free public transport plus discounted entry to most attractions. Public transport is easy to figure out from the maps at all bus and tram stops.

Sights & museums

Altes Rathaus

Am Alten Markt (0331 289 6336/ www.altesrathauspotsdam.de). Tram X98, 90, 92, 93, 96 Alter Markt. **Open** 10am-6pm Tue-Sun. **Admission** free.
Potsdam's former town hall is a mid 18th-century baroque building with Corinthian columns and a stepped dome. Badly damaged in the war, it was rebuilt in the 1960s and is now used for exhibitions and lectures.

Filmpark Babelsburg

August-Bebel-Strasse 26-53, entrance on Grossbeerenstrasse (0331 721 2750/www.filmpark.de). S1 Babelsberg, bus 601, 602, 618, 619, 690 to Filmpark. **Open** Apr-Oct 10am-6pm daily. **Admission** €19; €16 reductions. No credit cards.
In the 1920s, the Babelsberg film studio was the world's largest outside Hollywood and it was here that Fritz Lang's *Metropolis* and Josef von Sternberg's *The Blue Angel* were produced. These days there are state-of-the-art facilities for film and TV production. The only part open to the public is the Filmpark, which has an assortment of largely tawdry attractions, ranging from themed restaurants and rides to set tours and stunt displays.

Gedenkstätte Lindenstrasse

Gedenkstätte Lindenstrasse

Lindenstrasse 54 (0331 289 6136/ www.potsdam.de). Tram 94, 96 Dortusstrasse. **Open** 10am-6pm Tue, Thur, Sat. **Admission** €1.50. No credit cards.

Built in 1737, this former palace was later used first by the Nazis and then by the Stasi to hold and interrogate people. There is a warrenous complex of cells; the building is now a memorial against political violence.

Haus der Brandenburgisch-Preussischen Geschichte

Kutschstall, Am Neuen Markt 9 (0331 620 8550/www.hbpg.de). Tram X98, 90, 92, 93, 96 Alter Markt. **Open** 10am-5pm Tue-Fri; 10am-6pm Sat, Sun. **Admission** €5; €4 reductions. No credit cards.

Opened in 2003, the permanent exhibition here charts 900 years of Prussian history from the Middle Ages to the modern day. The Kutschstall was originally a royal stables.

Nikolaikirche

Am Alten Markt (0331 270 8602/ www.nikolaipotsdam.de). Tram x98, 90, 92, 93, 96 Alter Markt. **Open** 9am-7pm Mon-Sat; 11.30am-7pm Sun. **Admission** free.

This 19th-century church, with its huge dome, was inspired by St Paul's in London and is one of the most dominant buildings in Potsdam. It was the last work by Berlin's most famous architect, Karl Friedrich Schinkel.

Sanssouci

Potsdam (0331 969 4202/ www.spsg.de). Bus X15, 695. **Open** *Palace* Apr-Oct 10am-6pm Tue-Sun; Nov-Mar 10am-5pm daily. *Park* 9am-dusk daily. **Admission** *Palace* €8; €5 reductions. *Park* free. No credit cards.

An elegant legacy of Frederick the Great, this is Potsdam's biggest tourist magnet. Located atop terraced vineyards, Sanssouci ('without worries')

is the result of the king's desire for an exquisite sanctuary to pursue his philosophical, musical and literary interests. You could spend an entire day wandering around the park, where the Drachenhaus (Dragon House), a pleasant pagoda-style café, and the Chinesisches Teehaus (Chinese Tea House), with its collection of porcelain, are two of the attractions.

Schloss Cecilienhof

Im Neuen Garten (0331 969 4244/ www.spsg.de). Bus 692. **Open** *Apr-Oct* 10am-6pm Tue-Sun. *Nov-Mar* 10am-5pm Tue-Sun. **Admission** €6; €5 reductions. No credit cards.

Built from 1913 to 1917, this mock-Tudor mansion was spared wartime damage and, in summer 1945, hosted the Potsdam Conference, where Stalin, Truman and Churchill (and later Clement Attlee) met to discuss the future of Germany. You can even see the round table where the settlement was negotiated.

Getting there

By train

There are frequent S-Bahn and Regionalbahn trains to Potsdam. Regionalbahn trains take about 25 minutes from Hauptbahnhof, S-Bahn trains (S1) about 40 minutes. From some parts of Berlin it's easier to take the S7 to Wannsee, and change to the S1 there. There is also a direct, hourly Regionalbahn train to Babelsberg that takes just 20 mins from Mitte.

Tourist information

Potsdam Tourismus Service

Brandenburger Strasse 3 (0331 275 580/www.potsdam-tourism.com). Tram 94, 96/bus x15, 695 Luisenplatz. **Open** *Apr-Oct* 9.30am-6pm Mon-Fri; 9.30am-4pm Sat, Sun. *Nov-Mar* 10am-6pm Mon-Fri; 9.30am-2pm Sat.

Essentials

Artist Riverside Hotel & Day Spa

Hotels

As Berlin gets used to its position as the third most-visited city in Europe (after London and Paris) – something that would have been unthinkable a generation ago – new hotels have been appearing in all shapes and sizes. Additions at the top end have included the cool and elegant Hotel Ellington on Nürnberger Strasse in the west end, and the 364-room Meliá by Friedrichstrasse station, lending its cool, modern silhouette to the Spree. Just across the river, meanwhile, stands the Artist Riverside Hotel, offering an affordable and delightfully over-the-top spa experience. To complement the city's abundance of hostels, a new breed of smart hotels with an emphasis on design has also begun to appear at the budget end of the market; see box p165.

The distribution is far from uniform. The most fashionable area to land in is Mitte, centre of sightseeing and nightlife, and that's where most new hotels are appearing. But central Charlottenburg, the city's west end, also features some funky new establishments as well as a complement of characterful old pensions – if you want a taste of the kind of history that was wiped out in the east, this is the area for you. Some districts, such as Friedrichshain, Prenzlauer Berg or Schöneberg, have hardly any hotels at all.

Note that smoking is now forbidden in all German hotels – both in public spaces and in the rooms.

Money matters

The good news is that Berlin still ranks among the least expensive European capitals,

ESSENTIALS

with hotel beds on average less than half the price of those in London or Paris, and considerably cheaper than those in Moscow, Rome or even Amsterdam. It's wise to reserve in advance wherever possible: on any given weekend in Mitte or Prenzlauer Berg many hotels are extremely busy, and decent rooms can be impossible to find at short notice during big cultural events such as February's Berlin International Film Festival. The best bargains are probably found in Charlottenburg.

Berliner Tourismus Marketing (p186), the city's privatised tourist information service, can also sort out hotel reservations. It provides a free listings booklet of over 400 hotels – but note that these have all paid to be included.

Mitte

Arte Luise Kunsthotel

Luisenstrasse 19 (284 480/www.arte-luise.com). U6, S1, S2, S5, S7, S9, S75 Friedrichstrasse. €€€.
In a neoclassical former palace just a short walk from the Reichstag and Brandenburger Tor, this 'artist home' is one of Berlin's more imaginative small hotels, with each of its 50 rooms decorated by a different renowned artist. There's graffiti artist Thomas Baumgärtel's 'Royal Suite', a golden room spray-painted with bananas; and Angela Dwyer's 'Room Like Any Other', whose surfaces are covered in stream-of-consciousness scrawlings. Some rooms get a little noise from the S-Bahn trains, but this is still a great place to stay.

Artist Riverside Hotel & Day Spa

Friedrichstrasse 106 (284 900/www.great-hotel.com). U6, S1, S2, S5, S7, S9, S75 Friedrichstrasse. €€€.
See box p168.

ESSENTIALS

Art'otel Berlin Mitte

Wallstrasse 70-73 (240 620/
www.artotels.de). U2 Märkisches
Museum. €€€.

This delightful hotel is a creative fusion of old and new, combining restored rococo reception rooms with ultra-modern bedrooms designed by Nalbach + Nalbach. As well as highlighting the artwork of Georg Baselitz – originals hang in the corridors and all 109 rooms – the hotel's decor has been thought out to the smallest detail, from the Philippe Starck bathrooms to the Breuer chairs in the conference rooms. The staff are pleasant, and views from the top suites across Mitte are stunning.

Baxpax Downtown Hostel Hotel

Ziegelstrasse 28 (278 748-80/www.
baxpax-downtown.de). U6, S1, S2,
S5, S7, S9, S75 Friedrichstrasse. €.

This new, third addition to the Mittes Backpacker Hostel empire is an excellent place to stay, with a brilliant location. Clean, contemporary and well designed, it has all the usual amenities, from baggage room to darts, with the additional luxury of a fireplace lounge, courtyard and rooftop terrace. There's a dorm just for women, 24-hour reception and keycard access for security, and a friendly, relaxed atmosphere.

Casa Camper Berlin

NEW *Weinmeisterstrasse 1 (2000*
3410/www.casacamper.com). U8
Weinmeisterstrasse. €€€.

'Walk, don't run' has long been the credo of Camper – yes, the same Spanish company that makes the shoes. Its second Casa Camper hotel (the first is in Barcelona) opened in September 2009 and offers the same eco-meets-cool atmosphere. The 51 rooms are cleverly minimal and painted in warm, cheery Camper red; offbeat amenities include a top-floor snack lounge open 24/7, a tapas-style Asian restaurant downstairs, and bikes to rent. A place for grown-up hipsters with a heart.

Circus Hostel

Weinbergsweg 1A (2000 3939/
www.circus-berlin.de). U8 Rosenthaler
Platz. €.

The Circus is a rarity – simple but stylish, warm and comfortable. And the upper-floor apartments have balconies and lovely views. The laid-back staff can help get discount tickets to almost anything, or give directions to the best bars and clubs, of which plenty are nearby. Deservedly popular, this place is always full, so book ahead. Just across the Platz, the owners have also opened the moderately priced Circus Hotel (below). Reservations and information are available on the above number.

Circus Hotel

NEW *Rosenthaler Strasse 1 (2000*
3939/www.circus-berlin.de). U8
Rosenthaler Platz. €€.

See box p165.

CityStay Hostel

Rosenstrasse 16 (2362 4031/
www.citystay.de). S5, S7, S9, S75
Hackescher Markt. €.

On a small, quiet street, but as central as you can get, this is a great modern hostel for the price. The rooms are clean and simple, and there are showers on every floor. Security is top-notch here, with access cards for the video-monitored entrance and floors. The helpful staff are friendly. The breakfast buffet features fresh organic bread, and the kitchen will fix your eggs any way you like 'em.

Dietrich-Bonhoeffer-Haus

Ziegelstrasse 30 (284 670/www.hotel-
dbh.de). U6, S1, S2, S5, S7, S9, S75
Friedrichstrasse or S1, S2
Oranienburger Strasse. €€€.

Named after the theologian executed by the Nazis for alleged participation in the 1944 Hitler assassination attempt, this hotel sits on a quiet corner behind the Friedrichstadtpalast. It was originally built in 1987 as a meeting place for Christians from East and

ESSENTIALS

West; as such, the atmosphere is warm, and the staff helpful. The rooms are large, the breakfast is pretty good and the location is excellent.

Heart of Gold
Hostel Berlin
Johannisstrasse 11 (2900 3300/ www.heartofgold-hostel.de). S1, S2 Oranienburger Strasse. €.
The prime location aside (it's only 50m from Oranienburger Strasse), this member of the Backpacker Germany Network (www.backpacker network.de) is an enjoyable place to stay. The rooms are bright and cheerful, all newly done with parquet floors. Lockers are free, and individual bathrooms and showers and a keycard system guarantee security. The laundry is cheap, as are the €1 shots in the bar.

Helter Skelter Hostel
Kalkscheunenstrasse 4 (2804 4997/ www.helterskelterhostel.com). U6 Oranienburger Tor. €.
Right behind the Friedrichstadtpalast in the historic Kalkscheune ('chalk barn') cultural centre, this centrally located hostel is a wonderful, relaxed place to stay, with amiable and international English-speaking staff. There are apartments for longer stays, and kitchen facilities in the communal room. The rooms are curiously decorated, but fun – one has a pool table on the ceiling. You're close to practically everything, and Friedrichstrasse station is handy to reach anything else.

Honigmond Garden Hotel
Invalidenstrasse 122 (2844 5577/ www.honigmond.de). U6 Zinnowitzer Strasse. €€€.
Along with its nearby sister Honigmond Restaurant-Hotel (see below), this is one of the most charming hotels in Berlin, and it doesn't cost an arm and a leg. Choose between large bedrooms facing the street, smaller ones overlooking the fish pond and Tuscan-style garden, or spacious apartments on the upper floor. The rooms are impeccably styled with polished pine floors, paintings in massive gilt frames, antiques and iron bedsteads. There's also a charming sitting room overlooking the garden. A stay here is highly recommended.

Honigmond
Restaurant-Hotel
Tieckstrasse 11 (284 4550/ www.honigmond.de). U6 Oranienburger Tor. €€€.
The 40 rooms in this beautiful 1899 building are spacious and lovely, and although some of the less expensive ones lack their own shower and toilet, this is still probably the best and prettiest mid-price hotel east of the Zoo. The reception area has comfy chairs around a gas fireplace, and breakfast is served in the Honigmond restaurant (p74). The friendly staff speak English, and the hotel is perfectly situated within walking distance of the Scheunenviertel and Hackescher Markt.

Hotel Adlon
Kempinski Berlin
Unter den Linden 77 (226 10/ www.hotel-adlon.de). U55, S1, S2 Brandenburger Tor. €€€€.
Not quite the Adlon of yore, which burnt down following World War II, this new, more generic luxury version was rebuilt by the Kempinski Group in 1997 on its original site next to the Brandenburg Gate. Although it's still considered one of Berlin's finest hotels – popular with movie stars, royalty and anyone keen to make an impression – the 409 rooms (including three bullet-proof presidential suites) are decorated in a generic international-executive style. The staff can be frosty if you don't look the part.

Hotel Amano
NEW *Auguststrasse 43 (809 4150/ www.hotel-amano.com). S1, S2, S25 Oranienburger Strasse.* €€.
See box right.

Budget design

For a long time, high-concept accommodation in Berlin came at correspondingly high prices. But at last – and seemingly all of a sudden – a scad of new hotels with cool design and innovative services has opened for budget travellers who want good looks along with the basics.

In the heart of Mitte, the owners of the infamous Circus Hostel have created **Circus Hotel** (p163), a downright classy older sibling. In two corner buildings on a busy intersection, it offers 60 airy, minimalist rooms, (truly) friendly service, clever touches such as iPods charged with a selection of Berlin music, a plush restaurant serving modern German fare and prices starting at around €70. The clientele skews toward the young, creative set.

Just up the street at the brand-new **Hotel Amano** (p164), a sexy lounge and streetside bar beckon

to guests and even locals through large-pane windows. Standard rooms are on the small side, but Amano also has apartments (up to 90 square metres/970 square feet, and equipped with washing machines) for longer stays. With clean lines and muted colours throughout, the design here looks terrifically expensive, but it isn't. Singles start at €70 a night.

Further east, near the Ostbahnhof, **OSTEL** (p171) replicates communist-era design in a real *Plattenbau* building, right down to wildly graphic wallpaper and ubiquitous orange lamps (rooms with en suite bathroom start at €30.50 per night).

Then there's the long-awaited **Michelbergerhotel** (p171) in Friedrichshain. Created by German designer Werner Aisslinger (www.aisslinger.com), its cheerful rooms and casual-chic public areas are studies in clever use of space under sky-high ceilings. The Michelberger captures Berlin's multi-use vibe in other ways, too: the construction site was used as a club before opening in September 2009. Prices start at €59.

So at last, affordable hospitality in the German capital for guests who've doffed their backpacks but were never interested in – or could afford – upscale luxury. Why so many new, inexpensive yet clever, attractive hotels all at the same time? 'Hoteliers and investors were finally ready to create properties that reflect the city,' says Birgit Schmoltner, spokesperson for the Michelberger. Even here, it's all about poor but sexy.

Circus Hotel

Hotel Am Scheunenviertel

*Oranienburger Strasse 38 (282 2125/
2830 8310/www.hotelas.com). U6
Oranienburger Tor or S1, S2
Oranienburger Strasse.* **€€**.
This simple, unpretentious 18-room
hotel sits right in the middle of the old
Jewish Quarter and the historic heart
of town. If just a bit dark, the rooms
are clean and comfortable, each with
a toilet and good shower. The friendly staff will gladly help you plan your
walking tour of the nearby sights. Be
sure to request a room in the back if
you're a light sleeper, as the bar downstairs can get noisy.

Hotel de Rome

*Behrenstrasse 37 (460 6090/
www.roccofortecollection.com). U6
Französische Strasse.* **€€€€**.
In 2006, this 19th-century manse, originally built as the headquarters of
Dresdener Bank, was transformed by
Rocco Forte into a grand and sumptuous affair. All 146 rooms are state-of-
the-art if somewhat generic plush, with
plenty of polished wood, marble and
velvet. The former basement vault now
houses a pool, spa and gym. The lobby
restaurant, Parioli, specialises in
Mediterranean cuisine, with al fresco
dining in summer, and lighter fare is
available in the sleek Bebel Bar &
Lounge or the Opera Court, where
afternoon tea is served.

Hotel Gendarm Nouveau

*Charlottenstrasse 61 (206 0660/
www.hotel-gendarm-berlin.de). U2,
U6 Stadtmitte.* **€€€**.
If you fancy a five-star location but
don't want to spend a fortune, then this
place is just the ticket. The 39 rooms
and two suites are smart and comfortable, and the whole place recently
underwent a modernising makeover.
It's close to the Gendarmenmarkt,
Friedrichstrasse and the State Opera.
At rates around half those at the nearby Sofitel or Hilton, you can't really
go wrong.

Hotel Hackescher Markt

*Grosse Präsidentenstrasse 8 (280
030/www.loock-hotels.com). S5, S7,
S9, S75 Hackescher Markt.* **€€€**.
This elegant hotel in a nicely renovated
townhouse avoids the noise of its central Hackescher Markt location by cleverly having many rooms face inwards
on to a tranquil green courtyard. Some
have balconies, all have their own bath
with heated floor, and the suites are
spacious and comfortable. The pleasant, helpful staff speak good English,
and, while you don't necessarily get the
most atmosphere for the money, you
can't beat the address.

Hotel Pension Kastanienhof

*Kastanienallee 65 (443 050/www.
kastanienhof.biz). U8 Rosenthaler
Platz or U2 Senefelderplatz/tram
M1, 12.* **€€€**.
Ideally located at the bottom of
Kastanienallee, this is a warm, cosy,
old-fashioned hotel. The pastel-
coloured rooms are generously propor-
tioned and well equipped, and there are
three breakfast rooms and a bar. The
English-speaking staff are friendly.
Book ahead for weekends.

Lux 11

*Rosa-Luxemburg-Strasse 9-13 (936
2800/www.lux-eleven.com). U2 Rosa
Luxemburg-Platz.* **€€€**.
A member of the Design Hotels group,
this former apartment house for the
DDR secret police is a stylish, no-non-
sense apartment-hotel with an emphasis on wellbeing. The cool, modern
white-walled apartments are elegant
and well appointed, with everything
from intercom for visitors to
microwave and dishwasher in the
kitchen, and queen-sized beds in
between. There's an in-house Aveda
salon, and the restaurant, Shiro i
Shiro, serves wholefood breakfasts.
The location is perfect for the fashionable sites of Mitte.

River beds

Some places simply defy categorisation. Take the **Artist Riverside Hotel & Day Spa** (p161), which confounds expectations at every turn. The building looks nothing special – a prefabricated structure that until recently housed a car dealership. But it's in a fabulous Friedrichstrasse location on the bank of the Spree, handy for just about everything, and all of the suites and several of the rooms offer views over the river.

Despite the name, this isn't an 'artist hotel' in any conventional sense, but the warm interior has been designed by owner Uwe Buttgereit with a theatrical panache and love for art nouveau ornament.

Is it a budget hotel or a luxury establishment? Well, it's both. Or neither. Rooms come in five categories, from basic 'tourist' accommodation to fabulously over-the-top suites with waterbeds, whirlpool baths and fancy mirrors. One suite has a bronze bathtub on a podium, from which you can gaze upriver while taking an extravagant soak. Another is available with access to its own jacuzzi on the balcony. If all this wasn't wellness enough, there's the Balinese-style Day Spa with a multicultural menu of treatments and massage, a sauna cabin with a Spree view, and a clamshell floatarium for two.

The Riverside is, in short, a unique and somewhat eccentric establishment offering watery pleasures aplenty for travellers on any budget. All this, and the Grill Royal (p67) downstairs too.

Meliá Berlin

NEW *Friedrichstrasse 103 (2060 7900/ www.meliaberlin.com). U6, S1, S2, S5, S7, S9, S75 Friedrichstrasse.* €€€.
Just across the street from Friedrichstrasse station, this new corner building by the Spree is a huge link in the Spanish Sol Meliá chain. All 364 rooms are similarly and tastefully appointed, many with fine views of the river and Reichstag beyond, but the rich wood units and headboards seem a little incongruous. The rooftop restaurant offers reasonably priced theatre and business lunch menus, while the tapas bar off the lobby provides lighter dishes. It's a good stopover for the harried business traveller, but for folk in search of atmosphere, there's better fare for the money to be found elsewhere.

Miniloftmitte

Hessische Strasse 5 (847 1090/ www.miniloft.de). U6 Zinnowitzer Strasse. €€€.
A brilliant alternative to the hotel hustle, these 14 flats – housed in a combined renovated apartment building and award-winning steel-concrete construction – are modern, airy and elegant. Each comes with a queen-sized bed, couch and dining area, with warm-coloured fabrics, organic basics in the kitchen, and lots of light. The owners/ designers/architects are a young, friendly couple who live and work on the premises. Highly recommended.

MitArt Hotel

Linienstrasse 139-140 (2839 0430/ www.mitart.de). U6 Oranienburger Tor. €€€.
In a beautifully restored printing house, this warm, simple and unpretentious hotel is perfectly situated for hopping the area's galleries, and – as evidenced by the paintings and sculpture that decorate the rooms – the owner is well versed in the scene. Rooms are frill-free, warm and bright, and without TV, so you're pretty much

forced to kick back and relax. The breakfast buffet is served each day in the hotel's organic café.

Park Inn Hotel

Alexanderplatz 7 (238 90/www. parkinn.de). U2, U5, U8, S5, S7, S9, S75 Alexanderplatz. €€€.

With 1,012 rooms overlooking Alexanderplatz, Berlin's largest (and tallest) hotel is something of a mixed bag. Although the views are spectacular, the vibe is a little cold and impersonal considering the price. There are special package deals – and a casino – for the convention groups that fill the lobby, and easy access to public transport for a business stopover, but for the traveller in search of warmth and atmosphere, there are better choices nearby.

Platte Mitte

Rochstrasse 9 (0177 283 26 02/ www.plattemitte.de). S5, S7, S9, S75 Hackescher Markt. €€.

Proudly calling itself a 'No Hotel', these four apartments on the 21st floor of a 1967-built *Plattenbau* are airy and well designed, each with spectacular views of the city around Alexanderplatz. Colourfully decorated and eclectic, the furnishings mix original pieces of the period with fanciful touches such as poster-plastered walls and mannequins by the bed. And as most of the neighbours are original tenants, this is a wonderfully unique way to experience Berlin.

Radisson Blu Hotel

Karl-Liebknecht-Strasse 3 (238 280/ www.radissonblu.com/hotel-berlin). S5, S7, S9, S75 Hackescher Markt. €€€.

With interiors by German designer Yasmine Mahmoudieh, the 427 rooms here are fresh, uncluttered and free of chain-hotel blandness. The Radisson's claim to fame, however, is 'the tank' – a 25m- (82ft) high aquarium with a million litres of salt water housing 2,500

varieties of fish that dominates the hotel's atrium. Many of the bedrooms have a view of it.

Westin Grand

Friedrichstrasse 158-164 (202 70/ www.westin.com/berlin). U6 Französische Strasse. €€€€.

Despite its East German prefabricated exterior, the Westin Grand is pure five-star international posh. The decor is gratifyingly elegant, with lots of polished crystal and brass and a grandiose foyer and staircase. The rooms are tastefully traditional, and the 35 suites are individually furnished with period decor themed after their names. There's also a garden and patio, plus a bar and restaurant, and the elegant haunts of the Gendarmenmarkt are just outside the door.

Prenzlauer Berg

Ackselhaus & Bluehome

Belforter Strasse 21 (4433 7633/ www.ackselhaus.de). U2 Senefelder Platz. €€€. *No credit cards.*

Just doors apart, what ties these two establishments together – aside from their shared reception desk – is a wonderfully realised 'modernised colonial' style. In Ackselhaus each apartment has a bedroom, sitting room, bathroom and kitchenette, with old wooden floorboards, white walls, antique furniture and a Mediterranean feel. The pricier Bluehome (at no.24), with its blue façade and balconies, is home to the Club del Mar restaurant, which offers a breakfast buffet and open fireplace. There's also a delightful garden out back, complete with lawn chairs in summer.

Hotel Greifswald

Greifswalder Strasse 211 (442 7888/ www.hotel-greifswald.de). Tram M4 Hufelandstrasse. €€.

The Hotel Greifswald is tucked away in a quiet rear courtyard just a short distance from both Alexanderplatz

ESSENTIALS

and Kollwitzplatz (and the nearby Knaack and Magnet clubs), and is a favourite among artists and musicians. The rooms are tasteful and cheery without the fluff, the staff friendly and helpful. But the highlight is the excellent breakfast buffet, served from 6.30am till noon. During the summer you can have it al fresco in the back. Apartments are also available.

Hotel Transit Loft
Immanuelkirchstrasse 14A (4849 3773/www.transit-loft.de). Tram M4 Hufelandstrasse. €€.
This loft hotel in a renovated factory is ideal for backpackers and young travellers. The rooms all have en suite bathrooms and there's a private sauna, gym and billiard room with special rates for hotel guests. The staff are friendly and well informed, and there's good wheelchair access too.

Lette'm Sleep Hostel
Lettestrasse 7 (4473 3623/ www.backpackers.de). U2 Eberswalder Strasse. €.
Just off the Helmholzplatz, this small hostel has new floors and bathrooms, and a beer garden in the back. There's free tea and coffee but no breakfast, which you can either make yourself in the kitchen or enjoy at one of the many decent cafés around the corner. All rooms have basins, and hot showers are always available. The three large apartments can sleep up to ten people each.

Myer's Hotel
Metzer Strasse 26 (440 140/www.myershotel.de). U2 Senefelderplatz. €€€.
This renovated 19th-century townhouse sits on a tranquil street. There's a garden and a glass-ceilinged gallery, and the big leather furniture invites you to light up a cigar. The rooms, however, seem a bit over-priced. Still, the beautiful Kollwitzplatz is just around the corner, as are a bunch of decent bars and restaurants.

OSTEL Das DDR Design Hostel

Friedrichshain

A&O Hostel & Hotel Friedrichshain
Boxhagener Strasse 73 (809 475 400/www.aohostel.com). U5 Samariterstrasse or S3, S5, S7, S8, S9, S41, S42, S75, S85 Ostkreuz. €.
This branch of the nationwide chain has something of a school camp atmosphere, but the rooms are clean, the pine furniture inoffensive, and there are cooking facilities. There is also the budget 'Easy Dorm': no shower, no booking – just a bed. During the summer, everyone hangs out in the courtyard, but you can also rent a bicycle and head down the street to the shops and cafés.

Eastern Comfort
Mühlenstrasse 73-77 (6676 3806/ www.eastern-comfort.com). U1, S3, S5, S7, S9, S75 Warschauer Strasse. €.
Berlin's first 'hostel boat' is moored on the Spree by the East Side City Hotel Berlin (below). The rooms – well, cabins – are clean and fairly spacious (considering it's a boat), and all have their own shower and toilet. If you need to get up and stretch there are two common rooms, one lounge and three terraces offering beautiful river views. The owners have now done up a

second boat, the Western Comfort, which is moored over the river on the Kreuzberg bank.

East Side City Hotel Berlin
Mühlenstrasse 6 (293 833/www. eastsidehotel.de). U1, S3, S5, S7, S9, S75 Warschauer Strasse. €€.
This modest hotel has a certain funky charm, not to mention a fabulous view of one of the last remaining stretches of the Berlin Wall. Get a room in the back if you want peace and quiet, although this will mean missing sunset over the Oberbaumbrücke. Each double room comes with a bathroom and bath, there's a huge breakfast buffet, and easy access to public transport.

Gold Hotel
Weserstrasse 24 (293 3410/www.gold-hotel-berlin.de). U5 Samariterstrasse. €€.
This is a moderately priced alternative for young travellers who've outgrown the hostel scene but aren't yet ready to splurge on the frills. Perfectly situated just off the main drag on Wismarplatz, this family-run hotel is clean and comfortable with standard rooms and standard decor, and there's a beautiful winter garden for coffee. All 35 rooms have showers, toilet and cable TV.

Michelbergerhotel
NEW *Warschauer Strasse 39-40 (2977 8590/www.michelbergerhotel.com). U1, S3, S5, S7, S9, S75 Warschauer Strasse.* €€.
See box p165.

Odyssee Globetrotter Hostel
Grünberger Strasse 23 (2900 0081/ www.globetrotterhostel.de). U5 Frankfurter Tor. €. No credit cards.
Down a dark wooden corridor and up the backyard stairs, this is the metal and tat version of a good old-fashioned youth hostel. The place has a little edge to it, with a dimly lit reception area and lounge for a change. The rooms are

clean, the showers are good and there's billiards and table football, although the neighbourhood also has lots of alternative clubs and bars.

OSTEL Das DDR Design Hostel
Wriezener Karree 5 (2576 8660/ www.ostel.eu). S1, S2, S5, S7, S9, S75 Ostbahnhof. €. No credit cards.
The owners scoured Germany for the original wallpaper, furniture, lamps, radios and clocks that decorate this cheeky six-floor homage to communist-era design. There are 33 rooms, each with its own bathroom, and the hotel also has an apartment that sleeps up to six in DDR style just a few streets away at Andreasstrasse 20. The hostel shop sells East German items such as plastic egg cups and official portraits of former head of state Erich Honecker.

Kreuzberg

Angleterre Hotel
Friedrichstrasse 31 (2021 3700/ www.gold-inn.de). U6 Kochstrasse. €€€.
The Berlin hotel group Gold Inn has scrubbed the graffiti off this former squatted building and the original 1871 façade now fronts a warmly furnished mid-range hotel offering a touch of Englishness near Checkpoint Charlie. There's a Speaker's Corner restaurant, and the Commonwealth bar/lounge serves Newcastle Brown Ale. The deluxe rooms have balconies, and the hotel's proximity to the heart of Berlin's major gallery scene also makes it an attractive option.

Baxpax Kreuzberg Hostel
Skalitzer Strasse 104 (6951 8322/ www.baxpax.de). U1 Görlitzer Bahnhof. €.
This second hostel by the owners of Mittes Backpacker has a rather more refined aesthetic than its predecessor, but the English-speaking staff are just as friendly and the party

atmosphere still prevails. There's a self-service kitchen and a barbecue balcony, and the rooms are creative, to say the least (one has a bed made from a converted VW).

Die Fabrik
Schlesische Strasse 18 (611 7116/ www.diefabrik.com). U1 Schlesisches Tor. **€**. No credit cards.
Bang in the middle of a newly invigorated Schlesiche Strasse, this former telephone factory – hence the name – with turn-of-the-19th-century charm, has 50 clean and comfortable no-frills rooms. No kitchen, no TV and no billiards. Just a bed and a locker. But with the café next door for breakfast, and plenty of restaurants and bars nearby, you don't need much more.

Hotel Riehmers Hofgarten
Yorckstrasse 83 (7809 8800/ www.hotel-riehmers-hofgarten.de). U6, U7 Mehringdamm. **€€€**.
In a historic building with one of Berlin's prettiest courtyards, is this lovely hotel. The 22 exquisitely styled rooms are airy and elegant, the staff are charming, and Thomas Kurt, chef at the restaurant, e.t.a. hoffmann, was highly praised in 2008's Gault Millau guide. Although the location is somewhat off the beaten track, the neighbourhood has many charms of its own, with Victoria Park and Bergmanstrasse's shops and cafés nearby.

Hotel Transit
Hagelberger Strasse 53-54 (789 0470/ www.hotel-transit.de). U6, U7 Mehringdamm. **€€**.
Located in one of the most beautiful parts of Kreuzberg, this former factory is now a bright and airy hotel with 49 basic but clean rooms, each with a shower and toilet. There's a 24-hour bar on the premises, and the staff speak good English. With Victoria Park around the block and a wealth of bars, cafés and restaurants in the area, it's often full – so it's wise to book ahead.

Motel One Berlin-Mitte
Prinzenstrasse 40 (7007 9800/ www.motel-one.de). U8 Moritzplatz. **€€**.
Who'd have thought that such a seemingly anonymous chain could produce such a smart hotel? The 180 rooms, all recently remodelled and refreshed, are basic but done with flair: check out the large dark wood headboards, flat-screen TVs and modern free-standing sinks. Even that appliqué on the curtains and pillows is bearable. Throw in the bargain rates and you have a winner.

Rock 'n' Roll Herberge
Muskauer Strasse 11 (6162 3600/ www.rock-n-roll-herberge.de). U Görlitzer Bahnhof. **€**. No credit cards.
Having recently celebrated its second birthday, the Rock 'n' Roll Herbage is a great place with all the trimmings on a quiet stretch just blocks from the main drags of Kreuzberg. The downstairs rooms are small, but some have bathrooms. The staff are nice and friendly, there's a cocktail party every Wednesday and the bar/restaurant is popular with colourful locals.

Tiergarten

David's Cozy Little Backpacker Hostel
Bredowstrasse 35 (3988 5394/ www.david-berlin.de). U9 Birkenstrasse. **€**. No credit cards.
This funky little hostel is ideal for those who prefer a familial atmosphere over the usual anonymity of other digs, and it's especially good for people travelling alone. Groups are discouraged, and a minimum stay of three days is preferred, all to assure the relaxed familiarity. The rooms are slip-shod cosy (there's a dorm just for girls as well) and David and co are warm, friendly hosts. Just a couple of streets away at Waldenser Strasse 30, their John's Cozy Little Backpacker Hostel (3940 4594) is ready to handle the overspill.

Grand Hotel Esplanade

*Lützowufer 15 (254 780/www.
esplanade.de). U1, U2, U3, U4
Nollendorfplatz.* €€€€.
With an entry wall of gushing water lit
overhead by glittering lights, this is one
of Berlin's better luxury hotels, overlooking the Landwehr Canal and close
to the Tiergarten. The lobby is equally
grand, spacious and beautifully decorated, while the rooms are tasteful and
gratifyingly free of frilly decor. There's
also a fitness centre and a triangular
swimming pool, plus three restaurants
and a Harry's New York Bar.

Grand Hyatt Berlin

*Marlene-Dietrich-Platz 2 (2553 1234/
www.berlin.grand.hyatt.com). U2, S1,
S2, S9, S26 Potsdamer Platz.* €€€€.
The Grand Hyatt Berlin is a classy
joint. The lobby is all matt black and
sleek wood panelling – a refreshing
change from the usual five-star marble
or country villa look. The rooms are
spacious and elegant; the internet TV
is also a nice touch. The rooftop spa
and gym has a splendid swimming
pool with views across the city. The
ground-floor restaurant, Tizian, is
excellent, offering a choice of international classics and a top wine list.

Hotel Altberlin

*Potsdamer Strasse 67 (260 670/
www.altberlin-hotel.de). U1
Kurfürstenstrasse.* €€€.
This 'turn-of-the-19th-century-Berlin'
hotel doesn't actually date quite that
far back, nor do the seemingly 'retro'
furnishings. But the rooms are comfortable, and the restaurant downstairs, as
cluttered as a museum, serves up
hearty, traditional Berlin food. Across
the street from the Wintergarten
Theatre, and only a short walk to the
New National Gallery and Potsdamer
Platz, it's a useful location.

Hotel Intercontinental

*Budapester Strasse 2 (260 20/
www.berlin.intercontinental.com). U2,
U9, S3, S5, S7, S9, S75 Zoologischer
Garten/bus 200.* €€€€.
The extremely plush and spacious
'Interconti' exudes luxury. The airy
lobby, with its soft leather chairs, is
ideal for browsing the papers, and the

Motel One Berlin-Mitte

ESSENTIALS

Ellington Hotel

rooms, overlooking the Zoo and western edges of the new diplomatic quarter, are large and tastefully decorated, right down to the elegant bathrooms. Thomas Kammeier, Berlin master chef, whips things up in the restaurant, Hugo's (p135), while the huge gym and spa has everything a body could possibly need to exercise off the meal.

Mandala Hotel

Potsdamer Strasse 3 (590 050 000/ www.themandala.de). U2, S1, S2, S9, S26 Potsdamer Platz. €€€€.
This privately owned addition to the Design Hotels portfolio is an oasis of calm, luxury and taste. The 144 rooms and suites, most of which face their glass walls upon an inner courtyard, are designed for space and light, decorated in warm white and beiges, with comfortable minimalist furnishings and flat-screen TVs. A sheltered path through the fifth-floor Japanese garden leads to Facil, the world-cuisine restaurant now vying for its second Michelin star, and the rooftop wellness centre offers spectacular views.

Ritz-Carlton

Potsdamer Platz 3 (337 777/ www.ritzcarlton.com). U2, S1, S2, S9, S26 Potsdamer Platz. €€€€.

It's flashy, it's trashy, it's Vegas-meets-Versailles. The Ritz-Carlton is so chock-a-block with black marble, gold taps and taffeta curtains that the rooms seem somewhat stuffy, small and cramped. It's supposedly art deco style but feels more like some upscale shopping mall. Still, the oyster and lobster restaurant is deliciously decadent, and the service is fantastic.

Charlottenburg

Berlin Plaza Hotel

Knesebeckstrasse 63 (884 130/www. plazahotel.de). U1 Uhlandstrasse. €€€.
Despite a rather plain minimalist decor and colour scheme in the rooms, there's something posh about the Plaza. All double rooms, and even some singles, have both shower and bath. The restaurant and bar serve regional German specialities, and the breakfast buffet is excellent. Children under 16 can stay with parents for free.

Ellington Hotel

NEW *Nürnberger Strasse 50-55 (6831 50/www.ellington-hotel.com). U1, U2, U3 Wittenbergplatz or U1 Augsburger Strasse.* €€€.
This new hotel is the classiest, most sophisticated joint in Berlin. Hidden

within the shell of a landmark art deco dance hall, it combines cool contemporary elegance with warmth and ease. The rooms, mostly white with polished wood accents, are brilliantly simple, offering absolute calm behind their original double windows. An ambitious menu is served in the Duke restaurant, and there are Sunday jazz brunches in the central courtyard. All this and KaDeWe (p126) just around the corner.

Hecker's Hotel

Grolmanstrasse 35 (889 00/ www.heckers-hotel.com). U1 Uhlandstrasse or S5, S7, S9, S75 Savignyplatz. **€€€**.
This is a sleek, smart, high-quality hotel; stylish, with an air of privacy. The rooms are spacious and comfortable, if not minimally styled, with sparkling marble in the bathrooms, while the suites come with air-conditioning and Bang & Olufsen DVD-TVs. Other highlights include a rooftop terrace and the Cassambalis restaurant, serving Med cuisine.

Hotel Art Nouveau Berlin

Leibnizstrasse 59 (327 7440/ 7434/www.hotelartnouveau.de). U7 Adenauerplatz or S5, S7, S9, S75 Savignyplatz. **€€€**.
This is one of the most charming small hotels in Berlin. The rooms are decorated with flair in a mix of Conran-modern and antique furniture, each with an enormous black and white photo hung by the bed. The en suite bathrooms are well integrated into the rooms without disrupting the elegant townhouse architecture. Even the TVs are stylish.

Hotel Askanischer Hof

Kurfürstendamm 53 (881 8033-4/ www.askanischer-hof.de). U7 Adenauerplatz or S5, S7, S9, S75 Savignyplatz. **€€€**.
Despite standing on one of Berlin's best-known streets, the Askanischer

Hof is a well-kept secret, and chock full of atmosphere. Walk down the hall, filled with yellowed drawings, and you can almost see the ghosts of actors and literary types who visited long before World War II. The bedrooms are a fanciful mix of styles spanning a century of European interiors, from heavy Prussian desks and 1940s wallpaper, to over stuffed leather chesterfields.

Hotel Bleibtreu

Bleibtreustrasse 31 (884 740/ www.bleibtreu.com). U1 Uhlandstrasse or S5, S7, S9, S75 Savignyplatz. **€€€**.
The Bleibtreu is a friendly, smart and cosy establishment. The rooms are on the smaller side, but they're all very modern, and decorated with environmentally sound materials. The restaurant is famed for its no-sugar menu, and there's the Deli 31 for a bagel and coffee. The hotel also offers private yoga classes, as well as reflexology. A wonderful choice for the health-conscious, certainly, but good service with lots of pampering and attention will appeal to anyone.

Hotel Bogota

Schlüterstrasse 45 (881 5001/ www.bogota.de). S5, S7, S9, S75 Savignyplatz. **€€**.
Though the attractive foyer of this characterful two-star belies rooms more functional than fancy, it's still a wonderful place and terrific value. The history is remarkable too: there's a bit of ornate parquet near the lobby on which Benny Goodman once tapped his feet at a party. The photographs in the fourth-floor foyer were shot by the fashion photographer Yva, who had her studio on the very spot. Her assistant, Helmut Newton, learned his craft here before fleeing Germany in 1938 (Yva died in the Majdanek concentration camp four years later). Half the doubles have their own showers and all have at least a sink.

Q!

Hotel Concorde Berlin

*Augsburger Strasse 41 (800 9990/
http://berlin.concorde-hotels.com). U1,
U9 Kurfürstendamm.* €€€€.
Designed by Berlin architect Jan
Kleihues, this new French-owned five-
star is grandly proportioned with a
refreshingly minimalist and contemporary approach. Its 311 rooms (including 44 huge suites) are decorated in
warm woods and colour tones, intimate
lighting and modern art, to elegant and
under-stated effect. The Restaurant
Saint Germain will serve your breakfast, the Brasserie Le Faubourg your
French/Med dinner and the Club Étoile
on the top floors offers a wonderful
panorama of the city.

Hotel Pension Columbus

*Meinekestrasse 5 (881 5061/www.
columbus-berlin.de). U1, U9
Kurfürstendamm or U2, U9, S3, S5,
S7, S9, S75 Zoologischer Garten.* €€.
This pension next to the Ku-damm is a
charming and unique place, with children in mind. Kids' drawings line the
walls, and there are two larger rooms
with an optional adjoining two-bed
room, perfect for families. Prices are

unbeatable for the area, and the owners are extremely kind and friendly.
The breakfast room is a quaint place to
enjoy a bowl of home-made yoghurt.

Hotel-Pension Dittberner

*Wielandstrasse 26 (884 6950/
www.hotel-dittberner.de). U7
Adenauerplatz or S5, S7, S9,
S75 Savignyplatz.* €€.
From the ride up the 1911 elevator and
into the sitting room, this is a grand
place, stylish and eclectic, and a labour
of love. It's filled with fine original artworks, enormous chandeliers and
handsome furnishings. Some of the
rooms and suites are truly palatial (one
has a winter garden around the courtyard, for example). Frau Lange, the
owner, goes out of her way to make
guests feel at home. Truly one of the
best pensions in the city.

Hotel-Pension Funk

*Fasanenstrasse 69 (882 7193/
www.hotel-pensionfunk.de). U1
Uhlandstrasse.* €€.
Despite the fancy surroundings, this
wonderful pension offers really good
value. Built in 1895, this was once the
apartment of silent film star Asta
Nielsen, and the proprietor does his best
to maintain an ambience of graceful pre-
war charm. The 14 large, comfortable
rooms are furnished to cosy effect with
elegant pieces from the 1920s and '30s:
satinwood beds and matching
wardrobes. The only niggle is that some
of the showers are rather antiquated.

Hotel-Pension Modena

*Wielandstrasse 26 (885 7010/www.
hotel-modena.de). U7 Adenauerplatz
or S5, S7, S9, S75 Savignyplatz.* €€.
Just a floor below the Dittberner (p176),
this thoroughly unassuming 19-room
pension is charming, sweet and cheap.
The staff are very friendly, accommo-
dating and speak English, and the
atmosphere is relaxed. A top choice if
you're travelling as part of a group and
want to be in the west end.

Kempinski Hotel Bristol Berlin

Kurfürstendamm 27 (884 340/ www.kempinskiberlin.de). U1 Uhlandstrasse. €€€€.

Berlin's most famous hotel, and the well-aged mother of all Kempinskis, was first a celebrated restaurant before being rebuilt in its present form in 1951. While the rooms aren't as plush as you might expect at these prices, the generally grand atmosphere, friendly staff, original Berlin artwork and wonderful pool and saunas make up for it. A new restaurant, Reinhard's, has added a regional menu to the proceedings.

Pension-Gudrun

Bleibtreustrasse 17 (881 6462/ www.pension-gudrun-berlin.de). S5, S7, S9, S75 Savignyplatz. €€. No credit cards.

This simple, tiny pension has huge rooms and friendly, helpful owners who speak English, French, Arabic and German. The rooms are decorated with lovely turn-of-the-19th-century Berlin furniture, and for families or small groups, it's a marvellous deal.

Pension Kettler

Bleibtreustrasse 19 (883 4949). U1 Uhlandstrasse or S5, S7, S9, S75 Savignyplatz. €€. No credit cards.

Amid the collection of art that owner Isolde Josipovici has amassed over the past 35 years, she has created the warmest, most eclectic pension imaginable. Each of the six rooms, five of which have their own shower, is wonderfully decorated as inspired by the historic figure it is named after. There's golden brocade, say, for Goethe. The neighbourhood is fantastic, public transport is right at hand and breakfast is brought to your room each morning.

Q!

Knesebeckstrasse 67 (810 0660/ www.loock-hotels.com). U1 Uhlandstrasse or S5, S7, S9, S75 Savignyplatz. €€€.

This young and friendly hotel is almost worth staying in just for the spa downstairs, complete with Japanese washing room, two saunas, a sand lounge and optional massage. Rooms have their own temperature control, and are ingeniously designed: both bed and bath are part of the same wooden unit, so that you can literally roll into bed after a soak. There's a separate shower and toilet as well. The bar is red from floor to ceiling, with a beautiful gas fireplace.

Savoy Hotel Berlin

Fasanenstrasse 9-10 (311 030/www. hotel-savoy.com). U2, U9, S3, S5, S7, S9, S75 Zoologischer Garten. €€€.

Erected in 1929, and a favourite of author Thomas Mann, this is a smart, stylish hotel with lots of low-key flair. The rooms are elegant and understated, but for a little zing in the suites, such as the white Greta Garbo suite and black marble Henry Miller suite. The Weinrot restaurant serves a well-thought-out modern menu. A further bonus is the location, set back just far enough from the hustle and bustle of Zoologischer Garten to be quiet and convenient.

Savoy Hotel Berlin

ESSENTIALS

Getting Around

Arriving & leaving

By air

Until the new Berlin-Brandenburg International Airport is ready in 2011, Berlin is served by two airports: Tegel and Schönefeld. Information in English on both of them (including departure and arrival times) can be found at www.berlin-airport.de.

Tegel Airport

Airport information: 0180 500 0186/www.berlin-airport.de.
Open 4am–midnight daily.
Most scheduled flights use the compact Tegel Airport, just 8km (5 miles) north-west of Mitte. The airport contains tourist information, exchange facilities, restaurants, bars, shops and car rental desks. A cab can drop you right by the check-in desk and departure gate.

Buses 109 and X9 (the express version) run via Luisenplatz and the Kurfürstendamm to Zoologischer Garten (also known as Zoo Station, Bahnhof Zoo or just Zoo) in western Berlin. Tickets cost €2.10 (and can also be used on U-Bahn and S-Bahn services). Buses run every five to 15 minutes, and take 30-40 minutes to reach Zoo. From there, you can connect to anywhere in the city (same tickets are valid). You can also take bus 109 to Jakob-Kaiser-Platz U-Bahn (U7), or bus 128 to Kurt-Schumacher-Platz U-Bahn (U6), and proceed on the underground from there.

The JetExpressBus TXL is the direct link to the new Berlin Hauptbahnhof and Mitte. This runs from Tegel to Alexanderplatz with useful stops at Beusselstrasse S-Bahn (connects with the Ringbahn), Berlin Hauptbahnhof (regional and intercity trains, as well as the S-Bahn) and Brandenburger Tor S-Bahn (north and south trains on the S1 and S2 lines). It costs €2.10, runs every 15 or 20 minutes between 6am and 11pm, and takes 30-40 minutes.

A taxi to anywhere central will cost around €20-€25, and takes 20-30 minutes, depending on traffic and precise destination.

Schönefeld Airport

Airport information: 0180 500 0186/www.berlin-airport.de.
Open 24hrs daily.
The former airport of East Berlin is 18km (11 miles) south-east of the city centre. It's small but is used by UK budget airlines. The usual foreign exchange, shops, snack bars and car-hire facilities are found here.

Train is the best way into the city. S-Bahn Flughafen Schönefeld is a five-minute walk from the terminal (a free shuttle bus runs every ten minutes between 6am and 10pm; at other times, bus 171 also runs to the station). From here, the Airport Express train runs to Mitte (25 minutes to Alexanderplatz), Berlin Hauptbahnhof (30 minutes) and Zoo (35 minutes) every half hour from 5am to 11.30pm. Be warned that the final destination of the trains varies, so check the timetable for your stop. You can also take S-Bahn line S9, which runs into the centre every 20 minutes (40 minutes to Alexanderplatz, 50 minutes to Zoo) stopping along the way. The S45 line from Schönefeld connects with the Ringbahn, also running every 20 minutes. Bus 171 from the airport takes you to Rudow U-Bahn (U7), from where you can connect with the underground.

ESSENTIALS

Tickets from the airport to the city cost €2.80, and can be used on any combination of bus, U-Bahn, S-Bahn and tram. There are ticket machines at the airport and at the station. A taxi to Zoo or Mitte is expensive (€30-€35) and takes 45-60 minutes.

By bus

Zentraler Omnibus Bahnhof (ZOB)

Masurenallee 4-6, Charlottenburg (information 301 0380). **Open** 6am-9pm Mon-Fri; 6am-3pm Sat, Sun. Buses arrive at the Central Bus Station, opposite the Funkturm and the ICC (International Congress Centrum) in Charlottenburg. From the nearby Kaiserdamm station, U-Bahn line U2 runs east to the centre. There's also a left-luggage office.

By train

Berlin Hauptbahnhof

118 61/www.hbf-berlin.de.
Since June 2006, the new Berlin Hauptbahnhof has been the central point of arrival for all long-distance trains, with the exceptions of night trains from Moscow, Warsaw and Kiev, which start and end at Berlin Lichtenberg (U5, S5, S7, S75).

Hauptbahnhof is inconveniently located in a no-man's land over the River Spree just north of the government quarter, and is linked to the rest of the city by S-Bahn (S5, S7, S9, S75). The line U55, running just two stops to Brandenburger Tor station (formerly Unter den Linden) where it connects with S-Bahn lines S1 and S2, was opened in August 2009. Eventually, the line will supposedly extend to connect to the U5 at Alexanderplatz.

Hauptbahnhof is the largest railway interchange in Europe, and equipped with a whole mall's worth of shops, restaurants and services,

as well as banks, rail and tourist information offices, left-luggage facilities and car-rental agencies.

On their way in and out of town, intercity and international trains also stop at Nordkreuz (formerly Gesundbrunnen), Südkreuz (formerly Papestrasse) and Spandau, depending on destinations.

In town

The city is served by an efficient and comprehensive network of buses, trains, trams and ferries, which all interlink. Services are usually regular and frequent, timetables can be trusted and one ticket can be used for two hours on all legs of a journey and all forms of transport. The Berlin transport authority, the BVG, operates the bus, U-Bahn and tram networks, and a few ferry services. The S-Bahn (overground railway) is run by its own authority, but services are totally integrated within the same tariff system.

The BVG website (www.bvg.de) has a wealth of information in English. The S-Bahn has its own website at www.s-bahn-berlin.de.

The Liniennetz, a map of U-Bahn, S-Bahn, bus and tram routes for Berlin and Potsdam, is available free from info centres and ticket offices. It includes a city centre map. A map of the U- and S-Bahn can also be picked up free at ticket offices or from the grey-uniformed *Zugabfertiger* – passenger assistance personnel – who can be found wandering about the larger U-Bahn and S-Bahn stations.

The BVG publishes its own *Berlin Atlas*, with detailed maps of the city including every last public transport route, station and bus stop. It costs €11 and is available from newsagents and bookshops at the larger stations. You can also look at the BVG

ESSENTIALS

Atlas online, where you can type in any address and view all transport connections. It's at www.fahrinfo-berlin.de/Stadtplan.

Fares & tickets

The bus, tram, U-Bahn, S-Bahn and ferry services operate on an integrated three-zone system. Zone A covers central Berlin, zone B extends out to the edge of the suburbs and zone C stretches into Brandenburg.

The basic single ticket is the €2.10 (€1.40 for 6-14s) *Normaltarif* (zones A and B). Unless going to Potsdam or Schönefeld Airport, few visitors are likely to travel beyond zone B, making this, in effect, a flat-fare system. For €1.30 (€1) you can buy a short-journey ticket, called a *Kurzstrecke*, which is valid for three U- or S-Bahn stops, or five stops on the bus or tram, without any changes. A *Tageskarte* (day ticket) for zones A and B costs €6.10 (€4.40) and can be used until 3am the day after validating.

Tickets can be bought from the yellow or orange machines at U- or S-Bahn stations, and by some bus stops. The machines take coins and sometimes notes, give change and have a limited explanation of the ticket system in English. There are also ticket offices in some stations. Once you've purchased your ticket, validate it in the small red or yellow box near to the machine. Tickets bought from the drivers on buses are usually already validated. Many trams have ticket machines.

There are no ticket barriers or turnstiles, but if an inspector (*Kontrolleur*) catches you without a valid ticket, you will be fined €40 on the spot. Ticket inspections are frequent, particularly at weekends and at the beginning of the month, and are carried out by non-uniformed personnel who travel in pairs and might look like anything from skinheads to businessmen until they whip out their ID.

U-Bahn

The first stretch of Berlin's U-Bahn consists of nine lines and 170 stations. The first trains run shortly after 4am; the last between midnight and 1am, except on Fridays and Saturdays when trains run all night on lines U1, U2, U3, U5, U6, U7, U8 and U9. The direction of travel is indicated by the name of the last stop on the line.

S-Bahn

Especially useful in eastern Berlin, the S-Bahn covers long distances faster than the U-Bahn and is a more efficient means of getting to outlying areas. The 2002 completion of the Ringbahn, which circles central Berlin in around an hour, was the final piece of the S-Bahn system to be renovated.

Buses

Berlin has a dense network of 150 bus routes, of which 54 run in the early hours. The day lines run from 4.30am to about 1am the next morning. Enter at the front of the bus and exit in the middle. The driver sells only individual tickets, but all tickets from machines on the U- or S-Bahn are valid.

Trams

There are 21 tram lines (five of which run all night), mainly in the east, though one or two have now been extended a few kilometres into the western city. **Hackescher Markt** is the main tram terminus. Tickets are available from machines on the trams, at the termini and in U-Bahn stations.

Travelling at night

Berlin has a comprehensive *Nachtliniennetz* ('night-line network') that covers all parts of town via 59 bus and tram routes running every 30 minutes between 12.30am and 4.30am. Before and after these times the regular timetable for bus and tram routes applies.

Night-line network maps and timetables are available from BVG information kiosks at stations, and large maps of the night services are usually found next to the normal BVG map on station platforms. Ticket prices are the same as during the day. Buses and trams that run at night are distinguished by an 'N' in front of the number.

Truncated versions of U-Bahn lines U1, U2, U5, U6, U7, U8 and U9 run all night Friday and Saturday, every 15 minutes. The S-Bahn also runs on weekend nights, with S1, S2, S3, S5, S7, S8, S9, S25, S26, S41, S42, S46, S47 and S75 in service.

Boat trips

Getting about by water is more of a leisure activity than a practical means of getting around the city, but the BVG network does include a handful of boat services on Berlin's lakes. There are also several private companies offering water tours.

Reederei Heinz Riedel

*Planufer 78, Kreuzberg (693 4646).
U8 Schönleinstrasse.* **Open** *Mar-Sept*
6am-9pm Mon-Fri; 8am-6pm Sat; 10am-3pm Sun. *Oct* 8am-5pm Mon-Fri; 8am-6pm Sat; 10am-3pm Sun. *Nov-Feb*
8am-4pm Mon-Fri.
This company operates excursions that start in the city and pass through industrial suburbs into rural Berlin. A tour through the city's network of rivers and canals costs €8.50-€16.

Stern & Kreisschiffahrt

*Puschkinallee 15, Treptow (536 3600/
www.sternundkreis.de). S8, S9, S41,
S42, S85 Treptower Park.* **Open**
9am-4pm Mon-Thur; 9am-2pm Fri.
Offers around 25 different cruises along the Spree and lakes in the Berlin area. Departure points and times vary. A 3hr 30min tour costs €16.

Taxis

Berlin taxis are pricey, efficient and plentiful. The starting fee is €3.20 and thereafter the fare is €1.65 per kilometre (about €3 per mile). The rate remains the same at night. For short journeys ask for a *Kurzstrecke* – up to two kilometres for €4. These are only available when you've hailed a moving cab rather than taken one from a rank. There are many taxi stands in the city, especially in central areas near stations and at major intersections.

You can phone for a cab 24 hours daily on 261 026. Most taxi firms can transport people with disabilities, but require advance notice. Cabs accept all credit cards except Diners Club, subject to a 50¢ charge.

Most cabs are Mercedes. If you want an estate car (station wagon), ask for a *Combi*. As well as normal taxis, Funk TaxiBerlin (261 026) operates vans capable of transporting up to seven people (ask for a *Berliner Taxi*) and has two cars for people with disabilities.

Driving

Despite some congestion, driving in Berlin, with its wide, straight roads, presents few problems. Visitors from the UK and US should bear in mind that, in the absence of signals, drivers must yield to traffic from the right, except at crossings marked by a diamond-shaped yellow sign. Trams and buses always have right of way.

ESSENTIALS

An *Einbahnstrasse* is a one-way street. Watch out for cyclists.

Since January 2008, a so-called *Umweltzone* ('environment zone') has been implemented in central Berlin. It means that any car entering Berlin's city centre (defined as the area inside the S-Bahn ring) has to display a windshield sticker called an *Umweltplakette* that shows the vehicle's emission status. Prices vary between €5 and €10. Cars driving in the *Umweltzone* without a badge will be fined €40. You can order this *Umweltplakette* and/or obtain more information at www.car-germany.eu.

Parking

Parking is free in Berlin side streets, but spaces are hard to find. On busier streets you may have to buy a ticket (€1-€2.40 per hour) from a nearby machine. Without a ticket, or if you park illegally, you risk getting your car clamped or towed.

There are long-term car parks at Schönefeld and Tegel airports (p178). Otherwise, there are various *Parkgaragen* and *Parkhäuser* (multi-storey and underground car parks) around the city, open 24 hours, that charge around €2 an hour.

Vehicle hire

Car hire in Germany isn't expensive and all major companies have offices in Berlin. There are car hire desks at Hauptbahnhof and both of the city's airports. Look under 'Autovermietung' in the *Gelbe Seiten* (*Yellow Pages*).

Or you could try CityMotion (0900 124 0120, www.city-motion.at), which provides Smart cars to rent for just €1 per day. The only catch is that you have to drive a minimum of 30 kilometres (19 miles) within the city limits – the cars are plastered with advertising.

Cycling

Berlin is great for cycling, especially on the western side. East Berlin has fewer cycle paths and more cobblestones and tram lines. But throughout the city, cyclists are fully integrated into the transport network with cycle paths, cycle lanes and lights at many junctions.

Cycles can be taken on the U-Bahn, up to a limit of two at the end of carriages that have a bicycle sign on them. Bikes may not be taken on the U-Bahn during rush hour (6-9am and 2-5pm). More may be taken on to S-Bahn carriages, and at any time of day. In each case an extra ticket (€1.50) must be bought for each bike. The *ADFC Fahrradstadtplan*, available in bike shops (€6.90), is a good guide to cycle routes.

DB (Deutsche Bahn) operates a fleet of 'CallBikes'. They're silver with a child seat bearing the red DB logo. To rent one, you need a mobile phone and a credit card number. Register by calling 0700 0522 5522 (operators speak English). You will be billed at a rate of 8¢ a minute up to a maximum of €9 for 24 hours.

For more conventional bike hire, try the companies below or see 'Fahrradverleih' in the *Yellow Pages*.

Fahrradstation

Dorotheenstrasse 30, Mitte (2838 4848/www.fahrradstation.de). U6, S1, S2, S5, S7, S9, S75 Friedrichstrasse. **Open** *Summer* 8am-8pm daily. *Winter* 10am-7pm Mon-Sat. **Rates** from €15/day; €35/3 days. **Other locations:** Bergmannstrasse 9, Kreuzberg (215 1566); Leipziger Strasse 56, Mitte (6664 9180).

Pedalpower

Grossbeerenstrasse 53, Kreuzberg (7899 1939/www.pedalpower.de). U1, U7 Möckernbrücke. **Open** 10am-6.30pm Mon-Fri; 11am-2pm Sat. **Rates** from €10/day. No credit cards.

Resources A-Z

For information on travelling to Germany from within the European Union, including details of visa regulations and healthcare provision, see the EU's travel website: www.europa.eu/abc/travel.

Accident & emergency

For the **police** dial 110; for an **ambulance** or the **fire brigade** it's 112. If you need a doctor, call the **Medizinische Notdienst** (Medical Emergency Service) on 310 031. A list of the nearest **pharmacies** open on Sundays and at night should be displayed in the window of every pharmacy, and a list of pharmacies can be found online at www.apo110.de. Type in your district or postcode.

Hospitals are in the *Gelbe Seiten* (*Yellow Pages*) under 'Krankenhäuser/Kliniken'. These are the most central:

Charité
Schumannstrasse 20-21, Mitte (450 50/ www.charite.de). U6, S1, S2, S5, S7, S9, S75 Friedrichstrasse/bus 147.

St Hedwig Krankenhaus
Grosse Hamburger Strasse 5, Mitte (231 10). S5, S7, S9, S75 Hackescher Markt or S1, S2 Oranienburger Strasse.

Vivantes Klinikum Am Urban
Dieffenbachstrasse 1, Kreuzberg (130 229 530). U7 Südstern.

Age restrictions

The legal age for drinking alcohol is 16; for smoking it is 16; for driving it is 18; and the age of consent for heterosexual and homosexual sex is 16.

Credit card loss

American Express *069 9797 2000.*
Diners Club *0180 507 0704.*
MasterCard/Visa *0800 819 1040.*

Customs

EU nationals over 17 years of age can import limitless goods for personal use, if bought tax-paid. For non-EU citizens and duty-free goods, the limits are:

- 200 cigarettes or 50 cigars or 250 grams of tobacco
- 1 litre of spirits (over 22% alcohol), or 2 litres of fortified wine (under 22%), or 2 litres of wine
- Other goods to the value of €300 for non-commercial use
- The import of meat, meat products, fruit, plants, flowers and protected animals is restricted

Non-EU citizens can claim back German VAT (*Mehrwertsteuer* or *MwSt*) on goods purchased in the country. Ask to be issued with a Tax-Free Shopping Cheque for the amount of the refund and present this, with the receipt, at the airport's refund office before checking in bags.

Dental emergency

Medeco Zahnkliniken
01805 942 941. **Open** 7am-9pm Mon-Fri; 9am-7pm Sat, Sun.
Call the emergency number above and staff will tell you which is the nearest of their six clinics around Berlin.

Vivantes Klinikum im Friedrichshain
Landsberger Allee 49, Friedrichshain (130 231 437/www.kzv-berlin.de). Tram M5, M6, M8 Klinikum im Friedrichshain. **Open** 8pm-2am daily.

ESSENTIALS

Disabled travellers

Only some U- and S-Bahn stations have wheelchair facilities; the map of the transport network indicates which ones; look for the blue wheelchair symbol.

Drugs

Berlin is quite liberal in its attitude towards drugs. In recent years, possession of hash or grass has been decriminalised. Anyone caught with under ten grams is liable to have it confiscated, but nothing more. Anyone caught with small amounts of hard drugs will be fined, but is unlikely to be jailed.

Electricity

Electricity in Germany runs on 220V. Change the plug or use an adaptor for British appliances (240V); US appliances (110V) need a converter.

Embassies & consulates

Australian Embassy *Wallstrasse 76-79, Mitte (880 0880/www.germany. embassy.gov.au/beln/home). U2 Märkisches Museum.* **Open** 8.30am-5pm Mon-Thur; 8.30am-4.15pm Fri.

British Embassy *Wilhelmstrasse 70, Mitte (204 570/http://ukingermany. fco.gov.uk/de). S1, S2 Unter den Linden.* **Open** 9-11am, noon-4pm Mon-Fri.

Irish Consulate *Friedrichstrasse 200, Mitte (220 720). U2, U6 Stadtmitte.* **Open** 9.30am-12.30pm, 2.30-4.45pm Mon-Fri.

US Consulate *Clayallee 170, Zehlendorf (832 9233/visa enquiries 0190 850 055/ http://germany. usembassy.gov). U3 Oskar-Helene-Heim.* **Open** *Consular enquiries* 8.30am-noon Mon-Fri. *Visa enquiries* 8.30-11.30am Mon-Fri.

US Embassy *Pariser Platz 2, Mitte (830 50/http://germany. usembassy.gov). S1, S2 Unter den Linden.* **Open** 24hrs daily.

Internet

Plans to cover the whole of Berlin with one gigantic free wireless network via routers positioned upon and powered by 5,000 traffic lights around the city have foundered on a combination of aesthetic, technical and financial problems. There are free wireless networks at the Sony Center, Hauptbahnhof, Ostbahnhof, the Amerika-Gedenkbibliothek (Blucherplatz 1, Kreuzberg) and the Berliner Stadtbibliothek (Breite Strasse 30-36, Mitte), plus at scores of hotels and cafés around town. Of the city's 17 McDonalds 12 have free Wi-Fi, and Starbucks offers an hour of free access.

For an ISP, try www.snafu.de or www.gmx.de.

Sidewalk Express

Dunkin' Donuts, Sony Center, Tiergarten (www.sidewalkexpress.com). U2, S1, S2, S26 Potsdamer Platz. **Open** 7am-11pm Mon-Thur, Sun; 7am-midnight Fri, Sat.
Dozens of computers, no staff, mechanised system to buy time online, and plenty of doughnuts. Other branches are similarly lodged with Dunkin' Donuts or Burger King.

Opening hours

Most banks are open from 9am to noon Monday to Friday, and 1pm to 3pm or 2pm to 6pm on varied weekdays.

Shops can stay open until 10pm Mondays to Saturdays, although most places close at 8pm. Most big stores open their doors at 9am, newsagents a little earlier, while the majority of smaller or independent shops open at around 10am or later.

An increasing number of all-purpose neighbourhood shops (*Spätkauf*) open at around 5pm and close at around midnight. Many Turkish shops open on Saturdays and Sundays from 1pm to 5pm. Most 24-hour fuel stations also sell basic groceries.

Opening times of bars vary, but many are open during the day, and most stay open until at least 1am, if not through until morning.

Police stations

You are unlikely to come into contact with the *Polizei*, unless you commit a crime or are the victim of one. There are few pedestrian patrols or traffic checks.

The **central police HQ** is at Platz der Luftbrücke 6, Tempelhof (466 40). Police will be dispatched from the appropriate local office if you dial 466 40.

Postal services

Most post offices (simply *Post* in German) are open from 8am to 6.30pm Monday to Friday, and 8am to 1pm Saturday.

For non-local mail, use the *Andere Richtungen* ('other destinations') slot in post-boxes. Letters of up to 20 grams (7oz) to anywhere in Germany and the EU need 55¢ in postage. Postcards require 45¢. For anywhere outside the EU, a 20-gram airmail letter is €1.70, a postcard €1.50.

You can search for your nearest post office at www.deutschepost.de.

Postamt Friedrichstrasse

Georgenstrasse 12, Mitte. U6, S1, S2, S5, S7, S9, S75 Friedrichstrasse. **Open** 6am-10pm Mon-Fri; 8am-10pm Sat, Sun. Berlin has no main post office. This branch, actually inside Friedrichstrasse station in Mitte, has the longest opening hours.

Smoking

Smoking is banned in nearly all public spaces, but some larger restaurants have smoking rooms, and some smaller bars can allow smoking if they put up a sign and refuse entry to under-18s.

Telephones

All telephone numbers listed in this guide are local Berlin numbers (other than in the **Day Trips** chapter), but note that numbers beginning with 0180 have higher tariffs. To call from outside the city, see below.

Dialling & codes

To phone Berlin from abroad, dial the international code (00 from the UK, 011 from the US, 0011 from Australia), then 49 (for Germany) and 30 (for Berlin), followed by the local number. To call Berlin from elsewhere in Germany, dial 030 and then the local number.

Making a call

Calls within Berlin from 9am to 6pm cost between 5¢ and 12¢ per minute, depending on the provider and time of day. Numbers prefixed 0180 are charged at 12¢ per minute.

Prices for international calls vary enormously, and there are numerous prefixes you can dial for budget connections. Look in local newspapers or visit www.tariftip.de.

Public phones

At post offices you'll find both coin- and card-operated phones, but most pavement phone boxes are card-only.

Phonecards can be bought in newsagents and at post offices for various sums from €5 to €50, and you'll find phonecard machines in Alexanderplatz and Zoo stations.

ESSENTIALS

To make international calls, look for phone boxes marked 'international' and with a ringing-bell symbol.

Operator services

For online directory enquiries (available in English), go to www.teleauskunft.de.
Alarm calls/Weckruf 0180 114 1033 (automated, in German)
International directory enquiries 118 34
Operator assistance/German directory enquiries 118 33 (118 37, English-speaking only)

Mobile phones

German mobile phone networks operate at 900MHz, so all UK and Australian mobiles should work in Berlin (if roaming is activated). US and Canadian cellphone users should check whether their phones can switch to 900MHz. If they can't, you can rent a 'Handy' (as the Germans call them) at www.edicom-online.com. They'll deliver to your hotel, and pick the phone back up from there when you're gone.

Time

Germany is on Central European Time – making it one hour ahead of Greenwich Mean Time – and uses a 24-hour system. 8am is '8 Uhr' (usually written 8h); noon is '12 Uhr Mittags' or just '12 Uhr'; 5pm is '17 Uhr' and midnight is '12 Uhr Mitternachts' or just 'Mitternacht'; 8.15 is '8 Uhr 15' or 'Viertel nach 8'; 8.30 is '8 Uhr 30' or 'halb 9'; and 8.45 is '8 Uhr 45' or 'Viertel vor 9'.

Tipping

In a restaurant or café, it's common to leave a tip of around 10%; hand the money over when you're paying the bill, rather than leaving it behind on the table. In a taxi round up the bill to the nearest euro.

Tourist information

Berlin Tourismus Marketing (BTM)
Hauptbahnhof (250 025/www.btm.de). **S5, S7, S9, S75 Hauptbahnhof. Open** 8am-10pm daily.
Berlin's official (though private) tourist organisation. There are other offices at the Brandenburg Gate (p55), the Reichstag (p132), the Fernsehturm (p82), the Neues Kranzler Eck Passage at Kurfürstendamm 21, and the Europa-Center, Budapester Strasse 45.

EurAide
DB Reisezentrum, Hauptbahnhof, Tiergarten (www.euraide.de). **U55, S5, S7, S9, S75 Hauptbahnhof. Open** *May-Aug* 10am-7pm Mon-Fri. *Sep-Apr* 10am-6pm Mon-Fri.
This office offers tourist info in English, and can sell you rail tickets.

Visas & immigration

A passport valid for three months beyond the length of stay is all EU, US, Canadian and Australian citizens need for a stay in Germany of up to three months. EU citizens with valid national ID cards need only show their ID cards.

Citizens of other countries should check with their local German Embassy or consulate, or look on www.germanyinfo.com.

What's on in Berlin

Berlin has two fortnightly listings magazines, *tip* and *Zitty*, and *Exberliner* is a lively English-language monthly. The city is also awash with listings freebies which can be picked up in bars and cafés: *[030]* (music and nightlife) and *Siegessäule* (gay) are the best.

Vocabulary

Pronunciation

z – pronounced ts
w – like English v
v – like English f
s – like English z, but softer
r – like a throaty French r
a – as in father
e – sometimes as in bed, sometimes as in day
i – as in seek
o – as in note
u – as in loot
ch – as in Scottish loch
ä – combination of a and e, sometimes as in paid and sometimes as in set
ö – combination of o and e, as in French eu
ü – combination of u and e, like true
ai – like pie
au – like house
ie – like free
ee – like hey
ei – like fine
eu – like coil

Useful phrases

hello/good day *guten Tag;* goodbye *auf Wiedersehen;* goodbye (informal) *tschüss;* good morning *guten Morgen;* good evening *guten Abend;* goodnight *gute Nacht;* yes – *ja;* (emphatic) *jawohl;* no *nein, nee;* maybe *vielleicht;* please *bitte;* thank you *danke;* thank you very much *vielen Dank;* no thanks *nein danke;* excuse me *entschuldigen Sie bitte;* sorry! *Verzeihung!* I'm sorry, I don't speak German *Entschuldigung, ich spreche kein Deutsch;* do you speak English? *sprechen Sie Englisch?* can you please speak more slowly? *können Sie bitte langsamer sprechen?* my name is...

ich heisse... open/closed *geöffnet/geschlossen;* with/without *mit/ohne;* cheap/expensive *billig/teuer;* big/small *gross/klein;* entrance/exit *Eingang/Ausgang;* push/pull *drücken/ziehen;* how much is... ? *wieviel kostet... ?* I would like... *ich möchte...* a table for four *ein Tisch für vier;* can I/can we pay, please? *kann ich/können wir bitte bezahlen?* could I have a receipt? *darf ich bitte eine Quittung haben?* how do I get to... ? *wie komme ich nach...?* how far is it to... ? *wie weit ist es nach... ?* where is... ? *wo ist... ?* airport *der Flughafen;* railway station *der Bahnhof;* train/platform *Zug/Gleis;* petrol *das Benzin;* lead-free *bleifrei;* please leave me in peace! *lass mich bitte in Ruhe!* can you call me a cab? *können Sie bitte mir bitte ein Taxi rufen?* no problem! *kein Problem!* left *links;* right *rechts;* straight ahead *gerade aus;* far *weit;* near *nah;* street *die Strasse;* square *der Platz;* help! *Hilfe!* I feel ill *ich bin krank;* doctor *der Arzt;* pharmacy *die Apotheke;* hospital *das Krankenhaus*

Numbers

0 *null;* 1 *eins;* 2 *zwei;* 3 *drei;* 4 *vier;* 5 *fünf;* 6 *sechs;* 7 *sieben;* 8 *acht;* 9 *neun;* 10 *zehn;* 11 *elf;* 12 *zwölf;* 13 *dreizehn;* 14 *vierzehn;* 15 *fünfzehn;* 16 *sechzehn;* 17 *siebzehn;* 18 *achtzehn;* 19 *neunzehn;* 20 *zwanzig;* 21 *einundzwanzig;* 22 *zweiundzwanzig;* 30 *dreissig;* 40 *vierzig;* 50 *fünfzig;* 60 *sechzig;* 70 *siebzig;* 80 *achtzig;* 90 *neunzig;* 100 *hundert;* 101 *hunderteins;* 110 *hundertzehn;* 200 *zweihundert;* 201 *zweihunderteins;* 1,000 *tausend;* 2,000 *zweitausend*

Menu Glossary

Useful phrases

I'd like to reserve a table for... people *Ich möchte einen Tisch für... Personen reservieren;* Are these places free? *Sind diese Plätze frei?* The menu, please *Die Speisekarte, bitte;* I am a vegetarian *Ich bin Vegetarier;* I am a diabetic *Ich bin Diabetiker;* I am allergic to... *Ich habe eine Allergie gegen...* What is that? *Was ist das?;* We'd/I'd like to order *Wir möchten/Ich möchte bestellen;* We'd/I'd like to pay *Bezahlen, bitte*

Berlin specialities

Berliner jam doughnut; *Berliner Weisse mit Schuss* weak wheat beer with a 'shot' of either Himbeer (raspberry) syrup or Waldmeister (artificial woodruff-flavoured syrup), served in a goblet and often drunk through a straw; *Bulette* meat pattie that's Berlin's version of the hamburger; *Currywurst* pork sausage sliced and doused in warm ketchup and curry powder; *Eisbein* fatty pork knuckle usually served with pea purée; *Hoppel-Poppel* omelette-like breakfast dish made with eggs, smoked pork, potatoes and onions; *Königsberger Klopse* veal meatballs; *Senfeier* boiled eggs in a mustard sauce; *Strammer Max* bread fried in butter and topped with ham and fried egg; *Strammer Otto* same as *Strammer Max* only topped with roast beef

Basics

Frühstück breakfast; *Mittagessen* lunch; *Abendessen* dinner; *Imbiss* snack; *Vorspeise* appetiser/starter; *Hauptgericht* main course; *Nachspeise* dessert; *Belegtes Brot* open sandwich; *Brot/Brötchen* bread/rolls; *Butter* butter; *Ei/Eier* egg/eggs; *Essig* vinegar; *Honig* honey; *Käse* cheese; *Nudeln/Teigwaren* noodles/pasta; *Pfeffer* pepper; *Reis* rice; *Rührreier* scrambled eggs; *Senf* mustard; *Sosse* sauce; *Salz* salt; *Spiegeleier* fried eggs; *Zucker* sugar; *gekocht* boiled; *gebraten* fried/roasted; *gedünstet* steamed; *paniert* breaded/battered; *Gabel* fork; *Glas* glass; *Löffel* spoon; *Messer* knife; *Tasse* cup; *Teller* plate

Soups (Suppen)

Bohnensuppe bean soup; *Brühe* broth; *Erbsensuppe* pea soup; *Hühnersuppe* chicken soup; *klare Brühe mit Leberknödeln* clear broth with liver dumplings; *Kraftbrühe* clear meat broth; *Linsensuppe* lentil soup

Meat & poultry (Fleisch & geflügel)

Ente duck; *Gans* goose; *Hackfleisch* ground meat/mince; *Hirsch* venison; *Huhn/Hühnerfleisch* chicken; *Hähnchen* chicken (when served in one piece); *Kaninchen* rabbit; *Kohlrouladen* cabbage-rolls stuffed with pork; *Kotelett* chop; *Lamm* lamb; *Leber* liver; *Nieren* kidneys; *Rindfleisch* beef; *Rindwurst* beef sausage; *Sauerbraten* marinated roast beef; *Schinken* ham; *Schnitzel* thinly pounded piece of meat, usually breaded and sautéed; *Schweinebraten* roast pork; *Schweinefleisch* pork; *Speck* bacon; *Truthahn* turkey; *Wildschwein* wild boar; *Wachteln* quail; *Wurst* sausage

Fish (Fisch)

Aal eel; *Forelle* trout; *Garnelen* prawns; *Hummer* lobster; *Kabeljau* cod; *Karpfen* carp; *Krabbe* crab or shrimp; *Lachs* salmon; *Makrele* mackerel; *Matjes/Hering* raw herring; *Miesmuscheln* mussels; *Schellfisch* haddock; *Scholle* plaice; *Seezunge* sole; *Thunfisch* tuna; *Tintenfisch* squid; *Venusmuscheln* clams; *Zander* pike-perch

Pasta (Nudeln)

Maultaschen big pasta pockets (like giant ravioli) filled with meat or spinach; *Nudelauflauf* pasta bake; *Spätzle* Swabian noodles, often served with cheese (*Käsespätzle*)

Herbs & spices (Kräuter & gewürze)

Basilikum basil; *Kümmel* caraway; *Mohn* poppyseed; *Nelken* cloves; *Oregano* oregano; *Petersilie* parsley; *Thymian* thyme; *Zimt* cinnamon

Vegetables (Gemüse)

Austernpilze oyster mushrooms; *Blumenkohl* cauliflower; *Bohnen* beans; *Bratkartoffeln* fried potatoes; *Brechbohnen* green beans; *Champignons/Pilze* mushrooms; *Erbsen* green peas; *Erdnüsse* peanuts; *Frühlingszwiebeln* spring onion; *Gurke* cucumber; *Kartoffeln* potatoes; *Knoblauch* garlic; *Kichererbsen* chick peas; *Knödel* dumpling; *Kohl* cabbage; *Kürbis* pumpkin; *Linsen* lentils *Möhren* carrots; *Paprika* peppers; *Pfifferlinge* chanterelles; *Pommes* chips/fries; *Rosenkohl* Brussels sprouts; *Rösti* roast grated potatoes; *rote Bete* beetroot; *Rotkohl* red cabbage; *Salat* lettuce; *Salzkartoffeln* boiled potatoes; *Sauerkraut* shredded white cabbage; *Spargel* asparagus; *Tomaten* tomatoes; *Zucchini* courgettes; *Zwiebeln* onions

Fruit (Obst)

Ananas pineapple; *Apfel* apple; *Apfelsine* orange; *Banane* banana; *Birne* pear; *Erdbeeren* strawberries; *Heidelbeeren* blueberries; *Himbeeren* raspberries; *Kirsche* cherry; *Limette* lime; *Pfirsich* peach; *Trauben* grapes; *Zitrone* lemon

Drinks (Getränke)

Apfelsaft apple juice; *Alsterwasser* shandy; *Bier* beer (*dunkles/helles* dark/lager); *Glühwein* mulled wine; *Kaffee* coffee; *Kaffee mit Milch* coffee with milk; *Mineralwasser* mineral water (*mit Kohlensäure* sparkling, *ohne Kohlensäure* still); *Orangensaft* orange juice; *Rotwein* red wine; *Schnaps* any kind of spirit or short; *Saft* juice; *Tee* tea; *Tomatensaft* tomato juice; *Trinkschokolade* drinking chocolate; *Wein* wine; *Weinbrand* brandy; *Weisswein* white wine; *Weizenbier* wheat beer (*hefe/kristall* yeasty/clear)

Index

Index

ESSENTIALS

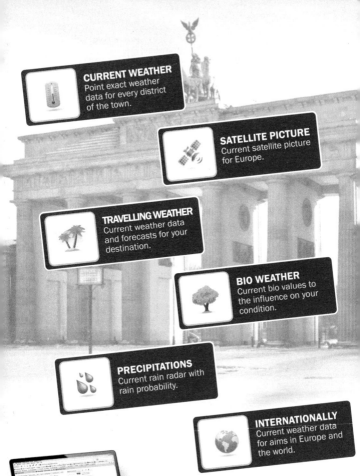